MEDGAR & MYRLIE

MEDGAR & MYRLIE

Medgar Evers and the Love Story That Awakened America

JOY-ANN REID

MARINER BOOKS
NEW YORK BOSTON

A hardcover edition of this book was published in 2024 by Mariner Books.

FIRST MARINER BOOKS PAPERBACK EDITION PUBLISHED 2025.

Designed by Jennifer Chung

Library of Congress Cataloging-in-Publication Data
has been applied for.

ISBN 978-0-06-306880-3

24 25 26 27 28 LBC 5 4 3 2 1

FOR PRUDENCE

Contents

PROLOGUE

Love

I don't know what to say, except that Medgar
was the love of my life.

—Myrlie Evers

The thing about love is that it has no chill. It takes no prisoners and makes no exceptions for the times or the environment or the dangers ahead. It has no situational awareness, particularly when it is true and intense and existential. At its best it is fearless. Love is why this book is.

In the 1950s, Myrlie Louise Beasley fell inextricably in love with Medgar Wiley Evers. She loved him the moment she laid eyes on him on her first day at Alcorn A&M College (later Alcorn State University), though at the time she wouldn't dare admit it. She was seventeen years old and intended to major in education, with a minor in music after being part of a locally famous girls singing group in high school. She was talented enough as a singer and pianist that her grandmother and aunt—who had raised her after plucking her out of the arms and home of her teenage mother—were certain that one day she might play in

New York's famous Carnegie Hall, despite her being a brown-skinned Black girl from segregated Vicksburg, Mississippi. At Alcorn, Myrlie pledged the historically Black sorority, Delta Sigma Theta, and she was driven to succeed by her grandmother and her namesake, Aunt Myrlie, despite the ugly realities of her state and country.

Medgar was twenty-five years old—a tall, dark, handsome football player and World War II veteran. He and his elder brother, Charles, had what you might call "attitude," which back then was risky for Black men in the South. Medgar had taken risks to register to vote, and he carried himself with a confidence and keen sense of the dignity he knew he was owed by the country he had defended against the Nazis in Europe. He believed in himself and what his education ought to bring him as a man in Mississippi. Medgar, to put it mildly, made an impression on the seventeen-year-old Black girl from Vicksburg.

Despite her family's determination that Myrlie focus on her education before matters of the heart, love turned her head. Medgar and Myrlie married a year after they met, on Christmas Eve, 1951. They embarked on a perilous, often contentious romantic journey that got swept up in Mississippi's civil rights struggle and ended in blood, tears, and a woman's quest not just for justice, but for vengeance.

This book is first and foremost, a love story.

It is not just about the love between two Black people in Mississippi, and their love for their children. It is also about the higher love it took for Black Americans to love America and to fight for it, even in the state that butchered more Black bodies via lynching than any other, and that ripped apart the promise of Reconstruction with a ferocity unmatched by any other place in this fragile and fractured nation. Despite all of that, Medgar Evers had a deep and unfaltering love for Mississippi. He loved its pastoral plains, deep rivers, and wooded areas where he could fish and hunt and feed his family with his physical labor. His love for the Black farmers and maids and butlers and strivers of this tormented state gave his life meaning.

Myrlie Evers demanded more than once that Medgar tell her if he loved her and his children more than his work. He pressed her to understand that he did his work *because* he loved her and their children. He didn't want them to live as he did, growing up walking by the bloody clothes of a lynched Black man on his way to school and seeing Black men and women abused and disrespected as a daily fact of life. He was determined to exorcise the ghosts in the trees that whispered to him and his brother that in Mississippi, and throughout America, people like them were something less than human. Medgar's work was a labor of love.

Francis H. Mitchell, in his November 1958 profile of Medgar for *Ebony*, noted a plaque hanging on the living room wall of the Evers home in Jackson. On it was a quote from President Abraham Lincoln that for Mitchell, a groundbreaking figure as a Black photographer and journalist of that era, seemed to sum up Medgar's relationship "with his God and with the white man at the same moment."[1] Lincoln's words on the plaque were published in *Harper's Weekly* in July 1865, three months after his assassination: "I have been driven many times to my knees by the overwhelming conviction that I had nowhere else to go. My own wisdom, and that of all about me, seemed insufficient for that day."

James Baldwin, the eminent Black American author, met Medgar Evers shortly after New Year's Day in 1963, as Baldwin embarked on a lecture tour throughout the American South for the Congress on Racial Equality, in response to the violent riots that accompanied James Meredith's integration of the University of Mississippi months before. Meredith's bid to enter "Ole Miss" had been backed by Medgar, who had himself been rejected by the state's premiere college simply because he was Black. Baldwin quickly became close to Medgar and decades later recalled him as "a great man . . . a beautiful man . . . and a troublemaker" in the way that Baldwin respected, and that he possessed "the calm of someone who knows they're going to die before their time—like Martin Luther King."[2]

Baldwin returned to the United States from self-exile in Paris in 1957 and dove into civil rights. He befriended each of the three men he declared to be the core triumvirate of the Movement: Dr. King, Malcolm X, and Medgar. All three were "troublemakers" in the eyes of the racist white Southern establishment and the federal government, particularly the FBI (which also kept a file on Baldwin). Medgar would be the first to meet the fate that the eminent author had perceived as all but inevitable.

In the early morning hours of June 12, 1963, Medgar Evers was shot in the carport of his home in Jackson, Mississippi, by an assassin with links to Mississippi's White Citizens' Council and the Ku Klux Klan. Medgar was just thirty-seven years old. Myrlie, who was only thirty, became the widowed single mother of three young children, and the frightened and despondent but determined author of her martyred husband's legacy.

Love had made Myrlie put up with the fear and dread that came with being the wife of a civil rights leader, who was continually on the hit list of the Mississippi KKK and hated by every racist in the state, Kluxer or not. Love made her put up with the threatening phone calls and the terror her children endured as they learned to drop to the floor if they heard gunshots and to hide in the bathtub if the bad men came for their daddy. And love would make Myrlie pick herself up off the bloody pavement where Medgar lay dying and turn her screams and rage into a determination to hunt the killer for decades, until she got justice for her slain husband and her family.

Evers's assassination came amid a national torrent of civil rights demonstrations, sit-ins, federal troops–backed college desegregations and demands from Black demonstrators across the South for an immediate end to Jim Crow segregation. As the highest-profile civil rights leader at that time to be killed in an act of racist violence, he soon became a national household name. News of Evers's assassination, two years before the murder of Malcolm X in Harlem and five years before Dr. King was cut down in Memphis, was splashed across the front pages of the country's newspapers, from Shreveport, Louisiana, and Waterloo, Iowa, to Portland, Maine, and Stockton, California.

Officials from Jackson, Mississippi, and Washington, D.C., expressed shock and outrage. Many feared mass racial violence in Jackson, as police arrested anyone attempting to march in mourning or in protest, including fourteen mostly Black clergy and a church layman, plus 146 protesters during a tense and angry June 12 march through downtown Jackson protesting the murder.[3] As far away as New Jersey, NAACP activists shifted their plans for a July 2 civil rights march in the wake of the slaying, with the Rockland County NAACP president issuing a statement saying, "The Negroes in Rockland County can no longer sit back and calmly watch the acts of barbarism against their brothers in the South."[4]

A statement from the White House declared that President John F. Kennedy, who within months would also fall to an assassin's bullet, was "appalled by the barbarity" of the Evers murder.[5] Kennedy called former president Dwight D. Eisenhower to the White House the day after the assassination to discuss the urgency of the country's "tense racial problem."[6] They were joined by Vice President Lyndon Johnson and Attorney General Robert Kennedy, who said he was "saddened and shocked" by the killing and announced that the FBI would begin a full federal investigation.[7] King and his deputies were galvanized by the Evers killing as they planned an August March on Washington, at which Myrlie Evers was to be among the few women slated to speak.

Yet today, much of that historical memory has vanished. When *Oprah Daily,* the Hearst publication and website launched by Oprah Winfrey, published its list of "30 Civil Rights Leaders of the Past and Present" in February 2023, they named many of the Movement's luminaries, such as King and Malcolm, W. E. B Du Bois, Julian Bond, A. Philip Randolph, Ella Baker, and Roy Wilkins. Medgar Evers wasn't on the list.[8] Likewise, PBS's 2013 catalog of civil rights heroes included the great Daisy Bates and Ralph Bunche, along with Chicago's legendary activist Fred Hampton and the more familiar names (Martin, Malcolm, Rosa Parks, John Lewis), but not Medgar. This is, in part, because Medgar's assassination was followed—and quickly overshadowed—by so many momentous events: the 1963 March on Washington; the 16th Street Baptist Church bombing that killed four little girls; the 1964 Freedom Summer protests throughout Mississippi, which were built on the youth activism Medgar erected through the NAACP Youth Councils; the disappearance of three civil rights workers in rural Mississippi and the discovery that they had been killed by the Klan; and Fannie Lou Hamer and the Mississippi Freedom Democrats' disruption of the 1964 Democratic convention. Not long after that, Malcolm X was killed in New York and Dr. King in Memphis, each man cut down in the prime of his life. The era also saw the assassinations of President Kennedy and Robert Kennedy, characterizing it by so much violence and death we sometimes struggle to sort through it all and preserve a comprehensive historical memory.

The fundamental argument of this book is that Medgar's activism, from his role in investigating the Emmett Till lynching and other racist murders of Black Mississippians to the boycott movement he orchestrated in Jackson, was the foundation upon which the later efforts by SNCC, CORE, and other organizations were built. James Baldwin had it right: Medgar Evers deserves a place alongside Malcolm X and Dr. King in our historical memory, as contemporaries who fought the same demons of white supremacy during the same perilous era, often with overlapping tactics. Medgar Evers, with Myrlie as his partner in activism and in life, was doing civil rights work in the single most hostile and dangerous environment in America: Mississippi.

Among other things, this book is a love letter to Myrlie Evers-Williams, whom I have been lucky enough to come to know and admire as a woman, a sorority sister, a civil rights leader, and an icon in her own right. Her independence, fighting spirit, and determination make her as captivating a figure as there is in American history. Her deep, resonant voice is almost musical—appropriate given her gifts at the piano. Her fierce love for her children, grandchildren, and great-grandchildren is inspiring, as was her determination to find love again and to build a new life for her family in California. I recorded more than a half dozen interviews with Mrs. Evers-Williams over the course of nearly a year, by telephone and in person.

The book extensively uses her words, her memories, and her stories, along with interviews with family members, friends, and neighbors of the Everses during the time they lived on Guynes Street in Jackson, Mississippi; historians from the Mississippi Delta community they resided in during their early marriage; and nearly a dozen men and women who as young activists, were influenced by and allied with Medgar. I have also drawn from Evers-Williams's two autobiographies (the first published just four years after her husband's assassination, and the second in 1999), the autobiography of Medgar Evers, co-edited by Evers-Williams and the late Manning Marable, and other reference materials, including the family archives at the Evers Institute in Jackson.

Throughout this book, I refer to Medgar Evers and Myrlie Evers Williams as "Medgar" and "Myrlie," but make no mistake: like all African American men and women, they deserve and always deserved the honorific of Mr. Evers and Mrs. Evers-Williams. A similar tack is taken in describing their friendships and closest relationships. The shorthand is meant to convey this love story in its purest form, and not to take away from my reverence for these historical figures and the dignity of their lives. The term "Negro" is occasionally used throughout the book to convey the way Black Americans referred to themselves, contemporaneously to the events described. And to the extent possible, the stories in this book are told through the voices of the people who lived them.

And now, to the love story.

CHAPTER 1

Mississippi *Goddamn* . . .

To understand the world, you must first understand a place like Mississippi.

—ATTRIBUTED TO NOVELIST WILLIAM FAULKNER

When Medgar Evers set foot back on Mississippi soil, it must have been like crashing through the atmosphere and returning to earth after spending time on a distant planet. It was the spring of 1946, and the stocky, handsome World War II veteran, who stood five feet eleven, with deep brown skin, a slight mustache, and a serious, studious demeanor, was twenty years old and brimming with ambition. He was the second of his parents' children together—the second of his father's four, including an older brother and two younger girls, and the fifth of his mother's seven—born into a blended family in the small town of Decatur, Mississippi, on July 2, 1925.

He had been born *again* in the world beyond Mississippi.

In that wider world—that distant planet called "Europe"—Medgar Evers was a man; a technician fifth grade in the Quartermaster Corps of the U.S. Army, with the rank of sergeant, after serving in England, at Liege and Antwerp in Belgium, and in France in La Havre, Cherbourg, and Omaha Beach. He was an American, who had seen more of the world than the vast majority of white Americans. He was a World War II veteran and a human being. Yet the moment he returned to Mississippi he was nothing but a nigger.

Having received an honorable discharge on April 16, he was flown back to Camp Shelby, near Hattiesburg, Mississippi, with the other returning servicemen. From there, the bus ride is more than six hours to Decatur. Still wearing his uniform, Medgar climbed aboard and took a seat near the front. The trouble started as soon as they got close to his hometown.

"When we were almost there, the driver asked me to move . . . to the back. Well, I wouldn't do it," he said. "Hell, I'd just been on a battlefield for my country. When we reached my hometown, the driver signaled to some men in town. They came on the bus and beat me within an inch of my life." Medgar actually told the story laughing. "It was the worst beating I ever had," he said. "But after that, I was a different man."[1]

Though he was young, Medgar was plagued by the questions raised by what he'd experienced in the war. "Why should I put my life on the line for my country, the place where I was born and reared . . . and even while I am here in Europe, I'm still treated [by the U.S. Army] as a second-class citizen," he told family members and friends. "And then when I return to the country of my birth, I'm treated not only as a second-class citizen, but a human being that they despise and want to see put down and kept on a lower tier than everybody else."[2] He told the story again and again.

He just couldn't let it go.

From the time of his induction on October 7, 1943, until his discharge in 1946, Medgar used his time in the military both to serve and, whenever he could find the time, to study. He developed a fascination with the African liberation movement in Kenya and its leader, Jomo Kenyatta, who had been engaged for more than a decade in the struggle to rid the country of British colonial rule. He had a deep respect for Kenyatta, who in 1945 attended the fifth Pan African Congress in Manchester, England—a meeting that brought together African leaders like Kwame Nkrumah and Black American intellectual leader W. E. B. Du Bois. Kenyatta later led the bloody Mau Mau rebellion against white colonial settlers (and eventually emerged as the independent nation's president).

"I admired the man," Medgar said. "He was intelligent, and he didn't believe in compromise. And while I never cared for brutality, I realized that just as the Africans followed Kenyatta, Negroes might have successfully followed someone like him."[3] He even dreamed at one stage of arming his own "black shirt Army" and mounting an uprising against the racist white system in Mississippi. His flirtation with ideas of armed revolution didn't last. "It didn't take much reading of the Bible," he said, "to convince me that two wrongs would not make the situation any different, and that I couldn't hate the white man and at the same time hope to convert him."[4]

Medgar also idolized his brother, James Charles Evers, whom everyone just called "Charles," and who was three years older and their father's firstborn. From childhood on, the brothers were close, with Charles acting as Medgar's protector. Charles warmed the bed they shared as children, before Medgar, who hated the cold, climbed under the sheets. A Mississippi civil rights attorney named Jack Young described the brothers by saying, "Charles was a rough and tumble guy, Medgar was a gentleman."[5] Mainly, though, they were inseparable. In high school, Medgar stood out for his athleticism on the football field and for his "zoot suit" fashion style (not unlike a contemporary, Malcolm Little—later Malcolm X—who was two months older), complete with baggy slacks and a brimmed hat tipped to the side, and for the large vocabulary that was a testament to his bookishness.

After America's entrance into World War II, Medgar followed Charles by dropping out of high school to enlist in the Army. He filled out his registration a month before his eighteenth birthday on June 3, 1943. In doing so he defied his mother's admonishment to her children that they beat the odds for Blacks in Mississippi and get their education, though he had every intention of finishing school after his service. He dreamed of becoming a lawyer and combatting the discrimination against Black Mississippians in the courts.

Medgar entered basic training at the strictly segregated Camp Shelby and was soon deployed to England and then to France, where he experienced the mass death and horror of the U.S. military assault at Omaha Beach in June 1944. U.S. troops from the First and Twenty-Ninth Infantry Divisions began landing across the six-mile stretch of the Normandy coast at 6:30 in the morning. From the start it was pure chaos. The assault on the Normandy coast was the largest amphibious invasion ever attempted in military history. Divisions of troops were mixing haphazardly as men raced to climb out of the ships and escape the "kill zone" along the beach, where German forces were raining fire at the assault, and get to a safe spot, on higher ground.[6] Medgar was assigned to the all-Black 325th Port Company as a designated "supply clerk." As part of the famed, and largely African American "red ball express," he loaded and unloaded weapons and supplies, and offloaded vehicles from transport ships onto trucks to keep the front lines supplied. The still-segregated Army allowed few Black men to participate in combat. But there was no escaping the gore of the 10,300 D-Day casualties among the 133,000 U.S. and Allied troops who crammed into 7,000 ships and landing craft or who strafed the beach from the air. Remaining in France after D-Day, Medgar joined the all-Black 3677th Quartermaster Company and the 958th Quartermaster Service Company.[7]

Like his elder brother, Medgar relished his experience in Europe despite the segregated service. The horror was real; seeing the bodies of dead soldiers littering Omaha Beach changed something in him, he later told Charles. It hardened him. He was moody and started doing uncharacteristic things, like swearing. Some of the white officers were deliberately cruel, bringing a touch of Mississippi overseas.[8] But Europe was not Mississippi. There was no Jim Crow system of formal racial segregation and no Ku Klux Klan. People in England, and especially France, often treated Black Americans with a normalcy that elided race. Medgar's military service gave him confidence and perspective, and it heightened the contradictions between the mission of fighting for liberty and freedom abroad, while at home as a Negro man he had none.

And there were the women. French women seemed particularly intrigued by Black American men; or at least, they were free to show it openly. Unlike in the American South, going around with them was neither illegal nor particularly frowned upon; as long as no white American soldiers were around. This allowed Medgar to experience something that would have been incredibly dangerous, even life-threatening in Decatur: a romance with a white woman. It happened in Cherbourg. The woman was the daughter of a French couple he'd befriended. Unbelievably to him, he could hold her hand and even kiss her in public without fear of reprisal. Her parents even approved of the union.[9] It was a mesmerizing change of status. Back home, he would likely have been lynched for such a romance.

In France, white U.S. servicemen frequently tried to prevent Black troops from interacting with white women. They spread rumors among French locals that Black men were rapists, or even that they had tails. The racist propagandizing didn't work. More than 350,000 Black men had served in France during World War I, nearly 100,000 of them seeing combat under French commanders, so Blacks were not viewed as alien in the country, which continued to operate a colonial empire that included countries like Guadeloupe, Niger, and the Ivory Coast. France was not free of racism, but it did not have institutionalized discrimination and terror based on color alone. Outside of American barracks, Black soldiers could move around freely.

And there was Paris.

Since the 1920s, the city had been a magnet for Black artists, such as Josephine Baker, and a hub for the popular spread of jazz, though many of these Americans left the country as the Nazis invaded and began to outlaw the "corrupt influence" of jazz. After World War II ended, Paris was still reeling from the physical and emotional ravages of war and Nazi occupation, and food rationing was still underway. Despite this, the city became an even greater magnet for African American artists, writers like Chester Himes, William Gardner Smith, James Baldwin, and Richard Wright, as well as musical performers who wished to escape the limitations of segregated venues in the United States.

Part of Medgar wanted to stay in France after the war, the way Baldwin and Richard Wright had done. Wright, like Medgar, was a Mississippi native and the grandson of slaves—born in 1908 on Rucker Plantation near Natchez, where his father was a sharecropper and his mother a schoolteacher. He called Paris "a place where one could claim one's soul."[10] Medgar shared Wright's impatience with the limits America placed on Blackness. He was proud of being Black and chaffed at the pressure on Black Americans to feel or act ashamed. He was in Cherbourg, less than two hours away from Paris, so it could be done. He could simply refuse to go home. He had a girl, whose family accepted him. He could have a life outside Decatur and racist Mississippi.

It was a temporary dream. He wrote to Charles that he saw no reason they should have to leave Mississippi in order to succeed. He wanted to put his foot down in his home state and raise Black children in freedom there.[11] "This is home," he later said. "Mississippi is a part of the United States. And whether the Whites like it or not, I don't plan to live here as a parasite. The things that I don't like I will try to change. And in the long run, I hope to make a positive contribution to the overall productivity of the South."[12]

Although Medgar shared some of the rage that drove Charles to declare his utter hatred and contempt for white people, his relationship with his Paris sweetheart convinced him it was possible for Blacks and whites to live together harmoniously. He told Charles that when they got home from Europe, they were going to fix things. Still, neither he nor Charles could bring their white girlfriends home as their wives. They knew better than that because they were returning to Mississippi. So they both came back alone. Still, Medgar saved his Paris girl's letters until he married.[13] Their mother begged them to stop writing to these women (Charles's girl was Filipino) for fear that local whites would accuse the Evers boys of "messing with white women."

MEDGAR, CHARLES, AND THEIR SIBLINGS HAD RECEIVED THE standard education of every Black Southern child—the realization that there were three kinds of white people: the ones who hated you but were too cowardly to do anything about it, the dangerous ones who would kill you just as soon as look at you, and the nice-acting ones who despite their kindness wouldn't do a damned thing about it.

This lesson started young. "My parents were poor, but not destitute," Medgar later told *Ebony* about growing up in Decatur, where Black and white families lived in close proximity, as in much of the South. He spoke of a white kid who lived next door, who "practically lived" at the Evers house. Seemingly oblivious to their divergent status in Mississippi, the boys would spend the long, sweltering summers playing hide-and-seek, bickering over favorite toys, sharing personal treasures, or telling each other what they wanted to be when they grew up. Neither could imagine in those moments that either of them couldn't be a fireman or ship's captain; a banker, boxer, or business tycoon; or that they wouldn't always be friends. They were just boys, dreaming. It was a blissful boyhood in what felt to a child like a close-knit community. Until it wasn't. Medgar told of the day, he didn't even recall at what age, that his friend stopped coming over. Then one day, Medgar saw his friend standing with a group of white friends. "He called me 'nigger,'" Medgar said. "The split had come. The lines were drawn, Blacks on one side, white on the other. I guess at that moment, I realized my status in Mississippi."[14]

The same split came between Medgar and the sons and daughter of the white woman their mother worked for. Their perfectly normal childhood friendship ended abruptly when they all reached school age—and especially puberty. It was then that the lines were most sharply drawn in the South, and the white children seemed to instinctively learn to fix their mouths into a sneer, to replace their Black friends' names with "nigger" and "boy," and to demand that these "friends" call them "sir" and "miss," especially in front of white adults. Suddenly, they were no longer allowed to run to the creek together or even to talk to each other—especially the white girls, who became instantly dangerous to even look at square in the eye.

Death arrived quickly for Black boys in Mississippi. Its specter began to hover the moment you were old enough to possibly catch the attention of the wrong white man's daughter, or if she flirted with you. One thing you could count on was that no white woman would ever admit to flirting with a Negro. She would let you hang instead. More than a few white men bragged about their "nigger women" on the colored side of town. Sometimes the ones who talked the loudest and the meanest quietly left land to those same children in their wills, producing a society of constant socioeconomic contradictions and inexplicably complicated social rules. It was a bitter irony. Slaveholders had raped enslaved Black women so routinely that they invented new racial categories to characterize the resulting offspring: *mulatto*, *quadroon*, and *octaroon*—based on the percentage of "white" the person was. Many of these children were put up for sale regardless of being their "owner's" child and were often the subject of confusion and wonder at how a "Negro" could look so white.

Slavery in Mississippi and throughout the South had been characterized by forced breeding and relentless sexual violence. Yet the sons and grandsons of the men who built that system, and who fought to defend it during the Civil War, built their postbellum Southern culture around the constant fear that *Black* men were fixated on raping white women. And even though the South's defeat at the war's end failed to stop the raping of Black women, these sons and grandsons of enslavers invented a palliative for their fears: lynching.

In Mississippi, and across the American South, Black life was cheap. A Black man, woman, or child could be killed for anything or for nothing: for looking at a white man wrong or testifying against him in court (Mississippi juries were of course, all white, and until 1968 all male); for brushing against a white woman on the sidewalk because you didn't jump into the gutter fast enough; for talking rudely to a white man or woman or even to a white child; or answering "yes" without the "sir" or "ma'am." Your life was in danger every minute of every day. You lived at the whim of any white person's momentary moods. And they knew the law, which was deeply enmeshed in white supremacy, wouldn't touch them. For the first hundred years after slavery officially ended, whites in the South got in bigger trouble for killing a pig or a dog than for killing a Black person. Slavery hadn't really ended for the sharecroppers still tied to white planters' land and for those trapped in the pernicious system of convict leasing that thrived in the loophole of the Thirteenth Amendment. Police existed solely to serve white people, to excuse their crimes, and to bully, bludgeon, and control Black bodies. The "peckerwoods," as the rich whites called poor whites, were the most dangerous whites. Their shops and feed stores served primarily Black customers, and the planter class and the sell-to-whites shopkeeper classes unleashed them to exorcise their frustrations on Black bodies.

"Slavery was seventy years gone," Charles Evers later wrote. "But the system I was raised in might as well have been slavery. White folk segregated 'the niggers' to hold us in line. They forced us to sharecrop, worked us like mules, walked on us like dirt. We lived in shacks and shanties, went down cheap, and grew old with nothing. Half of us died as children, and the other half were always in danger. You drank that in with mama's milk. You knew you were a nigger the very first time you rode in a car and couldn't use the bathroom at the service station and had to relieve yourself in the woods just off the road, hiding from passing cars."[15]

The white plantation owners who ran every rural Southern town closed the Negro schools during planting season so Black children could pick cotton in their fields. There was always work to be done: Mississippi cotton didn't stop being the finest-grade cotton in the world just because formal slavery ended. When Medgar and Charles made the miles-long trek to the ramshackle, one-room, all-Black school during the nonplanting season on foot, "white kids in their school buses would throw things at us and yell filthy things." Medgar called this the "elementary course" in white supremacy.[16]

For Blacks in Mississippi, as in every Southern state, everything in your life was separate. If you wanted to watch Hedy Lamarr and Tom Mix movies and work out the psychology of whether you should root for the cowboys or the Indians, you did so from a dusty balcony, while the white patrons watched from comfortable seats below. Every beautiful woman in the movies and advertisements was white. Black people were portrayed mainly as moronic, simple, and docile; Black men as dangerous to white women if let loose, as shown in 1915's *Birth of a Nation,* the wildly racist film that popularized and galvanized the Ku Klux Klan throughout the South—and was screened by President Woodrow Wilson in the White House.

If you wanted to eat outside your home, you had to wait for a plate to be shoved roughly into your hands from the back window of a local mom-and-pop restaurant, provided they would serve you at all. If you strayed downtown, you weren't welcome at the Woolworth's lunch counter at all, and to buy a pair of shoes or a dress you had to take it home without trying it on. When your mom dropped off the white people's washing, she entered the white family's house only through the back door and didn't go far into the house, even if the white family were nice. That was just the way it was. Once you learned to drive, you quickly learned never to let a car full of white men pass you, lest they run you off the road or shoot at you from the passenger or rear windows. Life was humiliation and threat, every day, all day. Slavery was technically gone, but the plantation class was determined to cling to as many of its social and economic features as possible, using every cruel means they could find.

"Just before I went into the Army," Medgar later said, "I began wondering how long I could stand it. I used to watch the Saturday night sport of white men trying to run down a Negro with their car, or white gangs coming through town to beat up a Negro."[17]

In 1932 or 1936, depending on which brother was telling the story, Medgar and Charles witnessed their first lynching. The murdered man was a friend of their father's named Willie Tingle. "I guess he was about forty years old, married, and we used to play with his kids," Medgar said. "I remember the Saturday night a bunch of white men beat him to death at the Decatur fairgrounds because he sassed a white woman. They just left him dead on the ground."[18]

That was all it took back then: an accusation by any white person could sentence any Black man, woman, or child to the rope, the pistol, or worse. As Charles Evers put it, in the Mississippi they grew up in, "killing Negroes was a white man's prerogative. They'd kill Negroes just like stepping on a bug."[19] And brag about it. "Negro bodies were found in rivers and creeks all over the South," Charles wrote. "For every Negro we knew was murdered, there were two others buried deep in the forest or fed to the gators."[20] In Willie Tingle's case, Charles wrote that before they beat him, they tied him to a wagon and dragged him alive through the streets of Decatur, as Black people watched helplessly and rushed their children off the street. After that torture, they hanged Mr. Tingle's body from an old tree in the fairgrounds and shot him full of holes, cut him down, and left the body lying there. It was Medgar and Charles's father, James, who collected Mr. Tingle's body and carried it to his uncle Mark Thomas's funeral home in the company hearse.[21]

Charles wrote that Medgar asked their father afterward why those men killed Mr. Tingle. The answer had to be as devastating to a young Black psyche as the murder itself: "just because he was a colored man." When Medgar asked his dad if white men could kill him, too, Mr. Evers told them the truth: "If I was doing anything they didn't like, they sure could kill me."[22]

James Evers, who drove the family hearse as a side vocation, worked mainly as a lumber stacker at the local sawmills and for the railroad. He also owned land in Decatur and ran a small cow, chicken, and pig farm, and he rented two small houses on it. He was a tough man, never one to bow and scrape before white people. He was known to buck white folks in Decatur so often, they labeled him "Crazy Jim."

Not much shook Mr. Evers the way Tingle's lynching and Medgar's question had. In answering his son, he had laid bare a Black child's ultimate vulnerability: that in the white South, in America, you had no protector, no matter how much your parents loved you and how tough they were. Medgar's mother echoed her husband's warning to her boys to always be careful around white folks. She chastised the feistier Charles, who complained loudly that the lynching was unfair, urging him to pray on it. Someday things would get better, she said. It was the kind of thing Black church ladies would say, but Charles didn't want to hear it. "Mama, we pray all the time," he told her. "What do it get us?"[23] The children had learned young that white folks hated nothing like they hated Negroes. "White hatred dogged your heels like a shadow," Charles would later write.[24]

For months, Charles and Medgar passed Tingle's bloody clothes as they passed the fairgrounds on the three-mile trek to their segregated school in the Decatur Consolidated School District. (The bright yellow-and-black school buses that carried white children to their modern, well-equipped schools were denied to Negro children.) The clothes had been deliberately left on display by the lynchers, to rot and stink of clotted blood and gore, so that every other "nigger" would remember their place. Worse, most everyone in town knew who the killers were; yet they had just gone on about their business.

For Medgar, the worst part was the silence from a Black community that had been terrorized into submission. "Everyone in town knew" what happened, Medgar said, but there was "never a word in public. . . . They left those clothes on a fence for about a year. Every Negro in town was supposed to get the message from those clothes and I can see those clothes now in my mind's eye. I saw them every time we ran rabbits near the fairground. Nothing was said in public. No sermons in church. No news, no protest. It was as though this man just dissolved, except for the bloody clothes."[25]

The lynching produced a desire for revenge among the Evers boys. When the school bus drivers tried to push them off the road into the muddy gutters by driving so close to them that they stumbled and dirtied the clothes their mother had carefully hand-washed for them, they retaliated by throwing rocks. A year later, they decided to start selling the Black newspaper the *Chicago Defender*. The paper offered positive stories about Black people and about Africa, a palliative to the ugly and dismissive coverage by papers like the *Clarion-Ledger*. When local white leaders shut down their trade, decreeing that only whites could be paperboys, Charles and Medgar secretly ambushed a couple of white paperboys with a hail of rocks, then destroyed their bundle of newspapers as they fled.

Despite their mother's deep disapproval and fear for her youngest boys, James Evers seemed to quietly approve of their bravado. He had long taught his sons that most racist whites were bullies but also cowards, only capable of harming you when they greatly outnumbered you or caught you out alone. A smaller number were truly dangerous, mostly because they had authority or associated with those who did. Every colored man or boy needed to know the difference. Charles was particularly eager to test that theory often. He was angry and rambunctious, and he and Medgar were constantly engaged at hijinks, often to make a buck. They swiped pecans or other small items from a local shopkeeper and sold them; always looking for little businesses to get into. Years after the *Defender* play fell apart, they started bootlegging, which was strictly illegal in "dry" Mississippi. Sometimes they drove the liquor to "wet" Tennessee in their great-uncle's hearse.[26]

Charles called Medgar the saint of the Evers family. He was as studious and serious as Charles was balled-up rage. Charles gave him the nickname "Lope"—a play on the name of an old Black preacher who used to come to the Evers house during revivals and eat up all the pies and treats Mrs. Evers whipped up for the pastors but couldn't afford to fix for her kids during an average week. The two brothers shared a deep resentment over the treatment of Blacks in Mississippi and were determined to make something of themselves. Even as children, Charles and Medgar moved with resoluteness. For Medgar, that included a drive to stay in his home state, come what may. It came from his natural stubbornness and from knowing that his family's blood ran deep into the Mississippi soil.

James Evers and his wife, Jessie Wright Evers, came from mixed-heritage families. Jessie's great grandfather was Medgar Wright, the namesake of Jessie's future son. The elder Medgar was a half-Black, half-indigenous slave whose reputation was one of incorrigibility. Jessie's father, Essiens Wright, was half white and born in Georgia in 1874. In 1893, at twenty years old, he married a Black woman one year his junior and they had a son; less than a year later, they moved to Washington, Mississippi, where their two daughters, Lessie and Jessie, were born in 1894 and 1897. According to family lore, what prompted the change of scenery was an incident in which Essiens Wright shot two white men after one of them called him a "half-assed mulatto."[27]

Jessie was no rabble-rouser. Instead, she was a holy roller who skillfully sewed her children's clothes and required them to be in church three times a week for Bible study and Sunday services. She encouraged them to be patient with white folks, pray for those who trespassed against them, and put their trust in the Lord. Like most Black women in the South, she worked for white families, taking in laundry and returning it through the back door, cleaning their homes, and minding their children. One of her older children, Eddie, became a hobo, hopping trains and living free. Charles admired his uncle and strived to one day achieve that kind of freedom.

James Evers was born in Lena, Mississippi, on September 6, 1882, according to his World War I draft card. He was one of four children of Mike Evers, a farmer who owned land near Decatur and who was born in 1845 in Georgia, and Mary Lizzie Horn, a Black and Creole Indian woman born in 1850 in North Carolina; both were likely formerly enslaved. Charles remembered his grandmother for her high cheekbones and long hair. As in most Black families at the time, there were no family photographs or portraits. Just memories and old folks' stories.

James and Jessie, who called each other "Jim" and "Grimm," married sometime around 1920. Jessie had been married before and brought three children into the marriage. They then had four more: Charles, Medgar, and two girls, Mary Ruth and Liz. Jessie Wright Evers ensured her children went to school every day, all four months of the

Negro school year. The schools barely passed for educational institutions. Decatur Negro schools were one- or two-room shacks that were freezing cold during the late winter months that comprised the school year for Negro children. The segregated schools were typically stuffed with one hundred or more students, presided over by just two or so teachers struggling to educate kids of all ages at once. There were few books and few resources. What passed for truth in the history books was little more than propaganda: denouncing Reconstruction as a shameful period and omitting the contributions of Black people to U.S. history. This was what white Southerners called "separate but equal," as their children attended school in modern, clean buildings with plenty of books, pencils, and globes, where they, too, were taught that Negroes had contributed nothing to the United States or to the world, other than what they could contribute with their backs or on them.

Despite the determination of whites to keep Southern Blacks dumb and docile, one Evers daughter finished high school, and both Medgar and Charles finished college, which was unusual for Blacks in that era, and both boys were determined to go to law school, determined to learn how to fight segregation and Negro subjugation via the law. The Evers kids had books at home, and Medgar in particular kept his nose in them.

Medgar and Charles idolized their father, whom they referred to as "Daddy" even as adults. They revered him for the same reason local whites respected him: because James Evers refused to bow and taught his sons not to, either. He was the rare Black man who refused to move off the sidewalk to let white folks pass, or to skin and grin and "yassa boss" to those who viewed themselves as his betters. The assumption by whites in Decatur that he had to be crazy to act the way he did afforded him and his family a measure of safety.

Charles loved to retell the story of the day their father was overcharged five dollars at the local sawmill commissary. James Evers couldn't read, but he could add in his head better than most. When the commissary manager, a white man named Jimmy Boware, sneered at him, "Are you calling me a liar, nigger?" James stood his ground and politely but firmly reiterated that Boware had got the math wrong. When Boware went for his pistol behind the counter, Evers, who stood over six feet and was broad and physically imposing, broke a Coca-Cola bottle and held out the sharp end, quietly explaining to the man that if he came around that counter, he was gonna get his brains bashed in. The Evers boys stood behind their father and refused to leave him, even grabbing Coke bottles of their own. As they walked home along the railroad tracks, Evers admonished his boys, who feared reprisal from the white men in the store, telling them, "Don't run, don't run. They're nothin' but a bunch of cowards."[28] Indeed, no one followed them. Evers told Charles and Medgar that night, "Don't never let anybody beat you. . . . If anyone ever kicks you, you kick the hell out of him."[29] White men in Decatur knew that if they were ever going to kill this "crazy nigger," he would take a couple of them with him. They left him alone. But that night, James Evers sat up with his .22 rifle, just in case.

BLACKS IN THE SOUTH WERE KEPT FROM THE BALLOT THROUGH A mix of trickery and terrorism—a crucial means of maintaining the status quo. Lynchings often targeted those who expressed a desire to vote. White newspapers published lists of Blacks who appeared before a voter registrar or who became members of the NAACP. Being on those lists could mean getting fired by your white employer, being evicted from your tenant farm, or even having the bank foreclose on your home. And because you had to be a registered voter to serve on a jury, the practice of keeping Blacks from voting served a double purpose.

Mississippi was in many ways the birthplace of the American creed that neither a Black citizen nor a Black voter should ever exist. The notion of limiting the franchise to "free white males" dates to the Tenth

Congress, which in 1808 amended the Organic Act that controlled the Mississippi territory, nine years before it became a state.[30] The number of free Blacks in Mississippi in 1808 was just 181, versus 14,523 enslaved Africans and 16,602 Whites.[31] The rich alluvial soil in Mississippi's Delta region made its planters exceptionally wealthy. "The Delta has probably the richest soil outside of Africa and therefore very conducive to the planting and the harvesting of cotton," Jackson State professor Cassie Sade Turnipseed said. The mass of Black labor required to run the wildly prosperous plantations of the American South resulted in several Southern states having populations that were almost equally Black and white or, in South Carolina and Mississippi, majority Black. Indeed, Mississippi emerged from the Civil War with a 55.3 percent Black majority that peaked at 58.5 percent in 1900.[32]

The planter class was determined to secure white minority rule through an aggressive system of American apartheid. After witnessing the election of Black statewide officials—including two United States senators: Hiram Rhodes Revels (1871) and Blanch Kelso Bruce (elected in 1874 and serving from 1875 to 1881), plus a Black lieutenant governor, Alexander K. Davis (1873–1876[33]), which made Mississippi, ironically, a model of Reconstruction—Mississippi's white Democrats vowed to beat back racial progress by any means necessary. When Reconstruction collapsed in the 1877 compromise made on the backs of the formerly enslaved, Mississippi was the most ferocious Southern state in forcing a total reversal. It was the first state to erect barriers like poll taxes and literacy tests to keep its Black majority from ever exercising the vote again.

Like most Southern states, Mississippi moved in 1902 to switch from a caucus system to a primary system to elect its candidates, which all but guaranteed white control. After the Civil War, the vast majority of Black Americans were Lincoln Republicans—members of the Southern "Black and Tan" party—so there was no need to block them from Democratic primaries, since no Republican could get elected dog catcher in any Southern state. That meant the Democratic primary effectively was the whole election. President Franklin Roosevelt's New Deal, despite the many ways it limited or even excluded Black participation, had drawn Black voters to the Democratic Party during the 1930s and '40s. Mississippi Democrats, along with those in other Southern states, came up with a new scheme to get around the Fifteenth Amendment. The "white primary" was predicated on the idea that a private political party had the right to make its own rules and choose its own candidates—in this case, white men.

For more than twenty years, the U.S. Supreme Court had begged to differ. In 1927 the nation's highest court struck down Texas's all-white primary in the landmark *Nixon v. Herndon* ruling, and it ruled that Congress had the authority to protect the right of all citizens to vote in primary elections in the *U.S. v. Classic* (1941) and *Smith v. Allwright* (1944) cases, ruling that a political party using the apparatuses of state government to run its elections was tantamount to state discrimination against Black voters.[34] The 1944 case, argued by NAACP lawyer Thurgood Marshall, revolved around a Black dentist from Houston, Texas, Dr. Lonnie E. Smith, who tried to register to vote in that state's Democratic primary but was denied because of his race. The Texas Democratic Party, like the one in Mississippi, argued that it was a "voluntary association" and therefore not subject to Fifteenth Amendment rules. His successful lawsuit marked the end of the "white primary" in every Southern state, including in Mississippi.

Two years later, Mississippi's Democratic-controlled legislature made a careless error; passing a law exempting soldiers returning from the war from paying the poll tax, perhaps forgetting about the tens of thousands of Black men from the state who had enlisted. That meant some eighty thousand Black veterans had, in theory, become eligible to register and vote. And Medgar and Charles were two of them. The brothers, who both revered Thurgood Marshall, were determined to test the rules. They gathered a group of fellow Black veterans and decided to become the first Blacks from Decatur to register and vote in the July 1946 Democratic primary, in which the flamboyantly racist demagogue Theodore G. Bilbo was seeking a third term in the U.S. Senate.

Bilbo was in many ways the ultimate Mississippi caricature. He was a career politician, standing no more than five feet two but with the persona of a plantation boss. And he dressed the part: "business suit, metal-rim eyeglasses, big white hat, [and a] diamond stickpin in his necktie,"[35] as Charles described him. Bilbo was elected to the Senate in 1934 following a stint in the Mississippi legislature and two terms as governor. He made a name for himself with his raucous, triumphantly racist stump speeches.

"He called his opponents 'liars,' 'hypocrites,' and 'buzzards on a fence, waiting for the good white folk of Mississippi to let down their guard,'"[36] Charles wrote. "Then Bilbo would warm to his favorite subject: The Nigger. He'd start shouting about how he was going to preserve racial purity by 'sending the niggers back to Africa" and claim "Negroes meant to mongrelize the white race." [37] It was the straightest ticket to victory in Southern politics. Never mind that Bilbo also boasted about the "Negro woman down in Poplarville who bore him Negro kids,"[38] or that he quietly donated to Alcorn A&M college and to funds for "Negro schools."[39] Politics in the South, and especially in Mississippi, hinged on white Democrats' proficiency at publicly and elaborately demonizing Blacks, vowing with all the earnestness they could display that they would save the good white Christian men, women, and children of the South from their sullying, dusky influence.

As teenagers, Medgar and Charles sometimes went to Bilbo's speeches when he came to town, just for the sheer entertainment value. They were often the only Black faces there. Charles wrote that during the 1934 race, as they sat on the front steps of the Newton County courthouse, Bilbo even pointed them out, telling the hooting audience of white "peckerwood" farmers, "If we fail to hold high the wall of separation between the races, we will live to see the day when those two nigger boys right there will be asking for everything that is ours by right. You see those two little niggers sitting down here? If you don't keep them in their place, then someday they'll be in Washington trying to represent you."[40]

Charles wrote that Medgar nudged him and whispered, "Ain't a bad idea."[41]

At a rally on May 9, 1946, in Pontotoc, Mississippi, Bilbo raged that one of his opponents, a ten-term congressman named Ross Collins, "is expecting a lot of niggers to vote in this election, and they're registering all over the state or in the city." Winding himself up on the stump, Bilbo railed that "the niggers are having meetings all over the state and they've got delegates in every congressional district ready to vote. . . . And then, the other day, the Negro Council in Chicago sent a telegram to Harry Truman, the President, saying to send the Army down to Mississippi and to see to it that these 100,000 niggers are gonna vote. You see, the GI boys don't have to pay any taxes, that's their basic right you know and there's 100,000 white people and about 70 or 60,000 Negroes in Mississippi. Mighty sure that Ross is figuring on getting that nigger vote."

Then in June, he delivered a stemwinder in the town of Starkville, in which he declared that white people would be justified in going to any extreme to keep Blacks from voting, even offering free legal counsel to any white citizen who "took the situation into their own hands" by committing murder to keep Blacks from the polls. He also said he was certain no white Mississippi jury would indict, nor would a trial jury convict, a white person who "committed violence on Negroes."[42] Bilbo ended the speech with a menacing flourish: "The best way to keep a nigger away from a white primary in Mississippi," he said, "is to see him the night before."[43]

On July 2, Primary Day (and Medgar's twenty-first birthday), the *Clarion-Ledger*, owned by brothers Thomas and Robert Hederman, both ardent white supremacists, ran a headline forecasting fair weather for the vote and pointing to Bilbo's warnings of "racial trouble" to come. "A late development, which is seen as a threat to Bilbo's strength," the paper wrote, "is the steady stream of World War II veterans to the registration desks all over the state. The veteran vote is expected to be mainly against Bilbo."[44]

Bilbo faced not just Collins, but Tom Q. Ellis, who was vowing to stand for a "white man's South" and two other candidates, a war veteran named Levings and Frank Harper, who accused Bilbo of financial wrongdoing and claimed to "have the goods on him." The *Clarion-Ledger* summarized Bilbo's platform: "It is true I'm a little colorblind in Washington, but I cuss the nigger vociferously in election years in Mississippi and [popular national syndicated columnist and radio announcer] Walter Winchell [who was Jewish] cusses me all the time. What other qualifications in a senator do the people of this state want?"[45] The paper also reported that U.S. Attorney General Tom Clark said he intended to put the full power of the Justice Department behind the U.S. attorney in Mississippi's announcement that all qualified Negro voters be allowed to register and vote in the state primary.

With that in mind, Medgar and Charles walked with four other veterans to the Newton County Courthouse, where they asked to be registered. Decatur had some nine hundred registered white voters, but not a single Black voter on the books. Local whites in the small town seemed determined to keep it that way—and to take Bilbo's advice to heart. When word got out about the Everses' plans, a man named Alton Graham, a white clerk who knew the brothers' family, showed up to warn James Evers that his sons had better stand down if they didn't want any trouble.[46]

When the six Black veterans arrived at the courthouse, a group of about twenty white men, armed with shotguns and pistols, were waiting for them. They blocked the door; screaming and hissing at the "niggers" to go home. Medgar and Charles recognized faces in that crowd, including some that on any other occasion might even be friendly. They also recognized Alton Graham, but Medgar and Charles were armed, too. The escalating tension frightened the small, elderly registrar, a man named Mr. Brand. He pleaded with the group to leave it alone, and that in time, things would change. Brand knew he couldn't legally prevent the six men from registering, but he feared bloodshed could occur on the courthouse steps that day. But the men would not be deterred. They declared that having fought for this country, they had a right to register, and they intended to do so. After a tense standoff, Mr. Brand walked the six men into the courthouse and to a private room where he registered them.[47] This victorious act of bravery was the beginning of the fight, but not the end.

Between registration day and Election Day, Graham and other Whites, who the Everses derided as "Kluxers"—that is, the Ku Klux Klan—visited the Evers house and warned James that his sons were asking for trouble. "The word was always the same," Medgar later recalled, "'Don't show up at the courthouse [on] voting day.'"[48] Charles said that even some local Negroes begged them to stand down, lest they unleash hell on every Black family in Decatur. "Take your names off the books before some other Negro gets hurt," they would say.[49] But Medgar and Charles had it in their heads that they would not just register, they would vote.

On Election Day, November 3, Medgar, Charles, and four of their old friends from the neighborhood—A. J. and C. B. Needham, Bernon Wesley, and a fourth man Charles recalled only as Hudson—walked back to the courthouse to cast their ballots. This time, the angry crowd that met them numbered more than two hundred, all conspicuously armed. Medgar and Charles, ever their father's sons, were armed as well, with pistols and Charles's switchblade; and they moved their jackets aside to make that known.[50] The threat of bloodshed was dire, but the county sheriff made it clear that he had no intention of intervening to assist the Black men. The threat of riot and massacre was heavy in the air. At one point, the men split up into three groups to try to outflank the mob and get inside the building. This time, their efforts wouldn't end in a quiet room with Mr. Brand. Though they managed to get inside, the would-be Black voters quickly realized the ballot box had been placed behind a locked door.[51]

Charles later recounted their interactions with a white man named Andy May, whose family drugstore the Evers family had frequented. Far from a friendly ally, May patted the pistol in his pocket and blurted, "Listen nigger, ain't nothing happened to you yet," to which Charles responded by showing his switchblade and telling May that nothing was going to happen to them, if May knew what was good for him.[52]

In the end, Medgar convinced his brother and his friends to stand down and fight another day. "We'll get them next time," he said. Medgar had likely saved his brother's life, because Charles had been itching for a fight. As they left, a white man screamed at them: "You damn Evers niggers gonna get all the niggers in Decatur killed."[53] Some of the men threatened to follow the men home or to come for them later. Charles and Medgar threatened right back, channeling their father's bravado.

"I had been on Omaha Beach," Medgar told reporters years later. "All we wanted was to be ordinary citizens. We fought during the war for America—and Mississippi was included. Now after the Germans and the Japanese hadn't killed us, it looked as though the white Mississippians would."[54] Medgar and Charles sat up all that night with their shotguns ready, but none of the cowards ever came.[55] There would be no hanged men named Evers that night.

When his sons came to the house in Decatur to visit days later, James Evers neither praised nor admonished them. But it was clear to Medgar and Charles that they had made him proud.

Despite the setback for the Evers men, about 1,500 Black Mississippians voted in the 1946 primary; the first time Blacks had ever voted in a Mississippi Democratic primary. Though they represented just

1 percent of the vote and were a fraction of the half million eligible Black voters in the state, it was a historic moment in the state. The *Jackson Advocate*, a prominent Black newspaper since its founding in 1938, ran an above-the-fold headline on July 6, announcing in all capital letters: "MISSISSIPPIANS VOTE—BILBO THREATS: No Incidences of Violence Reported."

Bilbo had defeated his primary opponents handily, assuring him a third term. But there would be a cost. He had become a media spectacle even outside his state, and the emblem of what Mississippi stood for, as far as the national press was concerned. His outright calls to racial violence to keep Black votes suppressed were an embarrassment to the national party—which, after all, was the party of FDR and Harry Truman, who was pushing to desegregate the U.S. armed forces (which he would begin in earnest with an executive order in 1948, though it was not fully accomplished until the Korean War two years later). FDR's New Deal contained concessions to the Dixiecrats that limited the benefits Black Americans could receive and specifically excluded farm workers from protection; even so, it had provided crucial, federally funded employment for millions of Blacks during the Great Depression, which had hit those just a generation out of slavery harder than most white Americans. And with the ongoing advocacy of his first lady, Eleanor Roosevelt, and the relative openness of the succeeding Truman administration, the Democratic Party for the first time in its history was competitive among Black voters outside the South. To *that* Democratic Party, Senator Bilbo was a liability.

Even before the election, in May 1946, a special campaign expenditures committee, empaneled to investigate election practices in U.S. Senate races, received a petition from a group of Black Mississippians, accusing Bilbo of running "an aggressive and ruthless campaign" to "effectively deprive and deny the duly qualified Negro electors . . . of their constitutional rights . . . to register and vote." The petitioners accused Bilbo of operating a "reign of terror" against Black would-be voters, and they named him as a member of the Ku Klux Klan. The petitioners called on the Senate to void Bilbo's election by refusing to seat him for a third term.

The committee sent investigators to hold public hearings in Jackson that summer; despite warnings from the National Negro Council president and from Republican senator Robert Taft of Ohio that "Negro witnesses who told the truth in Hattiesburg or Grenada would not live to return home from the courthouse."[56] A December 16 report in *Time* described a raucous atmosphere at the federal courthouse in Jackson, in which white spectators laughed and cheered on the senator, who was present despite being ill, with shouts of "Tell 'em, Bilbo!" as ninety-six witnesses recounted stories of "violence, jailing, bribery or 'friendly advice' from white folks," to scare them away from the polls. From the *Time* report:

> An early witness, a Negro veteran, said that white men had whipped him with a piece of cable after he had tried to register for Mississippi's white primary and had then given him a ride back to town. (This brought guffaws from the spectators.) Then a shoe repairman and a taxi driver admitted that they had each received $25 for warning fellow Negroes away from the polls. A white Catholic priest, who had asked polling officials why his parishioners were not allowed to vote, had received the answer: "No Negroes are going to vote in Pass Christian [Miss.] unless they paint their faces white."[57]

The *Time* report, which went out of its way to dismiss the accusations against Mississippi's senior senator as "silly," said that none of the testimony connected Bilbo himself to the violence with one exception: his now-infamous line from his July speech about "visiting niggers" the night before a vote.

Ultimately, the Senate committee dismissed accusations of campaign interference against Bilbo as nothing but over-the-top rhetoric from a politician concerned about the interference of "outside agitators" in his state, including the press. A second committee simultaneously investigating Bilbo was prepared to act on allegations that he had used his office for financial gain, including taking illegal gifts such as "a new Cadillac, a swimming pool, excavation of a lake to create an island for his home, construction of a private roadway, painting of his 'Dream House No. 1,' and furnishings for his 'Dream House No. 2.'" This second committee produced a scathing December report, just in time for the Eightieth Congress, controlled by Republicans for the first time since 1933, to act.

Before they could do so, the boisterous segregationist was silenced by fate. He withdrew from the Senate to be treated for cancer of the mouth, which he succumbed to that August. Bilbo was not the last Southern white supremacist "dead ender" to make a name for himself standing in the way of Black Americans' right to the franchise. Over time, he would be largely forgotten by history.

Meanwhile, the Evers brothers had officially become what segregationists of the time called "agitators." More positively, their efforts caught the attention of the national NAACP and of a prominent and ostentatiously wealthy Black Mississippi activist and physician named Dr. Theodore Roosevelt Mason (or T. R. M.) Howard. Medgar nurtured this connection until the day he died.

With that fight temporarily behind them, Medgar prepared to take advantage of the G.I. Bill and go to college. To complete his high school degree, he enrolled at the Alcorn College Laboratory School.[58] With the strictly segregated University of Mississippi (known in the state as "Ole Miss") off-limits to Black students, Medgar joined his big brother again, enrolling at all-Black Alcorn Agricultural and Mechanical College. They both played football, but it was Medgar who excelled as a half back, making all-conference (though white schools refused to play against the Alcorn Braves).[59] He quickly became a big man on campus—majoring in business administration, running track, joining the debate team, and becoming the editor of the school newspaper. He even sang in the glee club.

Of the two brothers, Charles was the hustler, constantly starting small enterprises, selling everything from peanuts to bootleg whiskey, and hassling Medgar to get in on the action. Medgar's head stayed in his books. He was constantly reading—everything from philosophy to history—and he cut an impressive figure that got him noticed not just by the NAACP but also by the Alcorn administration. He was committed to sticking to his plan to go to law school, and he had Ole Miss in mind, though he knew it would be a fight.

In 1950, Medgar was twenty-five years old and starting his junior year at Alcorn when his life plan received a significant adjustment. On the first day of classes, a demure, pretty freshman from Vicksburg, Mississippi, named Myrlie Beasley appeared before him.

CHAPTER 2

Medgar and Myrlie

Love does not begin and end the way we seem to think it does.
Love is a battle; love is a war; love is a growing up.

—James Baldwin

"You shouldn't lean on that electric pole. You may get shocked," said the tall, slim, handsome Black man with a thin mustache (and far too much confidence).

Myrlie Louise Beasley knew he dropped that line to make her smile. Like the good girl she was raised to be, she didn't give him what he wanted—at least not on the outside.

Instead, she raised one eyebrow, put on her haughtiest look, and tossed her long, pressed hair so it landed provocatively on one shoulder, as she'd seen Veronica Lake do in the movies. Then she turned her face away from his.

"Oh, I'm not worried," she said, with all the nonchalance she could muster. By the time she'd gotten through this routine, her would-be savior had trotted back to his team.[1]

This was Myrlie's first day as a freshman at Alcorn Agricultural and Mechanical College, in Lorman, Mississippi. "We freshman were gathered around what we call 'the bunk,'" she said. "They had sandwiches and hamburgers and Coca-Colas, et cetera. The football players were there, and we mostly very shy girls were gathered around this hamburger bin, and the football team came in, fully dressed" in their uniforms. "You could hear them running. It sounded like a beast running toward our little group."[2]

The Alcorn Braves players spent the first day sizing up the new freshmen, to see which girls were dating material. Myrlie was just seventeen years old, and she'd been raised by a family of women with certain standards, and this was a ritual she could do without.

"They came in fully in 'herd' and casually looked us over, as though we were something there to be sold, or to be chosen per their likings. And, very calmly, coolly, Medgar came over and said hello to me," before dropping his helpful warning.

Myrlie was raised by her grandmother and her aunt, and they had told her to stay away from those upper-class boys, particularly the ones who were war veterans. They were too brash and confident, being freshly home from Europe. Mama, as Myrlie called Annie McCain Beasley, her grandmother, and Aunt Myrlie, for whom she was named, had big plans for the girl they called "Baby Sister." From the time Myrlie was a child, taking her first piano lessons in Vicksburg, they told her she would be good enough one day to play Carnegie Hall in New York City. But first, she had to get her college degree in education. Mama and Aunt Myrlie were educators. Myrlie intended to minor in music.

She did not want to disappoint these women, but this brash football player intrigued her. She asked around about him. Initially, she thought his name was Medgar Evans. They made eye contact in the dining room, and he somehow would find himself walking by the piano room while she was practicing. It was pure chemistry. She soon learned his name properly, and that he was president of the junior class—and popular with the women on campus. None of that was good news to Myrlie.

One day Medgar strode up to her while she was having lunch with her friends and asked, "Would you like to come and sit with me over there?" He pointed to a bench near an old campus oak tree, and her heart seemed to stop. "One of my friends kicked me under the table," she later wrote. "And I managed to squeak out a barely audible: 'okay.'"[3]

Medgar told her about his time in the war, and Myrlie discovered he was more than just an arrogant footballer with an eye for pretty girls. She was particularly struck by his vocabulary: he didn't talk like the boys she'd grown up with in Vicksburg. He was deeper and more thoughtful. He had a mission beyond getting his degree, making some money, and getting by.

"I certainly was intrigued by his intelligence, by his poise, by his directness," she said. "Imagine a 17-year-old leaving home for the first time, and within an hour you have this encounter with that man? And I never forgot him. He stayed on my mind from that moment on. Who knows? It was destiny."

Myrlie was smitten. "He talked about current events. He talked about the future. I was accustomed to high school boys who talked about romance and all of that kind of stuff. But Medgar was subtle in his approach." He later told her, "I saw something in you the first time I saw you, and I decided to pursue it." "That's how we got started," she said.

Myrlie didn't dare tell Mama.

WHEN MYRLIE WAS JUST A FEW WEEKS OLD, SHE FELL INTO THE care of her grandmother, Mrs. Beasley, whom she simply called "Mama." Months after Myrlie was born, Mama had marched across the street to where her daughter-in-law, Mildred Washington Beasley, was staying and said she was taking Myrlie home with her. Mildred was just sixteen years old and had dropped out of high school. Mama's son, James Van Dyke Beasley, who folks called Jim, had married Mildred at his mother's insistence, to keep baby Myrlie from being illegitimate. Jim, a World War II veteran, had a room at Mama's house, but he mostly stayed in the streets when he wasn't at work or gambling and carousing with women.

Mama Beasley was a force in Vicksburg—a pillar of the Black community and the unofficial dean of Magnolia Street, where they lived. She believed that just because the people of Black Vicksburg weren't well off didn't mean they shouldn't be surrounded by beauty. Her small, white-painted modest house was what could be afforded on a Negro teacher's salary. It lacked indoor plumbing, but the outhouse had four pots, which made Myrlie as a child think they must have been rich. The house was surrounded by fruit trees, including a fig tree, Myrlie's favorite. It also had a front lawn, which was rare in the Negro section. Mama mowed the grass, so it had a beautiful cascade of lines. And you'd better not walk on it. Other families with grass lawns mowed their shapes, too, and the competition played out at Sunday services, or when the pastor came to visit.

Mama's grandparents on both sides had been enslaved women and the white planters who owned them. She was quite fair skinned and prim; stern, with her long, blondish hair always pulled back in a tight bun. She had two years of college at Hampton Institute and had been divorced twice. She brooked no nonsense. Her first husband, Jim's father, abandoned the family. Her second husband was sent packing.

The Black community revolved around its churches. Mama was a Mother of hers, and that, along with being a retired educator, placed her in high standing. Myrlie recalled growing up in a very religious community. "You went to church all day on Sundays," she said. "Mondays you missed. But Tuesday and Wednesday, Thursday and Friday there was something always going on at church, which I had to attend." A Black girl's social life in Vicksburg consisted of young people's meetings, Bible study, and choir practice, along with homework, chores, and for Myrlie voice and piano lessons. Mama wanted her to be refined, regardless of their economic station. She corrected Myrlie's diction and insisted that she be polite, direct, and chaste.

Besides Jim, Mama also had a daughter, Myrlie Louise, who was twenty-six years old when she brought Myrlie home. Because they shared a name, and had such a wide age gap, the two Myrlies became known to the family as Aunt Myrlie and Baby Sister. Aunt Myrlie was a teacher just like Mama, and she was young Myrlie's first piano instructor. She acted as a sort of second mother to Myrlie, while Mildred, who Myrlie called "M'dear," was more like a sister who lived in a separate house, and whom she saw only from time to time.

Myrlie knew that whatever Mama's house lacked in resources, the love made up for it. "I'm an only child," she recalled. "People say, 'Oh, you were spoiled.' No way. They demanded so much from me until occasionally as a young child I thought I was in prison. There were strict rules but an awful lot of love. High expectations of me in every area I could think of: music, piano, voice, always reciting some poem or reading something before a group of people. . . . But along with that, there was a mountain of love, and I knew that, so I didn't resist." And whatever the task, "they always told me, 'Baby Sister, you can do it. You can do it.' I remember that so well."

Until Myrlie was five years old, someone other than Ms. Beasley had been called "Mama." This was Ms. Beasley's grandmother, Martha Hoover, who was born enslaved in Carroll, Mississippi, around 1847. She completed the village of women who raised Myrlie in Vicksburg on Magnolia Street. Myrlie recalled curling up with her as she sat in her favorite rocking chair, making the seat rock slowly. She was legally blind but sharp as a tack. If little Myrlie ever got into trouble, Mama Hoover snuggled her close and told her granddaughter, "You're not beating this child today." She was Myrlie's protector, and her large, warm lap was a place of refuge.

When Martha Hoover passed, Ms. Beasley inherited the status of "Mama," a title that dates back to the frightful and fleeting family bonds of enslaved Africans in America during slavery—bonds that could be broken at the whim of a so-called master,[4] or when their debts prompted them to sell away the people they owned (some of whom were their own children).

Medgar may have learned to fight the Mississippi system at every turn, but Myrlie was taught to withstand it.

"Was I conscious of the racism and terror?" she recalled. "I was born in Vicksburg, Mississippi, in 1933. That was one of the most hateful parts of the state. I grew up in it. My little friends and I learned how to slip by it, crawl over it, dig under it, and we learned how to survive."

Vicksburg, like every town in Mississippi and throughout the South, was strictly segregated. Even white children knew what liberties they were allowed to take. "Almost every afternoon there was a fight between the Blacks and the Whites. . . . we small group of kids . . . came together and mapped out a war map . . . which way to go home, which way to avoid another racist group, how to stack rocks behind certain hidden places. We learned how to trip those who were trying to harm us in an alleyway and pelt them with those big rocks. It's a thing called 'survival.' I don't think that those who grew up with me . . . in that neighborhood would be surprised at anything that happened. We'd always be prepared for the surprise attack. We were just wondering when it would come along.

"We had signals," she continued. "We had certain ways that we walked home from school. We had groups of [Black] boys who broke off from us and stationed themselves somewhere along the route. We had certain whistles or songs that we sang that [the Black boys] could hear, and they knew exactly what those songs meant" so they could "suddenly come out of the bushes and be there to protect us."

Myrlie was a skinny kid who was timid and didn't fight unless she had to. When her father, Jim, did come around, he prodded his daughter to get tougher. "I would run from a fight, unless my dad was around," she said. He would tell me 'turn around. You go back out there and fight.' I would cry . . . but as he said that he would always unbuckle his belt and take it off. He said, 'fight or the belt.' I'll never forget that. Always ran back outside and fought, but that was the only way that I would do it."

James Van Dyke Beasley also fought in the war but, unlike Medgar, he came home despondent. "My father served in India," Myrlie said. "And I heard some of the stories he told, and it would turn my stomach. Medgar told some" of those stories, too, but "he would stop, and excuse himself from the room, because he was too choked up to talk, and tears ran down his cheeks."

Myrlie recalled the cries . . . not in the terms of tears, but cries of a broken heart, that the war produced in these men. "They served in other parts of the world, on behalf of America, but were treated like they were nothing, laughed at, all because of the color of their skin. Their bodies bled red blood, just like the others. Medgar's service in the Army was one of the driving forces that compelled him to do something about prejudice and racism in the country where he was born, in the country he served that treated him just one step above slavery."

MEDGAR AND MYRLIE TALKED ABOUT OTHER THINGS BESIDES THE wars at home and abroad. They both loved music, and Medgar was an excellent dancer. It was the era of Nat King Cole, Fats Domino, Chuck Berry, Ella Fitzgerald, and Sarah Vaughn. Medgar was also fond of provocation. He seemed to get a kick out of challenging Myrlie, frequently leaving her both annoyed and enraged. He surprised her one day, when out of the blue he said, "You're going to be the mother of my children." When she objected, considering they had never even kissed, his reply was equally blunt: "I'm going to shape you into the woman I want you to be."[5]

Myrlie was properly confused. Some days she wasn't sure this man really liked her "in that way" at all. "I was accustomed to the young boys who were always flirting," she said, "and he didn't." Her annoyance made her more intrigued, and she demanded to know: when was he going to tell her he loved her? He promised to let her know when he did.

Sometimes Myrlie felt that Medgar spent too much time challenging her and not nearly enough on wooing her. If she said it was a good day, he asked her why. If she told him they should turn right, he insisted on going left. He engaged her in political discussions so frequently that she found herself cramming through current magazines before meeting up with him. "He was testing me . . . which he later admitted, to see how intelligent I was," she said. "He was trying me, in terms of his discussions about worldwide areas of interest. I did a lot of research on my own because I wanted to talk about world events with him. And we became good companions just doing that. And one thing led to another."

Medgar and Myrlie would sit for hours, talking about the Mau Mau revolutionaries in Kenya, or about civil rights in Mississippi. He was "pro-Black" before there was such a term. In many respects he was radical. He challenged Myrlie about straightening her hair; something she pointedly refused to give up. Even though he sometimes enraged her, she loved that he loved his people and wanted more for them.

"He talked about how much he loved his country," she said. "And he questioned how much his country loved and respected him. Medgar was speaking for all of those people serving in the Army, the Navy, the Marines, whose skin color was the same as his, saying 'I'm here, willing to give my life for my country, yet my country doesn't love me enough to keep me from living a segregated life. Yet here I am, still here.'" To Myrlie, he seemed exceptionally focused and motivated. "He said, 'I served my country, I put my life on the line. . . . This is what I see is wrong with my country: the prejudice and the racism. I'm a citizen, and I'm going to do everything I can to change that.'"

Myrlie was fascinated and smitten. Medgar knew she was still seventeen, and there were lines he had no intention of crossing. "He didn't try to make passes at me," she said. "I was accustomed to teenage boys who had on their agenda, passes. Putting it nicely. As a teenager, I was accustomed to, 'oh, baby, you send me,'" and to rejecting them outright. Medgar "had none of that in his approach."

That changed, just a little, one day in the Alcorn piano room. Myrlie was practicing the classical music Medgar claimed he liked as much as rhythm and blues, though she was certain he was just saying that to charm her. She was well through her piece and trying to concentrate as he stood just behind and to the right of the bench, watching her play, when he gently tilted her head back and kissed her lips. But Medgar being Medgar, he pressed the back of his hand to his mouth and showed her the red markings left behind.

"You wear too much lipstick," he said flatly.

It was another challenge. Myrlie, freed from her grandmother and aunt, and their churchy ways, had begun sporting a bright red lip color. After that day, she went back to the paler shades. She wanted him to kiss her again.

By now, Medgar and Myrlie were officially an item, and she wanted the other women on campus to know it. She was afraid to tell Mama and Aunt Myrlie that she was doing exactly what they warned her not to: falling for an upperclassman and a veteran. When she finally built up the courage to tell them she was dating someone, she did so with double news. She and Medgar had decided to take summer jobs in Chicago, where he had family. She had gotten a job at an automobile sales and service company, and she would stay with her mom's half sister, Aunt Frances.[6] Medgar would stay elsewhere, of course. When she dropped the bombshells back home in Vicksburg, Mama and Aunt Myrlie were not pleased. They told her that a twenty-six-year-old man was entirely too old for her. His voting rights and civil rights involvement made them nervous. He was the kind of man who attracted too much attention, including from the Klan.

Medgar needed to meet the women who could stand between him and Myrlie. When he did, the ice began to thaw. "He was a gentleman," Myrlie said. "He could hold a conversation" with the two well-heeled educators. "They really liked that, and they appreciated it. Medgar knew exactly what he was doing. If he zeroed in on something, he was very strategic in his planning, and I think that's what happened" with Myrlie's family.

The Chicago trip was approved, though Mama insisted on accompanying Myrlie to make sure she was properly situated with Aunt Frances and safely separated from her eight-years-older boyfriend. Myrlie relished getting out of Mississippi and spending time alone with Medgar. "We argued like crazy," she said, and later recounted one dustup during a day trip to Lake Michigan, when he failed to warn her about the end of a sandbar in the lake where they were swimming. She found herself plunging below the surface. She was never in any danger, but she didn't appreciate the impromptu swimming trial. She didn't speak to him during the long drive home, nor did she appreciate how tickled he was by her momentary dive, which ruined her pressed hair.

The Chicago trip solidified for Medgar that Myrlie was it, despite their tendency to disagree. Myrlie decided to have it out. She pushed him to exasperation. "He said I was too young for him. I told him a few things about himself." He wound up telling her he liked the fire that burned in her, and that she didn't fall all over herself about him, as other women had done.

"The argument ended with him grabbing me and telling me how much he loved me, kissing me passionately, and telling me he wanted to make a life with me. I cried. I said, 'Yes, because I love you too.'"

Myrlie finally had the Veronica Lake moment of her dreams, but there was still a task at hand.

"I said, 'You have to go through my grandmother and my aunt. I can't talk about [marriage] without you talking to them." He promised to do so, 'as soon I can. As soon we can make that appointment to see them, that's it.'"

Even with this change in their relationship, Medgar continued to be a gentleman. "Whatever sexual inclinations he had, he kept them within bounds," she said. "And I found that so stimulating. My goodness, when he finally, finally did reach out to hold me and to kiss me, I nearly passed out. I was ready to push him away. . . . I was like, "Oh, no, no, no . . . And that was the beginning of the romantic part of our relationship because I found that I could trust him. I could listen to Medgar. I could learn from him. I could walk with him to those goals that he talked about. . . . I grew so much. I matured so much just knowing him as a friend—and then knowing him as someone I looked at on a romantic basis. I truly looked at him as someone who would be an excellent husband and father for my children, whenever I got to that point.

"He saw me as very young, someone he could teach, and have as a partner in his life's work. Medgar was . . . older than I, had served in the Army, had worlds of experience, and he knew what he had: someone he could shape."

Myrlie had no intention of being a quiet pupil. That time when he said he intended to shape her into the woman he wanted her to be, she shot back: "Well, you have a job on your hands, baby."

He also had a job convincing Mama and Aunt Myrlie about that wedding.

As the couple returned to Mississippi, the mission to gain the mothers' approval was on in earnest. "After making many moves to get my grandmother and my aunt to consider the possibility of his proposal to me, Medgar was being turned down flat." Their answer was blunt: 'Our child is too young to think about marriage. She is planning on a career, and you are too old for her. Goodbye.' Bless his heart, he never gave up."

Medgar went to Vicksburg several times, not to see Myrlie, but to court Mama and Aunt Myrlie. "They [just] thought I was too young to even think about love." For a time, Myrlie felt caught between the man she loved and these women who so deeply loved her. But slowly but surely, things changed. "Some way or the other, he persuaded them that he was right for me. I don't know what he said, I don't know what he did, but they gradually let him in the door . . . though always with strict rules and regulations to follow."

The one person who did seem to understand was M'dear—her mother Mildred—who enthusiastically supported the idea of Medgar and Myrlie getting married. When Myrlie described how Medgar made her "quiver," M'dear laughed knowingly and asked her daughter the only questions that mattered: "Do you love him?" And "Do you think he loves you?" Myrlie's tears were the only answer she needed. Mildred knew what Mama and Aunt Myrlie thought: they had once thought the same of her and Jim. She also knew that the heart does not suggest. It demands. M'dear understood that they wanted Myrlie to finish school, but in her mind, if Myrlie had something good she should hang on tight.

Myrlie later realized how right M'dear had been—long after she was gone, Myrlie would recall that "for all that Mama and Aunt Myrlie mean to me, the older I became, the more I realized that it was my mother who truly understood me. My grandmother and aunt gave me so much of what I needed in the world, but M'dear gave me so much of what I needed in my heart."[7]

Medgar and Myrlie spent the last weeks of the summer mostly apart, but Medgar did not stop traveling to Vicksburg. "I think he courted my family more than he did me," she said. In the end, his persistence paid off. "There was something about him they liked," Myrlie said. "They had a great deal of respect for him because he had so much respect for *them*. The one thing that was [still] a problem was that Medgar was a Civil Rights activist, even though he was in college. That frightened my grandmother and my aunt because they were schoolteachers and [knew that] anyone who talked about Civil Rights was [treated as] a threat."

Teachers had lost jobs just for speaking out about voting or for trying to register. Her grandmother and aunt were concerned about Myrlie being seen with a man like Medgar in a state like Mississippi. "Finally, they overcame that, and they saw the good parts of this man, and they told me, 'You're [still] too young to know what love is, but if you insist, we will give you two a wedding.' And that was it. In the end, they loved him. I sometimes accused them of loving him more than they did me."

Medgar and Myrlie were married on Christmas Eve, 1951. Jim didn't show. Charles stayed away as well. Myrlie was the first person to come between him and his brother. Medgar had chosen Myrlie, and love—which Charles didn't exactly believe in—over the plans the two of them had made together since childhood in Decatur.[8] He wasn't ready to handle that.

During the ceremony, Mama stood smiling as Myrlie walked down the aisle, and she joined her granddaughter at the alter when the preacher asked, "Who giveth away this woman?"

"I do," a proud Ms. Beasley said.

"Newlyweds on college campus are always being asked . . . how is it being married?" Myrlie recalled. "Tell us all the details, please!" She had no interest in sharing. She was a married woman, all of eighteen years old, but she and Medgar were also still college students, sharing an apartment with another couple. Being a wife in the 1950s meant doing more than just your homework. Myrlie typed her husband's homework and was responsible for cooking—and sometimes burning—dinner for two.[9]

As an only child, Myrlie "was accustomed to doing my thing, not checking with someone else," other than Mama and Aunt Myrlie, in their world of women. Medgar was also eight years older and far more worldly than his wife. "After a few arguments, we decided we'd make it work," she said. "Medgar was a very good student. I was a good student, [though] I had to study and study hard. We kept our grades up," she said.[10] Still, Myrlie couldn't wait to leave Alcorn, even though she wanted to complete her degree. As she saw it, she could finally have Medgar to herself.

When Medgar graduated in 1952, Myrlie had completed two years. She hoped they would settle in Chicago, or maybe even New York City—someplace new, and free of Southern white tyranny, and where she could return to school. Medgar objected. He was determined to stay in Mississippi; to make it a place where his wife would *want* to raise their Black children safely and free from the fear of Klan violence. Myrlie knew that Mississippi needed to change, but she was no activist. She was content with just being his wife. Medgar repeatedly told her: "You have so much more than that to give."

When Medgar told her he had accepted a job in Mound Bayou, Mississippi, deep in the Mississippi Delta, Myrlie was disconcerted. He had been offered a position with Magnolia Mutual Life Insurance. The company was owned by Dr. T. R. M. Howard, likely the wealthiest Black man in the state. Howard was so erudite and aggressive in promoting opportunity for the formerly enslaved and their descendants that he attracted attention and respect, even from Mississippi whites.

All Myrlie heard was that Mound Bayou was in "the middle of nowhere, down in the Delta." It was the oldest Black-founded town in the nation, created in 1887 by Isaiah T. Montgomery and his cousin, Benjamin T. Green, two former enslaved men. They were members of a group of enslaved Blacks who first took over the plantation owned by Confederate president Jefferson Davis's elder brother Joseph, when the planter and his family fled as Union troops closed in. That group was led by Montgomery's father, Ben.

Ben was a gifted mechanic, inventor, and office clerk who had kept Joseph Davis's books, run his shipping operation, and even saved up enough money from Davis's rental of his labor, from which Davis gave him a small stipend, to open a general store on the relatively liberal plantation. Joseph Davis styled himself a more evolved brand of slaveholder, who encouraged some of his bondsmen to read. He relied on their help, principally Ben's, to run his plantation, and he had agreed after the war to sell the land to his former servant for three hundred thousand dollars plus interest. Montgomery intended to use the land to build a community for the formerly enslaved. The little makeshift town, which they called Davis Bend, thrived for a time, with Montgomery appointed by the Reconstruction military government as its justice of the peace—making him the first Black person to hold public office in Mississippi.[11] The project eventually foundered in the wake of constant flooding and natural disasters, and when Jefferson Davis returned from exile after the war, he used the courts to reclaim his brother's property and wrest the land from the freedmen.

Ben Montgomery died soon after, so it was his son, Isaiah, who would achieve the dreams of his father. Isaiah Montgomery and Green ventured deep into the Delta looking for land to start again and found 840 acres of uninhabited swampland between Memphis and Vicksburg. They and the other former residents of Davis Bend undertook the laborious process of draining the swamps and cultivating the land. When it was complete, they had created Mound Bayou, a refuge for newly freed Black men, women, and children. They planted high-grade Delta cotton and built their own mill. Mound Bayou soon became the place where even white Southern planters preferred to mill their crop because, according to town historians, if they got the Mound Bayou label, they got the highest price.

President Theodore Roosevelt arrived in Mound Bayou in 1907, invited by the town's mayor, and declared the all-Negro town to be "the jewel of the Delta."[12] It had large homes, picket fences, Negro-run banks and, as Roosevelt pointedly noted, "not even one saloon." Alongside Oklahoma's Greenwood district, nicknamed Black Wall Street, and towns like Jackson Ward in Richmond, Virginia, Sweet Auburn in Atlanta, and Rosewood in Florida, Mound Bayou became an example of what formerly enslaved Black Americans could create and become. Booker T. Washington hailed Mount Bayou as a symbol of Negro promise despite segregation. In short, it was the dream.

Dr. Howard hoped to further that dream, and to take advantage of what Mound Bayou could be to better the lives of Blacks across the Delta.

Theodore Roosevelt Mason Howard was born in Murray, Kentucky, in 1908. His father, Arthur, labored as a tobacco "twister,"[13] but T.R.M. caught the attention of the white doctor who had delivered him, and who employed Howard's mother as a domestic. That man, a Seventh-Day Adventist named Dr. Will Mason, mentored Howard and gave him a job at the hospital at age fifteen. He nurtured the young man's ambitions by recommending and financially supporting him at three different Adventist colleges: the all-Black Oakwood University in Huntsville, Alabama; Union College in Lincoln, Nebraska, where Howard was the lone Black student; and the College of Medical Evangelists in Loma Linda, California. By then, he had added Mason's surname to his own as an honorific.[14]

In California, Howard stood out as an activist: a champion of Prohibition who won the American Anti-Saloon's League's 1930 national oratorical contest, the writer of a regular column called "Our Fight" for the *California Eagle* Black newspaper in Loma Linda, and a fierce advocate against segregation. He was an eager advocate of "Negro self-help," in terms of both health and prosperity. He even worked on the political campaigns of radio preacher Robert Schuller and socialist author Upton Sinclair.[15]

After attaining his medical degree, Howard married a Black California socialite named Helen Nela Boyd in 1935. He completed his residency in the Midwest and arrived in Mound Bayou in 1942 as the newly appointed chief surgeon at the Hospital of Knights and Daughters of Tabor—colloquially, the Taborian hospital. Once Howard was prosperous enough, he launched his own enterprises: his own hospital, the Friendship Clinic; and a construction firm that erected some of Mound Bayou's characteristic four-story buildings, a restaurant, a hotel, and a farm. Unlike other places throughout the South, Blacks in Mound Bayou could enter any establishment through the front door. Dr. Howard even opened a small zoo in Mound Bayou, plus a park and the first public swimming pool in Mississippi that was open to Black families.

Howard's Friendship Clinic was the only hospital anywhere in the Delta that treated Black patients without discrimination. Black infants from dozens of miles away bore Mound Bayou on their birth certificates. The hospital even offered an early version of an HMO, allowing the impoverished people of the Delta a way to afford health care. Friendship Clinic also provided abortions in a state where they were strictly illegal, dating back to when enslaved women sought them as resistance against a system where any children they bore, often due to rape by lascivious planters, were chattel.[16] Howard was also a vocal advocate for legalizing prostitution.[17] These were positions that would eventually lessen his support among the conservative Christian Black residents of the town.

By the 1950s, Howard—a flamboyant man with a receding hairline and narrow mustache who drove flashy Cadillacs, jetted to Africa for big-game hunting, and had a reputation for womanizing (he and Helen adopted a son, but he fathered several children outside the marriage)—was recruiting promising young Blacks to work in Mound Bayou for his maiden insurance company. He hoped his company could give financial security to Black men and women of the Delta, many of whom had grown up in slavery, and prevent them from wasting away as sharecroppers and tenant farmers, dying in poverty with nothing to leave to their children.

"Medgar had two missions" in going to work for Dr. Howard, Myrlie said. "Working for the company was something he really wanted to do because it was owned and operated by" Black people. Howard was looking for young, bright students to come in and help build the company. Medgar saw his opportunity not only to gain employment but also to help his people.

MEDGAR'S JOB WAS TO GO DOOR TO DOOR, EXPLAINING THE BENefits of insurance. Myrlie recalled that he also checked on the people who worked on the plantations, "to see that the rates that were paid to them were sufficient for them to live on."[18] Medgar quickly discovered firsthand the abuses and indignities the sharecroppers in the Delta suffered, often leaving them barely better off than their grandparents had been during slavery. He lamented to Myrlie that these sharecroppers "might as well be slaves."[19] They lived in inscrutable poverty, in shack housing on the plantation grounds, that became dangerous in flood times. They were often stuck due to the debts they accrued as tenant farmers, bound to a system of peonage that was tantamount to the old antebellum system. Financial, physical, and sexual abuse of women and children were as common as it had been before the Civil War.

"At least I can call these people Mr. and Mrs.," he told Myrlie. "I can give them a sense of dignity. I can help them when they need to escape."[20] There were more than a few times, Myrlie said, when Medgar, dressing in field hand clothes to attract less attention, sneaked Black families off plantation grounds to escape debts or a lynching, or a lascivious planter demanding that a farmhand bring his daughter to the big house after dark. He would put them on trains in the dead of night with enough train fare to get to Memphis, Atlanta, or Chicago, where perhaps they had family or friends.

Howard put Medgar's passion to work, inducting him as a founding member of the Regional Council of Negro Leadership (RCNL) in 1952, along with Aaron Henry, who would go on to lead the statewide Mississippi NAACP, and NAACP activist Amzie Moore, who owned a rare Black-owned gas station in the rural town of Cleveland. Among their first campaigns was a boycott of gas stations that maintained segregated restrooms. Black Mississippians put Don't Shop bumper stickers, meaning "don't shop where you can't use the facilities," on their cars as an act of defiance and courage, even though they knew that daring to challenge the status quo could cause them to lose their jobs, or be evicted or even dragged into the street and beaten. Everything Medgar, Dr. Howard, and the others were doing carried tremendous risk, but Medgar saw the work as meaningful and exhilarating.

"Medgar loved it there," Myrlie said of Mound Bayou. He finally had a mission, a mentor, and a fellowship of men who were passionate about changing things. "Dr. Howard was very attracted to Medgar and his forcefulness, his vision, and his capacity for action." Not only was Medgar selling insurance, he was building connections with the people on the Delta plantations. "Medgar built a strong network, and it was a silent one," Myrlie said. She called the Howard operation a kind of "secret society" that could operate in white supremacist Mississippi. Black maids and butlers, field hands, and drivers quietly shared news, opportunities, and plans for meetings, including of the NAACP. They made quiet plans to get Blacks registered and out to vote, as safely as they could. It was an exciting time for Medgar.

Myrlie, though, was struggling. "I was there because I loved my husband, and [because] we started our family there," she said. "I don't think I saw the possibilities that existed in that town." She was still a teenage girl, who often focused on what *wasn't* there—including her husband, whose work had him spending long hours on the road. She was far from home, lonely, missing her man, and deep down—and maybe not even that deep down—she was miserable in Mound Bayou, whatever its splendor as a Mecca for the Negroes of the Delta.

"I didn't like the heat, I didn't like the dust," she said.[21] Medgar sometimes took her to nearby Clarksdale or Cleveland, to a segregated movie or restaurant, but that did little to assuage her depression. She carefully hid her tears from Medgar, who had too much on his mind. They argued sometimes, and Medgar would demand that she get in the car, so he could drive her home. "I can't deal with you," he would say at those times. Once he even drove her all the way to Vicksburg, to Aunt Myrlie and her husband's house—with its upright piano that Myrlie had once taken lessons from Aunt Myrlie on—and where an aging Mama now lived.

"I'm bringing your child back to you," Medgar dramatically announced. When Baby Sister refused to get out of the car. Aunt Myrlie leaned into the window and asked what was wrong. "Nothing" was all she got as an answer.[22] Eventually, and after much negotiation and conversation with Mama and Aunt Myrlie, Medgar drove them back to Mound Bayou, but he later admitted to Myrlie that in those first few months: "Myrlie, you drained my soul."[23]

Medgar suggested that Myrlie go back to Alcorn in the fall to finish her degree. She feared that physically separating from him could be the end of them, but they pressed on with the plan. Medgar even got a summer job for Myrlie as a keypunch operator at Magnolia Mutual.[24] It gave her something to do, and some money in her pocket that wasn't an allowance, but it didn't ease her loneliness. Nor did it stop her tears or her worry about the risks Medgar was taking driving deep into the Delta late at night, going from plantation to plantation.

"Medgar's travels around the state, selling insurance and helping the people of color in their community, got him in trouble," Myrlie said. "His name became synonymous with 'troublemaker.' But I remember him saying to me, 'No one's going to turn me around.'" She begged him to stop selling insurance and civil rights at the same time. "You're going to get hurt," I said. "And I asked him, 'What about me?' and I will never forget how he looked at me . . . it was a look of disdain. It was 'Woman, you don't understand where I'm coming from.' My answer, truly, was no.[25]

"That was a rough time for us in our marriage because we couldn't see eye to eye on what he was doing, and I was definitely afraid that I would lose him, because I knew the Delta. I knew Mississippi. He did, too."[26]

Few people in Mississippi—Black or white—attempted to rock the boat because of the danger involved. Many Blacks in the Delta had resigned themselves to taking their troubles to church service on Sunday and leaving them in the hands of the Lord. Most were just one or two generations out of slavery, and if they hadn't fled North by now, they likely never would. Leaving meant disconnecting from family, church brethren, and the fragile bonds that Black Americans built with great difficulty in the face of constant separation and loss during enslavement. Others just stayed out of pure hopelessness. "And along comes this young man saying, 'You are receivable of your rights,'" Myrlie said. "And the question became, 'What rights?' So, there was an educational process. People were beginning to shake their heads and acknowledge, [that] yes, they could and *should* have more."

Myrlie's plan to return to Alcorn was upended in mid-1952 by the news that she was pregnant. She and Medgar were thrilled, but on one of those days when Medgar was far away in the Delta, selling insurance and civil rights, Mrs. Porter, the older woman who lived in the adjoining apartment, heard Myrlie's cries and moans and came to her aid. Myrlie was two months pregnant, bathed in sweat and in excruciating pain. When Medgar got home, Mrs. Porter flagged him down outside and urged him to get to his wife quickly. Medgar gently gathered a barely conscious Myrlie in his arms, carried her to the car, and drove her to the hospital, where she was told she had miscarried. She had lost an alarming amount of blood.

Myrlie sank into grief, believing the old wives' tales that she would never have a child after this. The hospital stay drained their savings, scuttling the Alcorn plans. Medgar now went from activist to caretaker and consoler. By the fall, Myrlie was pregnant again, and on June 30, 1953, their son was born at Friendship Clinic in Mound Bayou.[27]

Up to that time all the Evers grandchildren had been girls. Medgar and Myrlie gave James and Jessie Evers their first grandson.

Myrlie hoped to name the boy James, after her father. Medgar wanted his son to be named "Kenyatta" after his hero, Jomo Kenyatta, who had led Kenya's Mau Mau uprising against that country's British colonizers that April. Myrlie had experienced Medgar's keen interest in the nationalist movements in Africa since the day they met. He had mused that maybe revolution was the way Blacks in America could free themselves from the persistent wickedness and calcified structure of white supremacy. Perhaps the sons and daughters of slaves should stop asking politely and take up the rifle.

Martin Luther King Jr., who was four years younger than Medgar, had not yet emerged as a national leader. In 1953, King was still completing his graduate divinity degree at Boston University and crafting his Gandhian vision for social change through nonviolence. Medgar was not a believer in nonviolence. He'd seen too much violence in Mississippi for that, and he and Charles had needed to bear arms to make more than one racist Kluxer back down, including at that courthouse in 1946. In Mound Bayou, he carried a rifle in the passenger seat of his car whenever he ventured into the Delta. He told Myrlie how important it always was to be prepared. If a race war was coming, they'd better be able to shoot back. Medgar even sometimes wondered aloud about whether those who had been enslaved in America and their descendants should build a nation of their own, free from the whites who would not let go of the system they'd built for themselves during hundreds of years of American slavery.

On the day her son was born, Myrlie had no patience for Medgar's intellectualism. As far as she was concerned a Black boy named "Kenyatta" stood no chance of making it to manhood in Mississippi. He would be presumed to be "trouble" just from his name, and he might even face strange side looks from the churchgoing Black community for his lack of a "Christian" name. She put her foot down, instructing the hospital registrar to put the name Darrell first on the birth certificate, and to make Kenyatta their son's middle name.

Medgar had little choice but to go along. Medgar understood full well that when Myrlie decided something, there was no going against it. A year later, a daughter, Reena, was born. Suddenly, the Evers were a family of four, and Myrlie felt like her life was finally becoming complete.

CHAPTER 3

Emmett Till

Most men today cannot conceive of a freedom that does not involve somebody's slavery.

—W. E. B. Du Bois

Myrlie knew of only a few times when her strong, fearless husband broke down in sobs that made his whole body shake. One was when James Evers Sr. died in the "Negro ward" of a Decatur hospital that was more of a warehouse for the dying than a place where medicine was performed. Another was after the lynching of Emmett Till. Both incidents were part and parcel of the Mississippi way.

James's father, Mike Evers, was born a slave in 1845, and he lived until he was 113 years old, well into the twentieth century. James was born just seventeen years after the Civil War. Slavery was no distant memory for Black families in the 1940s and 1950s. James and Jessie had survived bouts of economic want, and threats against them and their family. Their youngest daughter, Mary Ruth, died of cancer in 1951, while Medgar and Charles were still in college. James had survived sixty-three years of being a Negro in Mississippi, which was achievement enough.

He had a stroke in 1954, and despite never trusting hospitals, James desperately needed one. Charles and Medgar carried their father to Decatur's segregated Newton County Hospital, where he was taken to the stuffy, poorly equipped basement wing that Negro patients were consigned to. He languished there for hours while the meager hospital staff assigned to the "colored wing" were distracted by events taking place outside.

"My Daddy was dying slowly in the basement of that hospital," Medgar explained years later. "At one point, I just had to walk outside so I wouldn't burst."

"On that very night, a Negro had fought with a white man in Union, and a white mob had shot the Negro in the leg," Medgar recalled. "The police brought the Negro to the hospital, but the mob was outside . . . armed with pistols and rifles," yelling for the Black man to be handed over, surely for the rope. Despite Charles's and Medgar's increasingly angry pleas, the hospital staff, amid the chaos, were not about to move their father to an upstairs bed or even to the emergency ward where he might get the care he needed. Instead, the injured man was brought into the "colored" wing, and what medical staff the hospital was willing to spare to treat Black patients oscillated between treating his gunshot wounds and watching the door. There were no resources spared for James Evers, in those crucial first hours after his stroke.

Medgar, stricken with grief, frustration, and a growing rage, walked out into the middle of the melee outside the hospital. "I just stood there, and everything was too much for me," he said. "It seemed that this world would never change. It was that way for my Daddy, it was that way for me, and it looked as though it would be that way for my children. I was so mad I just stood there trembling and tears rolled down my cheeks."[1]

James Evers languished in that basement for a week and died there, on August 29, 1954. Jessie Evers, who had brought two sets of children into the world via two husbands and molded them into one family, would die four years later.

Months before James died, Medgar had argued with his father over his announcement that he intended to apply to the law school at Ole Miss. His application sought to take advantage of the landmark *Brown v. the Board of Education* case, which sought to reverse the indignity of *Plessy v. Ferguson*'s "separate but equal" doctrine. The case, combining five lawsuits by Black litigants dating back to 1950 in South Carolina, then Virginia, Delaware, Washington, D.C., and Kansas, had wound its way for years through the courts until the cases were combined and elevated to the Supreme Court in 1952. The combined case was argued by the NAACP's premier young lawyer, Thurgood Marshall, producing two years of deadlocks among the justices including the chief justice, Fred Vinson, who had wanted to uphold *Plessy*.

Medgar was tired of waiting. He had been an active NAACP member since his college days and had been named in January 1954 as an officer in the new Mississippi statewide NAACP charter, with his name published in the *Jackson Advocate* along with the other organization leaders.[2] He'd been putting hundreds of miles on his Oldsmobile, opening chapter offices in Mound Bayou and other Delta towns, often with Myrlie alongside him as his ad hoc secretary, while also leading boycotts with T. R. M. Howard's Regional Council of Negro Leadership. In January he'd met with James "J. P." Coleman, Mississippi's attorney general, to be interviewed for his law school application on behalf of the State College Board. He was accompanied by an NAACP lawyer from New Orleans.

Coleman asked Medgar why he wanted to attend Ole Miss. Medgar said he wanted the best law school education he could get in the state. He batted down Coleman's suggestion that it was the NAACP who had put the notion of applying to the law school in Medgar's head and that it wasn't his own idea. Coleman quizzed Medgar on why he didn't prefer to pursue a business degree instead and on where Medgar intended to live as a law student. Medgar's answer dripped with the dry wit that could thrill and annoy his wife. "I plan to live on campus in a dormitory, eat in the dining hall, and use the library," he said. "But I assure you, I bathe regularly, I wear clean clothes, and none of the brown on my skin will rub off."[3]

When he told his father about the meeting not long before the elder Evers's death, the answer he got disappointed him. His father saw no point in trying to break into the state's impenetrable white citadel. Medgar walked out of his house that day; a rare rebuke of the man who had shaped his own audaciousness.[4] James and Jessie Evers weren't the only ones who disagreed with Medgar's plan. Myrlie knew all too well what white Mississippians would be willing to do to keep their universities white.

"I did *not* want him to apply," she said. "The NAACP did . . . others did. [But] I saw him being used as a guinea pig. I used that term once with him, and I recall the look that Medgar gave me. . . . He was infuriated with me."[5]

Myrlie saw Medgar's determination to try for Ole Miss as a rejection of his family, which now included two small children. "I was so fearful of Medgar losing his life. [Trying to enroll at a white university] was a very, very brave thing to do back then. He had already received threats from more minor things that he had done" to help Black sharecroppers in the Delta, "and I was not ready to say goodbye to my husband."

Despite the doubts from his family, and his grief over burying his father, Medgar pressed on, asking Alcorn to send his transcripts to the University of Mississippi, and even getting the requisite recommendation from a white citizen: Jim Tims, an Ole Miss alum and Decatur's postmaster.[6]

On May 17, 1954, Earl Warren, the new Chief Justice, appointed by President Eisenhower after Vinson's sudden death from a heart attack, delivered the unanimous ruling in *Brown v. Board of Education*, declaring that "separate but equal" was dead.

White Southerners erupted. The *Clarion-Ledger* in an editorial declared May 17 "a black day of tragedy for the South, and for both races." The *Jackson Daily News* said that "human blood may stain Southern soil in many places because of this decision, but the dark red stains of that blood will be on the marble steps of the United States Supreme Court building."[7] Congressman John Bell Williams, a future governor of the state, called May 18, 1954, "Black Monday," and Sen. James O. Eastland proclaimed that Mississippi would never abide by the ruling and submit to the mixing of the races in its schools.

Gov. Hugh Lawson White formed a Legal Education Advisory Committee to find ways to, in the words of the *Ledger*, "dodge the ruling," even inviting some ninety Black leaders, whom he deemed to be "good Negroes," to meet with him and the board to seek their cooperation in maintaining separate schools, which the governor and other white elites insisted was a majority view among Black Mississippians. The governor even offered to improve Negro schools to make them "truly equal," in return for Black leaders pledging to oppose integration.[8] The group, including NAACP head Dr. E. J. Stringer, summarily declined the governor's offer and fully supported the *Brown* ruling and integration.

On July 18, the *Ledger* reported that "segregation problems on the university level [had] skipped Mississippi so far, with one exception: Medgar Evers of Mound Bayou, an NAACP director, has applied for entrance to the University of Mississippi."[9] Medgar was now officially a public name, with all the risks that entailed.

Within months, Governor White and the Democratic state legislature called a special session to pass a state constitutional amendment that white voters ratified later that year, allowing the state government to dissolve any school district that accepted integration. The amendment also added teeth to Mississippi's already monstrous voter suppression laws, requiring that voters show "good moral character" as well as interpret arcane passages from the state's 1890 constitution, subjectively decided by each county registrar, all of whom were white. Several counties required voters to re-register, forcing many of the few already-registered Black voters off the rolls.[10]

In Sunflower County, Robert Boyd "Tut" Patterson gathered a group of fellow white bankers, business owners, and planters to create the first Association of Citizens Councils of Mississippi (ACCM), which used its collective economic power to keep segregation in place by punishing Blacks who stepped outside the Mississippi social code by registering to vote, joining the NAACP, or attending meetings about changing the status quo. The Citizens' Councils attempted to distance themselves from the "rednecks" in the Klan, but their hostility to change, and tendency to keep a minute account of the activities of Blacks who "stepped out of line," had its own brutal calculation.

Medgar's determination to enter Ole Miss Law School stalled amid that rancor.

By fall, Attorney General Coleman recommended that the Mississippi State Board of Education reject Medgar's law school application. Instead, they returned it, saying it lacked a second reference from a white citizen who'd known Medgar for ten years.

Medgar's instinct was to sue, especially with the *Brown* victories in hand. Dr. Howard and Thurgood Marshall had other plans. Soon, on Marshall's recommendation, Medgar was offered the job of statewide field secretary for the NAACP, a new position the organization created for him. Medgar accepted, letting his law school dream go for the time being.

Myrlie was thrilled—and horrified. The job offer meant leaving Mound Bayou, and the bugs and the heat of the Delta, and moving to the state capital of Jackson. It also meant ratcheting up Medgar's visibility and the risks to his life.

At their dinner table, after the babies were put to bed, Myrlie protested. "I told him about my fear for his life, for the lives of our children and myself. He shared just a little about *his* fear, but I remember Medgar telling me, 'I'll always be there for you.' And I said to him, 'What about your body if *it's* not?'" Her question was met with silence. "He got up and walked away from the table . . . walked out of the room. And when he came back in, he was different. I didn't understand what had happened. And he told me, 'Myrlie . . . this is something I have to do.' I said, 'What about me? What about our children?' And he said, 'This is *why* I have to do it.' It took me a long time to understand that. I gave in, of course, because I wanted our marriage to last. I wanted it to be a comfortable marriage, as comfortable as marriages can be."

In September 1954, the same month Medgar's application to Ole Miss was officially closed—and three days after his daughter Reena was born[11]—thirty NAACP members in Walthall, Mississippi, were hauled before a grand jury for signing a petition to desegregate their local schools. Others who signed similar positions had faced home foreclosures or had their personal or business records seized. The harassment campaigns included firings and threatening phone calls.[12] Soon, the allegedly peaceful White Citizens' Councils fueled a fresh surge of Klan violence.

The goal of seemingly every public policy in the South, and especially in Mississippi, as Medgar described it in his first report as NAACP field secretary in December 1954, was to keep "the Negro in his place . . . keep him out of white schools . . . keep the ballot out of his reach . . . [and] keep him dependent"[13] even though Black Mississippians comprised the majority in a number of counties, particularly in the Delta. The report noted that Mound Bayou had "19,000 whites and 46,000 Negroes, and of course Bolivar County," where Mound Bayou sat, "has one of the strongest [White Citizens'] councils in the Delta."[14]

These Black majorities throughout the state played almost no civic role. In 1950, 68 percent of Leflore county's population was Black—with 43 percent working in the plantation system—yet of the 18,000 Blacks who were theoretically eligible to vote, just 297 were registered. Sunflower County—home to the notoriously racist Senator

Eastland; and where another T. R. M. Howard acolyte, Fannie Lou Hamer, would be evicted from the plantation where she lived and did backbreaking work picking cotton, then jailed and beaten for trying to register to vote—had only 114 registered Black voters in 1950 out of 8,949 eligible. Sunflower County was 68 percent Black, with a full two-thirds of Black residents working on the plantations, with a median yearly income of just $744.

This system clung stubbornly to the economic facts of the slave era and was maintained via brute force, combined with a strict caste system that imprisoned white and Black Mississippians alike. Mississippi had four kinds of people: Blacks, who were trapped at the bottom of the caste system, no matter their income or education; the wealthy white planter and professional class, including state and federal politicians; the white shopkeepers and clerks who served white customers in the tidy shops in towns like Jackson and Natchez; and the "peckerwoods."[15]

The "peckerwoods" included not just the feed- and food-store owners who served Black customers but also the state's sheriff departments that were riddled with the night riders of the Klan. They typically got their hands dirty in the brutality and lynching that upended any sense of basic safety Black men, women, and children might feel. This enabled the upper echelons of white Southern society to maintain control of the workers who fed their way of life and what they saw as the "peaceful coexistence of the races" in the genteel South.

Southern segregationists saw everything as a threat to that order, from Jackie Robinson's 1947 integration of Major League Baseball to Black troops like the Tuskegee Airmen showing their mettle in war and coming home changed by their experiences. The planter class in the South and, by extension, the economically stricken white men and women they recruited to their cause, needed segregation to survive. And they vowed to maintain it by any means necessary. Nothing short of the continued existence of the white race was at stake, as far as they were concerned. By 1955, the ACCM had sixty thousand members operating in 253 councils throughout Mississippi.[16]

WHEN MEDGAR GOT THE CALL TO TRAVEL TO NEW YORK CITY TO discuss the field secretary offer, Myrlie seized on the opportunity to spend a few days with M'dear. Mildred had moved to nearby Yazoo City with her second husband, Lee Mack Sanders, after his discharge from the Marines.[17] In those two days, the two women talked more and more deeply than they ever had, and relished spending time together without Mama Beasley's intervention. Their conversations stretched long into the nights as Darrell and infant Reena slept, and Myrlie later wrote that she learned more about her mother than she'd ever known. M'dear's stories brought into sharp relief the ravages and dangers of being a Black girl and woman in a society built on the bedrock of slavery, a world in which the men in your life—your father, your brothers, and your husband—had no power to protect you from the whims of predatory white men, from violence or rape, or from daily humiliation.

Myrlie quoted Charles Silberman, who wrote in *Crisis in Black and White* that in 1890, the year the racist, Reconstruction-ending Mississippi constitution was written, "the policy of crushing out the manhood of the Negro citizens is to be carried on to success."[18] Indeed, no Black man in the South was meant to be a man at all in the construction of white society. To fail to submit to the whims of any white man, woman, or child was to risk death. The lot of so many Negro men, particularly the Delta during and after enslavement, was to watch their woman outearn them as servants in white people's homes, while they—often toiling beside their children—eked out a living in the fields that couldn't even support their families or give them a purposeful role in their lives. In talking with M'dear, who had strongly supported Medgar's decision to apply to Ole Miss, even as Myrlie and everyone else seemed to object, she came to understand why her mother so admired Medgar, and why she did, too.

"My two days alone with my mother . . . taught me something about myself and Medgar," Myrlie wrote. "For the first time really, I was able to admit openly my pride and admiration for some of the things he had done; things I had opposed because they frightened me. I had begun to understand how important it was for Medgar to have my approval and backing—important not just for him but for myself. . . . Even more important, I had at least the beginnings of an understanding of the conflict within myself that had kept us apart. Largely through these long talks with my mother I had begun to understand that it was the very qualities that I most admired in Medgar that frightened me. I had grown up in a family that never discussed race, that never complained about discrimination. Until I met Medgar, I had never heard a Negro challenge segregation. Now I was married to a man who did, openly and publicly."[19] Medgar, in his determination to challenge the status quo, was in every sense a man. And Myrlie loved and admired him for it. Much like his late father, he was a Black man who refused to bow.

When Myrlie left Yazoo City, M'dear cried, something she didn't normally do when they parted. Two days later, Myrlie was at work at the insurance office in Mound Bayou when a coworker called her to the phone. Her stepfather was on the other end of the line, and he had devastating news. M'dear—Mildred Washington Beasley Sanders—had died of heart failure. She was just thirty-eight years old.[20] Her death, so soon after Medgar had lost his own father, brought Medgar and Myrlie closer still.

After M'dear's funeral, the Everses packed up their belongings and their children and began the move to Jackson. They would not be done with Mound Bayou, though, because death was not done with the Mississippi Delta.

Amos Brown was fourteen years old and living in Jackson when, on May 7, 1955, he learned about a killing. "I heard everybody around the Farish Street Historic District . . . talking about how these evil white men of the Ku Klux Klan and the White Citizens' Council ambushed a Black Baptist preacher named Rev. George Washington Lee on a Saturday night when he was on his way home from his grocery store in Belzoni, Mississippi," said Brown, who later became a civil rights activist and a pastor himself.

Reverend Lee, who with his wife ran a small grocery store and printing press, was the cofounder, with a fellow grocer named Gus Courts, of the Belzoni chapter of the NAACP and a vice president of the Regional Council of Negro Leadership. Through those organizations he had helped to register nearly all the eligible Black voters in Belzoni. The month before his murder he spoke at the RCNL's annual meeting in Mound Bayou, to a crowd that reportedly numbered seven thousand, and he "electrified" the crowd, reported *Jet*.[21] And though the coroner ruled that the left side of his jaw had been shot clean off by "number 3 buckshot" from a shotgun, and an FBI investigation found that a car likely pulled up beside his and a gunman opened fire, the local sheriff suggested Lee might have died of a heart attack while driving and wrecked his car; and that the metal shrapnel inside his jaw might have been his fillings becoming dislodged in the crash.[22] No one was arrested.

Lee's funeral attracted some two thousand mourners, all of whom risked their lives by attending. Lee's widow, Rosebud, made the momentous decision to leave his casket open, so the horror of what the Klan had done to her husband could be seen. This was the first such open-casket burial resulting from a lynching that is known in the civil rights movement. And it was one of Medgar's first investigations as field secretary, which he conducted alongside Ruby Hurley, the NAACP's southeastern regional director.

Later that summer, on August 13, three white men shot and killed sixty-three-year-old voting advocate Lamar "Ditney" Smith, a World War II veteran, on the steps of the Brookhaven courthouse in front of dozens of witnesses, including local sheriffs.[23] "There in Lincoln

County, named for Abraham Lincoln," Brown said. "He was on his way to where? To the courthouse, to deliver some absentee ballots. And at 10:00 A.M. in the morning . . . broad open daylight," he was shot dead. "What was his crime? He just wanted to be enfranchised. He just wanted to exercise his constitutional right to vote."[24] A frenzy was growing among white Mississippians to stop the train of integration at whatever bloody cost. "That year, 1955, was a year of terror,"[25] Brown said. (Gus Courts would be shot outside his grocery store that November. He was treated at the hospital in Mound Bayou and survived, and soon left Mississippi for Chicago.)

One week after Smith's murder, fourteen-year-old Emmett Till stepped into this toxic, boiling atmosphere, when he got off the train from Chicago and set foot on the soil of Money, Mississippi. Hundreds of thousands of African Americans fled Mississippi for Chicago between World War I and the years after World War II, and more than 6 million left the South during those years. A one-way train ticket to Chicago cost $11.10, and though the neighborhoods and schools were segregated there, Blacks could exist in a way that was unlike their experience in Mississippi.[26]

Emmett's mother, Mamie Till (later Till-Mobley), was born in Tallahatchie County but later said: "Chicago was a land of promise, and they thought that milk and honey was everywhere. . . . [There was] a lot of excitement leaving the South, leaving the cotton fields. You could hold your head up in Chicago." The city became a refuge from the violence and racial terror for everyone from Ida B. Wells to Richard Wright. The cord pulled both ways, though—and young Emmett, an only child, had come back South a number of times to spend time with the young cousins who were close to his age.

Medgar and his family shared those Chicago ties. He had spent each of his college summers working in Chicago, where one of his half brothers, Eugene Graham, lived. Medgar and Charles went back and forth to the city nearly every year of their young lives. James and Jessie had raised their children with the *Chicago Defender* in their home, and they encouraged their children to read its depictions of Black people as full of dignity and promise rather than shame. Medgar and Myrlie had solidified their bond in Chicago, the summer before they were married.

When Medgar heard that a boy from *that* city, where Black boys could breathe free, was missing, he rose to action. He, Amzie Moore, and Aaron Henry, his compatriots from the gas station boycotts, along with Ruby Hurley, donned overalls to disguise themselves as field hands, as he had so often done during his investigations, and headed deep into the Delta, to the Grover C. Frederick Farm, where Emmett's great uncle, sharecropper Moses "Mose" Wright, who local folks called "Preacher," lived with his wife, Elizabeth, and their youngest son, near the tiny, whistle-stop town of Money.

Emmett and his sixteen-year-old cousin Wheeler Parker had taken the train with Wright from Chicago to nearby Greenwood on the weekend of August 20 after a family funeral. After a few days in Wright's three-room house, with his great-aunt and -uncle, his cousin, and Wright's twelve-year-old son, Simeon, he and a jovial group of seven boys and one girl went to Roy Bryant's grocery and meat market to buy candy and Coca-Colas after a long day helping Uncle Preacher pick cotton in the scorching Delta heat. At one point, Emmett bopped into the shop on his own to buy bubble gum. When he emerged, he allegedly threw a casual "wolf whistle" at the store owner's wife, Carolyn, a claim that would prove impossible to verify, but that had deadly consequences.

What Medgar and his team, and later the FBI, learned was that over the next four days an amateur manhunt ended with a posse arriving at Wright's small home after 2:00 A.M., on August 28. They demanded that the sixty-three-year-old walk them through the pitch-dark house and produce the boy "who did the talking." Wright pleaded with them to just "give him a whipping instead," and his wife, Elizabeth, begged them to leave the child alone. He wasn't from here. He didn't understand the Mississippi way. The group of kidnappers included several white and three Black men, one of whom stood guard by the door. The last time Mose Wright saw Emmett alive, four white men led by J. W. Milam and Roy Bryant forced the child into the back of a pickup truck, with two Black men riding in back with him.[27] The truck disappeared into the night.

As days turned into weeks and word got out about the missing Chicago boy, Dr. Howard said there would be "hell to pay in Mississippi" if Till wasn't found unharmed, and he called for an FBI investigation.[28] Mrs. Till traveled to Mississippi and stayed in Dr. Howard's Mound Bayou home where community leaders gathered around her. Just three weeks had passed since Lamar Smith's murder, and Black Mississippians were exhausted and on edge. Simeon Wright later recalled in a 2011 oral history, "I lay there that night, and every car that I would hear, I thought it was J. W. Milam and Roy Bryant bringing Emmett back."[29]

According to an FBI probe conducted fifty-one years after the events, the group took the terrified boy back to Bryant's store, where another of Milam's brothers, Leslie, lived in an adjoining apartment, and then to a barn on Milam's farm, located on the Shurden plantation near Glendora, where they beat him, shot him,[30] and, according to what one of the Black men later told local folks in a story passed to the other Black man's son, that they finally put the boy out of his misery by putting a drill through the top of his head. Then they threw him off a Glendora bridge, breaking part of the bridge railing in the process.[31]

A fisherman found Emmett's bloated body in the nearby Tallahatchie River on August 31. This child, whose mother had escaped the death grip of forever-enslaved Mississippi, had been dragged from his uncle's home, beaten, and tortured, leaving one eye on his once sweet and pudgy face bulging from its socket and his head misshapen like a bloated lump of clay. His killers had weighted his body by strapping an industrial fan to his mutilated corpse with barbed wire. All of this was for allegedly "sassing" a white woman. The only way authorities identified the monstrous corpse as Emmett Till was by the ring on one of his fingers, which Simeon, who had been sharing the bed with him, pointed out for the police.[32]

The ring, which Emmett never took off, had belonged to his father, who had fought in World War II as part of the Italian campaign and died there at just twenty-three years old.

Lynching had become all but commonplace in the former Confederate states, and especially in Mississippi, but the brutal execution of a child from the *North* appeared to crack a seam in the nation's quiet acceptance of an apartheid system operating openly in the United States, a country that had shed blood to liberate Europe from Nazism, only to countenance an American version of the same ideology at home.

Especially once there were photographs.

Emmett's body, which Mississippi officials had tried to quietly bury in a local Black cemetery, was instead placed on a train to Chicago at Mamie Till's insistence. The local sheriff had sought to hide the vicious truth of what a Southern lynching looked like by boxing the remains and nailing the makeshift wooden coffin shut. Mrs. Till would have none of it.

From the moment she met her son's remains as they arrived at the train station on Twelfth Street on September 2, Mamie Till was not alone. With Dr. Howard's help, two Black journalists, Moses Newson of the Black weekly newspaper the *Tri-State Defender*, and Simeon Booker of *Jet* magazine, were there to chronicle her agony. Booker's photographer, David Jackson was with Mrs. Till on the platform and accompanied her and Emmett's body to A. A. Rayner Funeral Home, where he captured the explicit photographs of Emmett's mutilation that would shock the conscience of the world.

Mamie channeled Rosebud Lee in insisting that the remains of her once-beautiful boy be on display in an open casket, so that the whole world had to reckon with what the State of Mississippi had done to him, through the hands of those soulless men. For three days, beginning September 3, 1955, nearly fifty thousand people jammed the streets in front of A. A. Rayner Funeral Home, where Till's mangled body was displayed under a Plexiglas cover. It was said that nearly one in five of those who passed through the building for the viewing required medical intervention, as women fainted and staggered onto chairs outside.[33]

All two thousand seats inside Roberts Temple were filled and thousands more gathered outside the church to listen to the September 6 funeral on loudspeakers. Bishop Louis Ford used his eulogy to call on President Eisenhower to "go into the Southern states and tell the people there . . . that unless the Negro gets full freedom in America, it is impossible for us to be leaders in the rest of the world."[34] He announced that the burial would not take place for two days so that Emmett Till's body could lie in state for forty-eight hours. By the time he was finally laid to rest, some one hundred thousand mourners had viewed the body.

Milam and Bryant were indicted by a Tallahatchie County, Mississippi, grand jury the day after the funeral. The charges, murder and kidnapping, could yield the death penalty in Mississippi.

Medgar began the painstaking work of convincing terrorized Blacks in the Delta not only to come forward and tell what they knew but also to testify in the upcoming trial. Few Blacks in the Delta dared to speak of the Till lynching above a whisper. The fear was palpable. Medgar displayed a public patience and calm that belied his stress. Myrlie remembers that when they were at home, when her husband didn't need to be an NAACP leader or to file a report to the leadership in New York, the tears came. "It was just devastating," Myrlie said. "I can't tell you how emotional all of that time was, because it was constant. . . . It was very seldom when there was a quiet and peaceful time. Quite honestly, I don't know how he lived through it without having a heart attack."

Medgar pressed ahead, including working to attract maximum press attention to the case. The NAACP's New York–based PR director, Henry Moon, had asked Medgar and the head of the Greenwood NAACP chapter for help in guiding reporters from the *New York Post*, the *New York Times,* the *Pittsburgh Courier,* the Associated Press, and the *Baltimore Afro American,* who were traveling to Mississippi to cover the case. Medgar wrote to him, "Do not ever think that I am too busy to give information to those persons who are going to, some way or the other, help our cause down here."[35] He also pressed the national NAACP to get more involved. Under its founding president, Walter White, who had passed away just that March, the organization had been pressing for federal antilynching legislation for a generation. Charles felt that Roy Wilkins, elevated to lead the national organization after White, was too slow to respond to the Till case, but Medgar remained patient with him, as did the other national NAACP leaders.[36]

THE TRIAL OF J. W. MILAM AND ROY BRYANT IN THE KIDNAPPING and murder of Emmett Till began on September 19, 1955. Four days before, David Jackson's blockbuster photos of Emmett Till's mutilated body and the story of the funeral had run in *Jet* magazine, searing the images of the fourteen-year-old's lynching into the souls of Black folk nationwide.

Yet the atmosphere inside the Mississippi courtroom was jovial. Local white families piled into the courthouse wearing their Sunday best, some bringing their children with them, ice cream cones in hand and picnic baskets in tow. Local reporters hailed Carolyn Bryant's looks, dubbing her the "crossroads Marylin Monroe." Roy Bryant and J. W. Milam were treated like celebrities, too, with pithy pieces written about Milam's love for cigars and Bryant's imposing height. They posed for pictures with their wives, all smiles and confidence. Knowing that in Mississippi, there was almost zero risk that the all-white male jury would convict them.

Black Mississippians who dared to attend the trial were relegated to the back of the courtroom, and to the fear and sorrow of foreseeing the likely outcome of the trial. Black journalists, and even African

American congressman Charles Diggs of Michigan, who had become the state's first Black congressman in 1954, were shunted off to a card table in the rear section. When Tallahatchie sheriff Clarence Strider strode into the courtroom each day, big-bellied, foul-mouthed, and in every way befitting the image of a Jim Crow, Dixie lawman, he'd brush by the "Black table" and greet the African American journalists with "Hello, niggers!" And with a stated goal of "sending a message to outsiders," all five practicing attorneys in Sumner, the Tallahatchie County seat, agreed to represent Milam and Bryant free of charge, and local white businesses raised $10,000 to fund the defense.

Dr. Howard housed Mrs. Till at his home in Mound Bayou and escorted her to court each day in the armed caravan he used for protection from the Klan.[37] Howard's stately three-story brick house buzzed daily with NAACP and RCNP activists, ministers, and the witnesses Medgar urged to come forward, as well as the pool of reporters who descended on Mississippi to cover the trial, and for whom Medgar had provided guidance and coordination. Never again, Medgar vowed, would a person like Willie Tingle or Emmett Till just evaporate into the air, leaving a mound of bloody clothes with never a mention in the community or the press.

The prosecution called twelve witnesses, including the undertaker who prepared Till's body and the two men who discovered the corpse and fished it out of the river. Despite his personal fear and intense pressure to remain silent, sixty-four-year-old Mose Wright bravely testified about what happened the night the men raided his home and took Emmett, whom the family called "Bobo," away. Mrs. Till-Mobely also testified, as did three "surprise" witnesses Medgar, Ruby Hurley, and their NAACP team had coaxed to come forward. They were: a Black field hand named Willie Reed, who testified that he heard screams coming from Milam's barn; a Black woman named Amanda Bradley, who said she saw four men near Milam's barn on the night of the murder; and Willie Reed's grandfather Add Reed, who testified that he heard "whipping and hollering" coming from inside the barn.[38] After their testimony, Medgar worked to get them quickly out of town. Mose Wright was especially relieved to follow his wife and son, Simeon, after receiving from Medgar Evers that precious $11 ticket to Chicago.

Not everyone who knew the details of the murder testified.

Johnny B. Thomas was not much older than Emmett Till was at the time of the Milam and Bryant trial, and he would grow up to be not just an NAACP man, but the mayor of Glendora, near the place where Emmett Till was killed. He insists that his father took part in Till's murder despite the elder man's denials. Black men back then wouldn't have had much choice, unless they wanted their children to be next. Often whites didn't want to do the beating and get "nigger blood all over themselves," so just as would be done to Fannie Lou Hamer for attempting to register to vote, they forced Black men to deliver the blows. Thomas said his father and the other man who assisted Milam and Bryant in the kidnapping and murder both disappeared from town, conveniently, until the trial was over. He saw his father just a few times a year after that.[39]

When it was the defense's turn, Carolyn Bryant swore under oath that Emmett made "ugly remarks" before "whistling" at her. Her story would change over time. Sheriff Strider testified that he figured the body pulled from the Tallahatchie River had been there too long to be Till's. He'd even told a newspaper before the trial, absurdly, that he believed Till was still alive.[40] A local undertaker testified that the body presumed to be Till was unrecognizable, so it couldn't be proven that it was him. The defense also presented character witnesses for Bryant and Milam, who was a World War II veteran.

When the all-white male jury acquitted both men after just ninety minutes of deliberation on September 23, with the predetermined outcome delayed only "to drink pop," the outrage was electric, and global. Protests erupted in Chicago and across the country. Dr. Howard railed that "a white man in Mississippi will get no more of a sentence for killing a black person as he would for killing a deer out of season." One international newspaper pronounced that "the life of a Negro in Mississippi" was "not worth a whistle."[41]

After the verdict, Dr. Howard loudly demanded that J. Edgar Hoover's FBI launch its own federal investigation, noting, "It's getting to be a strange thing that the FBI can never seem to work out who is responsible for the killings of Negroes in the South." Hoover responded in an open letter accusing Howard of launching "intemperate and baseless charges" against the bureau.[42] Howard was not about to stay quiet though—with Mamie Till-Mobley, he set out on an NAACP-backed speaking tour. Thousands gathered to hear them talk about Emmett and the seemingly unending violence against Blacks in Mississippi, aided and abetted by authorities.

The combustible situation led Mississippi authorities to believe they needed to convict Milam and Bryant of something, if for no other reason than to cool the national temperature and rescue some semblance of Mississippi's reputation. In November, a second grand jury was empaneled in nearby Leflore County, where Mose Wright's house was, this time to consider solely a charge of kidnapping. Nothing would come of it.

As it turned out, Emmett Till's father, Louis Till, had indeed died in Europe during World War II, just not in combat. The elder Till had been accused along with a fellow Black private in the Transportation Corps, Fred A. McMurray, of the rape of two Italian women and the shooting death of a third. The men were tried by Army officers in a military court-martial, based on the testimony of the surviving women, who initially identified a different number of attackers, and a third soldier, who was subsequently released. Both men insisted on their innocence to the end. They were hanged on July 2, 1945, five months after their convictions and ten years before Louis Till's only son would be lynched. Mamie Till, who had never been told the circumstances of her husband's death, learned of his decade-old execution along with the world, when his sealed military file was suddenly leaked to the press by Mississippi's two segregationist Democratic senators, James Eastland and John C. Stennis, just as the Leflore County grand jury was set to convene.[43]

Milam and Bryant soon discovered they could brag about the killing, safe from double jeopardy, to the national magazine *Look* for $4,000. The piece ran in January 1956. They could not, however, continue doing business with Black Mississippians. Not long after the trial, a boycott against Bryant's store forced its closure; he eventually found work as a welder, which left him legally blind. Milam, who owned no land, tried his hand at plantation work, renting a large parcel in Sunflower County. But since no Black sharecroppers would work for him, the business failed, and he wound up taking menial plantation work himself, and ultimately wound up on the welfare rolls. The men soon moved their families to Texas, only to eventually return, with Bryant facing trouble with the law for food stamp fraud.

The Till case prompted a wave of activism that soon rumbled across the South. Young Mississippians were incensed by the violence, and Medgar became their natural organizer. "When I picked up that *Jet* magazine . . . and saw that mutilated head of Emmett Till, I was naturally horrified," said Brown. "I was angry. I was upset. But Mr. Evers said, 'Amos, let's be smart. I know how you feel, but let's do the right thing. Let's organize a Youth Council of the NAACP so that you and your young friends will learn how to fight this evil of racism and injustice in a strategic, smart way." Under Medgar's tutelage, Brown organized the first NAACP Youth Council in Mississippi that fall, in September 1955, the same month Milam and Bryant were acquitted. The Youth Councils would become the bedrock of the civil rights movement in Mississippi, and its primary source of young activists.

On November 27, twenty-six-year-old Dr. Martin Luther King Jr., fresh from earning his divinity doctorate at Boston University, hosted Dr. Howard and Mrs. Till-Mobley at Dexter Avenue Baptist Church in Montgomery, Alabama, where he had begun his first full-time pastorship a year before. The young pastor called for every member of the church to join the NAACP and to become a registered voter.[44] Rosa Parks, already an NAACP activist, was there that night, and she later said the Emmett Till case gave her the strength to remain in her front seat in the bus, which launched the Montgomery bus boycott that made King a national figure. Eight years later, King and his associates fixed the date of the March on Washington on the anniversary of Till's slaying—August 28, 1963.

Till's slaying haunted Medgar for the rest of his life. He wrote to the governor of Illinois, William Stratton, on March 20, 1957, detailing a string of murders of Black men and boys in Mississippi, and calling the lynching of Emmett Till "the most infamous crime committed against Negroes."[45] The young Republican governor had been the first white man to call for an FBI investigation into the Till lynching. Medgar would refer to the killing often, in letters and in speeches, as well as the killings of Reverend Lee and Lamar Smith, to illustrate the reign of terror being waged against Blacks in Mississippi.

The Citizens' Councils were at the heart of that ruthless, relentless campaign to stamp out the hunger of Black Mississippians to live in a free, modern world. A 2006 FBI investigation revealed that ACCM members visited every juror in the Milam and Bryant trial to ensure that they came up with the "right" verdict.[46] In the immediate aftermath of the trial, banks and plantation owners, all controlled by council leaders, launched an all-out economic assault on anyone who tried to bring Till's killers to justice and on anyone connected to the NAACP. The banks targeted NAACP leaders with foreclosures on their homes and businesses, including Amzie Moore, Dr. Howard, and Charles Evers, prompting Medgar to send a string of letters to national NAACP leadership, including to Gloster Current, the national executive director, urging financial assistance for the men.[47]

By the end of 1955, Charles Evers's restaurant and cab service were facing canceled loans, and he was no longer deejaying at the Jackson radio station where he mixed calls for NAACP membership between songs. Council leaders forced the station's owner to fire him. Charles finally gave up on Mississippi and joined the great migration to Chicago.[48]

Till's slaying changed Mound Bayou, too. By December, Dr. Howard, whose name was included on a Klan "kill list" alongside Medgar's and the already assassinated Reverend Lee,[49] packed up his wife and their adopted son, sold most of his Mound Bayou property, and joined the Mississippi exodus on a one-way train to Chicago. By then, Medgar and Myrlie were working out of the statewide field office they'd opened in Jackson, with Myrlie serving as Medgar's secretary in an office of two, while Mama acted as babysitter at home. At work, they kept things strictly professional. "We were . . . a very good team when it came to working together," Myrlie said. "He addressed me as Mrs. Evers, I addressed him as Mr. Evers at work."[50] Despite her ongoing fears, and the ongoing horrors of Mississippi, she felt a certain excitement about this new taste of city life.

CHAPTER 4

The House on Guynes Street

I may be going to heaven or hell . . . but I'll be
going from Jackson.

—Medgar Evers

The house at 2332 Guynes Street had pale yellow-green vertical clapboard on one end and pale brick on the other. The small, ranch-style house was built to Medgar's specifications—and with his family's security in mind. Its flat top was covered in gravel; the better to hear any intruder who might alight on the roof. Unlike the other homes on the block—which had otherwise identical layouts, with a combined living and dining room, a cozy kitchen, three bedrooms, and a narrow bathroom—this house had no front door. Instead, you entered through a side door at the top of the long, concrete carpark. The idea of the side entrance was to prevent anyone from being seen going in or coming out, while letting those inside the house see who was coming by peeking through the blinds of the living room window.

The carpark was wide enough for two cars, including Medgar's Oldsmobile and the black station wagon he later bought for Myrlie. The house welcomed civil rights leaders, celebrities, and spillover attendees of the NAACP mass meetings at the Masonic Temple, who became frequent fixtures at the home. An overhang roof stretching across the carpark connected the home to a narrow storage shed that looked like a skinny little house of its own. Medgar installed a freezer in the shed that he filled with the proceeds of the hunting and fishing trips that were his treasured weekend relaxation. For Medgar, who was a country boy at heart, hunting and fishing were more than just diversions. He'd made a vow to Mama Beasley and Aunt Myrlie that he would always provide for Myrlie. That included making sure that she and their children would never go hungry.

The backyard fence posts were festooned with small, gray stone Native American heads, standing soberly in profile with their headdresses pointing straight back; the yard was filled with trees, which Myrlie loved, because they reminded her of Mama's house in Vicksburg. There were plum and oak trees, and the couple planted a hackberry tree that dropped sweet, pulpy berries and sometimes, annoyingly, its tangly limbs, too. There was plenty of room in the yard for their cocker spaniel named Blackie, who had been Medgar's surprise gift to Myrlie, and later, a fiercely protective German shepherd named Heidi.

Guynes Street, a single block in northwest Jackson that comprised the Elraine Subdivision three miles from downtown, was an oasis of hope and possibility. Elraine was the first subdivision of modern homes built for the Black middle class in Mississippi after World War II. Its thirty-six homes were erected starting in 1955 by two Black developers, Winston J. Thompson and Leroy Burnett. It quickly attracted Black professionals, mostly teachers and a handful of business owners. Margaret Walker Alexander, the esteemed Black poet and novelist, was the first to move onto Guynes Street, and she owned the lone two-story home at the top of the block. She formed a kind of one-woman welcoming and veto committee, tacitly approving new arrivals to Elraine. The children on the block knew not to stray from the safety of their Negro enclave and into the all-white streets and neighborhoods adjoining their quiet block. As long as they stayed on Guynes Street, they lived as close to a normal, carefree life as a Black child could in that era.

For Medgar and Myrlie, the house was a step up to the Black middle class. The small amount they had saved from Medgar's time with Magnolia Insurance in Mound Bayou was devoured by the medical bills from Myrlie's miscarriage, so they borrowed the down payment[1] for the $10,500 home and took advantage of VA loans, though they would sometimes struggle to meet the $56 monthly payment.[2] Still, for Myrlie, it was worth it.

The move—after first living in a small, two-bedroom apartment in Jackson—meant the end of twenty-one-year-old Myrlie's misery in Mound Bayou. Myrlie's maternal grandmother, Big Mama, even came along initially, to help care for the children.[3] When the house on Guynes Street was ready in 1956, it also meant friends, and a social life for this young mother of a two- and a three-year-old, and moments of respite from the constant din of activity, threats, and loneliness that went along with being the wife of a civil rights leader. Myrlie even joined Ms. Walker Alexander's gardening group.

Medgar's $4,500-a-year salary[4] plus the $2,000 a year the NAACP paid Myrlie as Medgar's secretary[5] stretched only so far, so the couple furnished the house modestly. They placed a sofa and a small upright piano in the living room, where Myrlie could keep up her practicing. They had a record player, and they often slow-danced to "their song"—Erroll Garner's "Misty"—or bopped and swung to up-tempo R & B tunes. As the kids grew older, they stood in the hallway, which a pocket door separated from the living room, to sneak a peek.

A telephone was just outside the kitchen, and it seemed to ring day and night with calls from the NAACP, from those needing Medgar's help, or from others with menace in mind. They had a television in the living room, where Medgar exercised every morning to *The Jack LaLanne Show*, often balancing little Reena, whom he nicknamed "Punkin" and "Sunshine," on his knees while he did leg lifts. On Saturdays, that was where Medgar, Punkin, and little Darrell, "his big boy,"[6] watched cartoons. And like a growing number of Americans in the mid-1950s, they had a second television in their bedroom, where Myrlie would sometimes cuddle up with the children for a snuggly nap while Daddy was away.

The living room TV was tuned to the news every evening. As the kids grew, Medgar watched with them and explained what they were seeing. Sometimes on Sundays after church, the family would take long drives and Medgar would point out to the children the parks and swimming pools, restaurants, and libraries where they were not allowed to go, simply due to the color of their skin. He promised them that he was changing that.

It was a wonderful, terrible time. Medgar spent long hours away from home, driving back into the Delta to conduct his investigations, with the interior or even the trunk of his car sometimes doubling as the hiding place for Blacks who had to get out of town quickly after offending a local white person.[7] Myrlie was regularly faced with reminders around her home of her husband's dangerous activities. Medgar had guns stashed in nearly every corner of their modest bedroom.

"We had a relationship of fun, of depth, of challenge, of love that I have never known," Myrlie said. "I can't explain it other than to say it was a blessed relationship. Did we have problems? You bet we did. And those problems arose around his work in the civil rights movement. It was not that I did not support him, but I was fearful all the time for his life. Medgar was the love of my life, and the father of my children. And I knew that if he continued to pursue civil rights justice and equality, and certainly at that time, that his life would be taken from him. And I could not imagine life without Medgar."[8]

In those moments, when his young wife raised her doubts and fears, Medgar was encouraging but clear about his commitment to the movement. "You're stronger than you think you are," he told Myrlie. "You know what I'm in. I'm not going to leave it."

"And I said to him, 'Well, why not? I'm your wife. These are your children.' And he said to me, 'That's exactly why I'm not going to do it. Because I'm fighting for you and my children, and other parents and their children.' I really had no answer for that because I knew how sincere he was."[9]

Myrlie prayed, day and night: "'God, please take care of my husband.' And I always added to that: 'Because I cannot live without him.' And something always said [back]: 'You *will*.' I lived with that every day, every day, every day . . ."[10]

Black families in Jackson during this time were largely denied the benefits of the city's postwar economic boom. They were banned from the sprawling developments springing up all over the city and its surrounding suburbs and relegated to undesirable corners of the capital. Downtown shops barred Black women from trying on clothes or donning the white gloves to work at the cash register. Everything from cafes to movie theaters was strictly segregated. And the nearly seventy chapters of the Association of Citizens' Councils of Mississippi, whose Jackson headquarters was down the street from City Hall, were determined to keep it that way, especially in the schools.

Some already living on Guynes Street were less than thrilled about sharing their quiet, peaceful block with the most prominent and active civil rights activist in the state. Teachers in Mississippi were especially vulnerable to the Citizens' Councils, who made it clear that joining the NAACP was a firing offense. Before Medgar and Myrlie moved in, they learned that some on the block had signed a petition to keep them from living there. This anxiety by their new neighbors was painful for Medgar and Myrlie, but also well-earned.

A few months after the Everses moved into their house, Grace Britton Sweet and her husband, Dennis, moved in three doors down. Medgar and Myrlie soon made an impression.

"One afternoon, the doorbell rang, and it was Medgar at my door," Mrs. Britton Sweet said.

"I'm your neighbor," said Medgar. "All of us need to meet each other and get together and support [each other]."

The Sweets agreed, but Medgar wasn't done. "He wanted to know did we vote? And of course, the answer was yes," Ms. Britton Sweet recalled. A Tougaloo College graduate, she was one of the few Black Mississippians to get past the literacy tests and registered to vote in 1953.

Medgar also asked if they belonged to the NAACP. "And, well, our answers were no," she said. "Well, why?" he asked. Britton Sweet explained something Medgar already knew: they were teachers, like many others on the block, and if they joined the NAACP, they would be fired. The Citizens' Councils had worked out a way to easily discover anyone's NAACP membership.

"You had to sign things" declaring whether you were a member of the civil rights organization, Ms. Britton Sweet said. "If you did . . . you did not belong in the Jackson public school system," as far as white authorities were concerned. "Of course, it was a tactic to keep Black Mississippians from voting."[11]

"Well, I can join because that issue hasn't come up where I am," Dennis chimed in.

When Mrs. Britton Sweet said she'd join, too, Medgar changed his tune. "No, no, no," he said. "What I need you to do is to pay your dues" without going onto the organization's membership rolls. "We need your money. And what I want you to do is to vote, which you say you already do." He asked them to encourage their students at the local high school to vote and to get their parents to do so. "There's no need of you joining and getting fired. If you don't have a job, that's not going to help you, and it's not going to help us," he said.

Britton-Sweet was impressed. And the couple chipped in their dues.

The Everses were finding their niche in the community, and Myrlie was gaining in confidence. Dennis Sweet and Medgar often went fishing on Saturdays. The three Sweet kids and the Evers children attended one another's birthday parties and were part of the "Guynes Street gang" of kids who spanned every age from toddler to high school senior. They played together and stayed out of trouble, and they formed a bond that would last for decades, since few families on the block ever moved away. Ms. Britton Sweet's brother, Dr. Albert Bazaar Britton Jr., the first African American physician admitted to the staff of Baptist Hospital in Jackson, became the Everses' family doctor, giving them a replacement for Dr. Howard, and Myrlie some needed peace of mind.

"We got to know them [both] quite well," Mrs. Britton Sweet said. "They were very nice, very accommodating. . . . Boy, you just couldn't ask for better people." And once they settled in, the block was like one big family; the kind where you'd ask a neighbor: "Do you have a cup of sugar? I need some sugar and I'll pay you back."

"My husband was working on his master's degree and . . . he had to do a whole year in Atlanta, Georgia," Britton Sweet said. "And Medgar told him, 'Hey, I'll look after Grace and the kids, while you go, I'll look in on them. You don't have to worry, you go do that.' And that's what he did. We had floor furnaces, and [mine] went out and it was cold. It was really bad. I called Medgar's house, twelve o'clock midnight or one o'clock in the morning and said, 'Hey, I have no heat up here. Can you help me?' And he said, 'I certainly can.' He got out of bed, came past two houses, to my house, and the pilot [light] was under the house. So, he crawled under the house with a flashlight and lit the pilot and got my heater going."

Johnnie Pearl Young, who lived directly across the street, met Medgar before the Everses' house was finished. He'd come by to check on things, knocked on her door and asked: "Neighbor, do you think I might have a glass of water, since ours is not connected yet?" When Myrlie arrived a few weeks later with little Darrell and Reena, the two women bonded over having daughters around the same age. Medgar became fast friends with Young's husband, Thomas, too.

Nearly every weekday Ms. Young, who Myrlie called "Bo," dropped by after a long day teaching at a local Negro public school, to relax a bit in Myrlie's living room and chat about their days. Ms. Young was always stylishly dressed in clothes she made from fashionable patterns from companies like McCall's. Myrlie would fix her a cool drink and pop a record on the player. "Let me play some music for you, maybe that will relax you," Myrlie would say.

Medgar and Myrlie also befriended Houston and Jean Wells, who moved next door to the Everses with their children and were among the last to join the block. Houston Wells owned a furniture store in Jackson, and he and his wife, who worked at the store with him, were quiet but active financial supporters of the NAACP. When Medgar and Myrlie knocked on the door to welcome them to the neighborhood, Medgar made his customary pitch for them to join, only to find they were already members.

THE MISSISSIPPI STATE NAACP OFFICE WAS LOCATED AT 507 Farish Street, and Medgar also kept an office at the Masonic Temple at 1072 Lynch Street, where regular mass meetings were held to grow and nourish the Black resistance in the state. Officially, Medgar's job was to increase NAACP memberships and add to Mississippi's Black voter registration rolls. Both tasks would prove to be extremely challenging, given the fears among Black professionals, particularly the teachers who formed the backbone of Mississippi's small Black middle class, that joining the NAACP would cost them their jobs or bring about financial retribution from the Citizens' Councils. Impoverished Black sharecroppers feared the Klan violence that could result from registering to vote. Meanwhile, Black collegians and high schoolers in Jackson and around the state were watching a nascent civil rights movement bubble up in other parts of the South, and they were increasingly eager to join it in the wake of the Till lynching. This growing movement was built on the direct action that belied the staid legal tactics of the NAACP. Increasingly, Medgar, just thirty-one years old, was siding with the impatient youth.

Medgar wrote to Dr. Martin Luther King Jr. in July 1956, nearly a year after the Montgomery Bus boycotts, inviting King to speak in

Jackson. "We, the NAACP here," Medgar wrote, "feel that your presence would do more to bring together our ministers and the people of Jackson than any other person or incident conceivable."[12] The two had met briefly that month at the NAACP national convention in San Francisco.

King had to decline Medgar's invitation this time as he was set to travel abroad, but he telegrammed his reply: "It was a real pleasure having you in Montgomery. . . . Your presence added much to the success of our meeting. You have my prayers and best wishes as you continue your struggle against the forces of evil and injustice in the State of Mississippi."[13] It would not be Medgar's last attempt at courting an alliance with Dr. King, and his determination to do so would make him no friends at New York headquarters.

That October, Medgar sent a telegram to President Dwight Eisenhower on behalf of the State Conference, after the president invited Russian observers to come to the United States and "observe our system of free and fair elections." He called on Eisenhower to send the Russian observers to Humphrey County, Mississippi, where Reverend Lee had been killed and Gus Courts was shot "because they tried to vote as Americans. Send them to Jefferson-Davis County, where more than one thousand who have been qualified voters from three to ten years, were disenfranchised because they were Negroes. Send them to Hattiesburg, in Forrest County, where there are less than twenty-five Negroes registered to vote when there are twelve thousand Negroes in the Country. Mr. President," he concluded, "we feel that a more accurate and objective view will be derived from a visit in these counties, and the majority of Mississippi counties where no Negroes are permitted to register and vote in our great democracy."[14]

Excerpts from the telegram were published by the Associated Press, and Jefferson Davis County clerk James W. Daniels responded that "no one here has been refused the right to vote because of race or color. They have been refused because they have failed to qualify under the laws of Mississippi." The Associated Press pointed to the 1956 constitutional amendment requiring would-be registrants to interpret a passage from the state constitution to the registrar's satisfaction, pointing out, "There are no Negro circuit clerks in Mississippi" and that when the bill was argued on the House floor in 1955 and 1956, "backers said the tighter regulations would help curb the Negro vote."[15]

Yet even with Medgar's frenetic pace and six-day workweek, Mississippi's NAACP memberships were collapsing, dropping in Jackson from 4,639 in 1955 to 1,436 in 1956. "It is not the lack of interest," Evers wrote to the national office, "but fear."[16] The terrorism and economic reprisal sometimes seemed too brutal to overcome. Medgar was under tremendous pressure from the national office to refocus on his prime directives: voter registration and NAACP memberships. And he faced near-constant attacks from local critics. He was frequently targeted by the racist editors of the *Clarion-Ledger* and even in editorials in the *Jackson Advocate,* the biggest Black newspaper in the city, whose editor, Percy Greene, was an agent of the status quo and uncomfortable with the "radical" young leaders of the NAACP.

Medgar's 1957 annual report described his travels to speak at a protest rally in Detroit that September, and subsequent speeches in St. Louis, Tampa, and Nashville. He participated in a conference with Roy Wilkins, Thurgood Marshall, and Ruby Hurley, the director of the organization's Washington bureau, in which he pleaded with Assistant U.S. Attorney General Warren Olney for federal intervention in Mississippi "for the assurance that the Civil Rights of Negroes of that state would not be abridged."

The report also said he had put 13,372 miles on his car, "visiting branches, keeping speaking engagements, making various kinds of investigations, organizing branches, etc."[17] The wear and tear on his Oldsmobile prompted him to disclose in a separate letter to Wilkins that he had spent $382.70 of the organization's "special fund . . . to replace a set of worn out automobile tires and to have worn mechanical parts replaced on my car." He stated that "it was my means of being able to keep going over the state without being caught out on some of these country roads with a flat tire or a 'conked out' engine"—something that, for a man of his growing profile, could very well mean winding up dead.

Despite New York's frequent displeasure with his emphasis on King-style activism, and their perception of his lack of focus on memberships and voter registration, Medgar's relentless travel around the state was having an impact. He was setting up or reviving defunct field offices and aiding Black Mississippians in crisis. And the various offices around the state, and particularly in the Delta, as well as the many Youth Councils Medgar established at Mississippi's Black colleges and even among high school students were communicating, and coordinating—creating what amounted to a civil rights underground network. Fellow activists like Amzie Moore recognized that this was more valuable and more audacious than Medgar meeting his national NAACP membership quota. But Wilkins and the national NAACP often seemed impatient with Medgar's aggressiveness, believing that civil rights battles would mainly be won in the courts, not in the streets. Charles never trusted Wilkins and viewed him as jealous of Medgar and contemptuous of Dr. King.

Charles recognized that Wilkins was smart, a strong speaker, and an excellent diplomat, but he wasn't a Southerner, so he didn't grasp what the growing Southern movement was up against—or how relentless Medgar could be.

In February 1957, Medgar drove to New Orleans for King's inaugural Southern Christian Leadership Conference, which sought to coordinate the various Southern protest movements and draw on the reach and influence of Black clergy to form a broad movement around the principles of nonviolence, to "redeem the soul of America." Medgar was excited to finally meet with King, as well as other ministers like Fred Shuttlesworth and C. K. Steele plus strategists like Bayard Rustin, who were moving toward a strategy of direct action in the mode of the Montgomery bus boycott. At the conference, Medgar was elected assistant secretary, with the responsibility of assisting the Baton Rouge SCLC secretary, Rev. T. J. Jemison. That drew a rebuke from Wilkins, prompting Medgar to write an apologetic letter to Wilkins the following month, saying he was unaware that joining the SCLC was against the "policy of the NAACP" and insisting he was solely "trying to do what I possibly could to bring first-class citizenship to our section of the country as hurriedly as possible."[18] Medgar's tenure in the SCLC ended quickly.

That August, Medgar spoke at Mount Heron Baptist Church in Vicksburg, where Myrlie grew up and where they were married. His theme: "man's obligation to God and to man."[19] He spoke of the "righteous struggle" he had committed his life to, saying, "let it not be said in the final analysis when history will only record these glorious moments and when your grandchildren will invariably ask: granddaddy what role did you play in helping to make us free men and free women? Did you actively participate in the struggle or was your support only a moral one?" Medgar praised the Montgomery bus boycotts and King as examples of men putting their preaching into practice. Montgomery had sparked similar boycott movements in Florida and other states. He desperately wanted to bring that energy to Mississippi.

In November 1958, *Ebony* magazine ran a splashy, six-page profile of Medgar titled "Why I Live in Mississippi" by Francis H. Mitchell. Beside a full-page photograph of Medgar, wearing a casual striped shirt and leaning, half smiling, against a wall, Mitchell wrote that "Evers had not always planned to be a productive member of Mississippi society. In fact, during his Army days, he read extensively of Jomo Kenyatta's Mau Mau reign of terror in Africa and dreamed of arming his own band of blackshirts and extracting 'an eye for an eye' from whites who mistreated their black brothers." Mitchell quoted Medgar's change of heart. "It didn't take much reading of the Bible though, to convince me that two wrongs would not make the situation any different, and that I couldn't hate the white man, and at the same time hope to convert him."

More photos showed the Evers family in silhouette, standing at the site of the Civil War battle of Vicksburg, Medgar in a cap, beside a man in rural Mississippi, Medgar fishing in a boat on a lake, and Medgar and a beautiful, smiling Myrlie, cuddling four-year-old Reena. The caption quoted Medgar: "Why do I live in Mississippi? I live here to better it for my wife and kids, and for all the wives and all the kids who expect and deserve something better than what they are getting from life."[20]

The article described a March protest when Medgar boarded a Trailways bus in Meridian and refused the driver's request that he move from the front section. "He was removed and taken to the police station for questioning," Mitchell wrote. When he was returned to the bus, he sat in the front, and as they neared the station, the bus was stopped and a cabbie boarded and hit Evers in the face. "Says Evers of his refusal to fight back: 'You can't let your emotions get away with you. If I had retaliated, I would have helped defeat the cause for which I was struggling.'"[21]

"You know, it may sound funny," Medgar told Mitchell, "but I love the South. I don't choose to live anywhere else. There's land here, where a man can raise cattle, and I'm going to do that some day [*sic*]. There are lakes where a man can sink a hook and fight the bass. . . . There's room here for my children to play, and grow, and become good citizens—if the white man will let them."[22]

The article ended with Medgar, whom Mitchell had photographed fishing, speaking with a Black farmer deep in the Delta, cuddling four-year-old Reena and standing in silhouette with Myrlie, Reena, and Darrell at Vicksburg, declaring: "I'll be damned if I'm going to let the white man lick me. There's something that I've got to do for my kids, and I'm not going to stop until I've done it."[23]

Myrlie had learned to smile for the photos and cook the meals for the NAACP leaders who frequented their home. She did her best not to argue or explode, but the strain was growing. A year after the *Ebony* article, which helped turn the spotlight on Medgar into a klieg light, Myrlie was pregnant again.

On January 10, 1960, Myrlie gave birth to a boy they named James Van Evers, in a tribute to both of their fathers—Medgar's late father, dear old "Crazy Jim," and Myrlie's too-often-absent but beloved father James Van Dyke Beasley. With the birth of their third child, whom the family called "Van," Myrlie quit her part-time job as Medgar's secretary and devoted herself full-time to being a mother and supportive, if apprehensive, wife of Mississippi's most prominent civil rights leader.

Mrs. Young, whom Myrlie chose as baby Van's godmother, often heard Myrlie playing the piano from across the street. "It just sounded beautiful," she said. Sometimes Myrlie taught music lessons to kids on the block, just as her aunt Myrlie had done for her, earning a bit of money to supplement her allowance. Even with her new domestic role, Myrlie's car gave her the freedom she craved and helped to solidify her relationships with some of her still-reticent neighbors. She would help to shuttle the neighborhood kids back and forth to all-Black Christ the King, the Catholic elementary school most of the school-age children on Guynes Street attended. And because she was the only housewife on the block, Myrlie soon became a kind of block mom. And when he could grab some rare time off, Medgar provided the fun.

On Sundays, when Medgar wasn't resting his weary mind fishing, he'd toss a football with seven-year-old Darrell and the other neighborhood boys, watching as they peeled up the street jostling to catch it and throw it back. Johnnie Pearl Young said theirs was a mostly "boy block," and the kids just "fell in love with Mr. Evers."

Dennis Sweet III, the second of the three Sweet kids, remembered, "Me, Chipper, Zach, Ted, Billy Henry. . . . There was a bunch of boys," he said. "It was a blast. We weren't really feeling the weight of who [Medgar Evers] was. He was a dad on the block [among] a lot of dads. We'd get in the street . . . throw a football, a baseball. It was a good neighborhood."

"It was fun," Dennis's sister, Denise Sweet Owens, agreed. "I was seven, eight years old. We didn't have air-conditioning. When the sun came up . . . we went outside. We'd meet up—all the kids—kind of halfway—and we'd just start playing. We'd start climbing trees. We'd create 'gangs.' Reena Evers, Darryl Evers, Paula Pitman, Reggie Pitman, Dennis, and I, we just ran the streets, having a lot of fun."

Sometimes Medgar piled the kids into his Oldsmobile and took them out to eat. Ms. Young said, "He'd play with them a while, and then he'd say, 'Let's go!' And you talking about running, wanting to get into his [car]? Oh, they were so happy."

The kids from Guynes Street interacted only occasionally with the white kids who lived in the adjoining community—just one street away. Invariably, it didn't end well.

Sweet Owens recalled a "nice white lady" who lived on that nearby block. She and her husband had a son and a daughter, and she was Sweet Owens's frequent playmate. "We had a lot of fun," she said, until the day the girl remarked on a passing car with a Black driver and spat out "That nigger." An astonished Sweet Owens asked, "What did you say?" to which the girl repeated, "'That's a nigger,' and I realized something was strange here." Before long, Sweet Owens's mother informed her and her brother that the "nice white lady" and her family were moving away. The woman had told Mrs. Sweet, "We have to move because of integration. It's coming."

Medgar was determined to make it come, but the effort was hard on his family.

Darrell and Reena waited up eagerly every night for their father to come home. When he arrived—so long as it wasn't too late, Darrell and Reena ran to the door. He remembered his dad saying, "Well, I have some gifts for you." He always brought them something, "usually it was Cracker Jacks or something like that. We jumped all over him."[24]

Sometimes Myrlie's patience faltered: when she cooked too many dinners for one too many impromptu meetings in their living and dining room, or when funds ran low. She reacted with long silences, and Medgar implored her not to hold things in. He knew the pressure his life's mission was putting on both of them. "Medgar used to tell me, 'Myrlie, you shortchange yourself. You have so much more to offer than that,'" she said. "I was proud of what he was doing, and I can't even explain to you how much I loved that man. But the thought of losing him, and my children's father, was almost more than I could take."

By then, Medgar's every move was being watched. White men no one recognized would stand silently inside the Masonic Temple during NAACP mass meetings, watching, or hang around outside, writing down license plate numbers. That information was turned over to the *Clarion-Ledger* and the *Jackson Daily News*, both owned by the staunchly racist Hederman brothers and which openly supported the Citizens' Councils and served as a de facto partner of the Sovereignty Commission—Mississippi's state-operated spy agency and propaganda arm, created by the state legislature in 1956 to protect segregation against federal interference and controlled by the governor. It had been enacted by the Mississippi state legislature after the *Brown* decision, and its reach included everything from a national speakers bureau, which sent white and even Black speakers around the country to tout the benefits of segregation, to surveillance of NAACP meetings and organizers. At the commission's behest, white newspapers published the names of anyone who attended a civil rights meeting, making them vulnerable to retribution from their employer or mortgage holder, likely Citizens' Council members or, worse, from the Klan. The teachers and professionals on Guynes Street were especially vulnerable.

While the existence of the commission was not widely known at the time, Medgar and Myrlie soon suspected that not only were *their* phones tapped, but their neighbors' phones were, too. "You'd pick up the phone to use it, and then you could hear the neighbors on the side of you," Ms. Young said. Sovereignty Commission spies and paid informants were always around, including FBI-trained or retired agents. The commission would compile extensive records for decades on civil rights "agitators" and integrationists, Black and white.

"We would always have a saying in the meetings, we don't ever have to worry about planning and people knowing, because by the time we leave here, and in the morning, they're going to know anyway," said Bennie Thompson, then a young activist and currently the only Black congressman from exquisitely gerrymandered Mississippi.[25]

The Sovereignty Commission didn't recruit just white spies. A July 1957 Associated Press investigation exposed Greenwood pastor H. H. Humes, head of the General Baptist State Convention—the state's largest Black Baptist group—and *Jackson Advocate* editor Percy Greene, for accepting Sovereignty Commission payments in exchange for supporting the segregated status quo and informing on NAACP members.[26] Greene's paper would run articles attacking the NAACP that were later discovered to have been written by the Commission and reprinted in the *Advocate* verbatim.

Myrlie recalled discussions at the house about whether Greene was "getting paid."[27] He was a conservative in the Booker T. Washington tradition of some in Mississippi's small Black middle class who saw the benefits for Black businesses of maintaining segregation and, with it, a captive customer base. He and Humes were frequent and enthusiastic critics of the NAACP.[28]

Medgar understood that the fight for Black Mississippians was a messaging war that couldn't be waged by Blacks alone. On December 16, 1961, he and an interracial group of civil rights activists and editors, including John Salter Jr., a half-Indigenous, white-presenting Army veteran and former labor organizer who was a social science professor at all-Black Tougaloo College, launched the *Mississippi Free Press,* a four-page weekly with the defiant subhead: "The Truth Shall Make You Free." The inaugural issue's opening editorial stated: "We believe that all men should be free—no man a slave. We believe in freedom of speech, freedom of worship, freedom of movement, and freedom from intimidation. These, among others, are the rights of all Mississippians, regardless of creed, color or religion."[29]

The paper covered news and politics from Black communities that were about things other than crime, plus coverage of the freedom struggle, "voting and political tips" on how to make sure poll taxes and other requirements were completed on time, and articles denouncing the poor treatment of Black shoppers in downtown Jackson.[30] It ran advertisements by Black-owned business like Houston Wells's furniture store and Smiths Supermarket, owned by Black entrepreneur R. L. T. Smith Jr., who was running to become the state's first Black congressman.

The *Free Press* had to be printed far outside of Jackson each week in Holmes County, by Hazel Brannon Smith—a white, Baptist woman, born in Alabama in 1914, who was the owner, publisher, and editor of the *Lexington Advertiser* and three other small weeklies that served majority Black towns in the Mississippi Delta. She had initially supported segregation and criticized the New Deal as an abandonment of Southern Democrats, but she reversed her position after the *Brown* decision and published sharp editorials opposing segregation and denouncing White Citizens' Councils' intimidation of Black Mississippians. Unsurprisingly, the local council initiated an advertiser boycott of her newspapers. They had her husband fired from his job at Holmes County Hospital, and when a prestigious journalism award brought her national attention, the Klan burned an eight-foot-tall cross on her lawn and her office was firebombed.[31]

This partnership was not Medgar's only foray into interracial cooperation. In addition to writers and editors at the *Mississippi Free Press*, Salter became one of Medgar's fiercest allies. Another ally, Rev. Ed King, who was white, also became a trusted member of Medgar's inner circle. The two had met when Medgar attended an interracial forum at Millsaps College, where King was an undergraduate student. King would in later years become (at Medgar's urging) Tougaloo's chaplain.

Like Myrlie, Ed King hailed from Vicksburg—though white Vicksburg might as well have been on the moon, it was so different. But perhaps because of his religious convictions, he deplored the treatment of Black people in Mississippi. Medgar's visit to Millsaps came after the Emmett Till case as he worked to open college NAACP chapters, and the encounter changed the trajectory of Ed King's life.

Medgar "was a good organizer and a quiet agitator and a good teacher," King said. "And he invited some of us who were sociology or history students to come to his NAACP office, [so] he would give us more information about poverty and race and topics like that." Medgar preferred to show rather than tell, King said, in demonstrating to this group of young white Mississippians what it meant to be Black in the state.

"Medgar talked about people not having electricity, water, and things like that. And he said, 'get the census data . . . and you will find that there are people without indoor plumbing within a block of the State Capital Building.' He made us find it out for ourselves, but it also meant we could trust the other things he was saying. . . . He was wonderful as a teacher."

King's friendship with Medgar evolved quickly. "I think he considered me a student. But it was more like I was a little brother that could be guided. And I vaguely understood [that] for him to trust a white man was not something to be taken for granted."[32]

King was in Montgomery, Alabama, in 1958, working with Dr. Martin Luther King Jr. and Ralph Abernathy to coordinate white support for the movement. When word got back to the white Citizens' Councils in Mississippi, pressure was put on King's parents in Vicksburg, who were forced to leave the state amid accusations that their son was a communist.[33]

Back in 1955, a friend of Medgar's, a Black veteran named Clyde Kennard of Hattiesburg, Mississippi, had filed repeated applications for admission to all-white Mississippi Southern College. When he attempted to enroll again in 1958 and was again rejected, Medgar wrote in an NAACP report, "Legal action is now pending."[34]

Kennard was also an NAACP member, which, as far as the Sovereignty Commission was concerned, made him a threat. But the "legal action" that he would soon face would raise the level of peril for every Black Mississippian who desired to see change. "Kennard's application to attend Mississippi Southern was seen as an attack on segregation and set into motion a swift response from the state," said Rick Bowers, author of the book *Spies of Mississippi*. The Sovereignty Commission conducted a thorough investigation of Kennard's background and were unable to produce anything it could use to reject his application. They needed a new tactic.

Kennard was arrested by state police and charged with stealing $25 worth of chicken feed from the county co-op that police had planted on his farm. He was charged with grand larceny and for "conspiring to burglarize the Forrest County Cooperative."[35] Mississippi's notorious "pig law," passed in 1876, made such a theft punishable as an act of grand larceny with sentences of up to five years.[36] The law led to the imprisonment of thousands of impoverished, formerly enslaved men and quadrupled Mississippi's prison population. Not uncoincidentally, the profits from working convicts at plantation prisons like Parchman State Penitentiary, and the leasing of convicts as free labor to local planters, effectively returned slavery to the state, bringing Reconstruction in Mississippi to an abrupt and hideous end.

Now, the Citizens' Councils and Sovereignty Commission were weaponizing those laws against integration. Kennard's trial began on November 21, 1960, and lasted one day. He was sentenced to seven years at Parchman, a place that was considered horrific, even for the South. Medgar attended Kennard's trial and reported to the national office about the charade he observed.

Evers also released a statement to the United Press International and the Associated Press, calling what happened to the thirty-three-year-old veteran—just two years younger than Medgar—"the greatest mockery to Judicial Justice." He railed, "In a courtroom of segregationists apparently resolved to put Kennard 'legally away,' the all-white jury found Kennard guilty as charged, in only ten minutes."

After his statement was published, Medgar was served with a subpoena by the Forrest County Circuit Court, demanding to know why he should not be cited for contempt of court for criticizing a proceeding for which he had been present. A hearing was scheduled for December 2. Medgar was found guilty of contempt and sentenced to thirty days in jail plus a $100 fine—twice his monthly mortgage.[37]

The attacks would not end with Kennard.

Tougaloo College, where Medgar had opened a strong NAACP Youth Committee, was the activist center of Jackson. Medgar had also opened Youth and Collegiate NAACP chapters at Jackson State, along with active organizations at Black high schools in the state capital. "His focus was to get in and encourage the NAACP chapters across the state of Mississippi to groom the next generation of leaders," Daphne Chamberlain, historian and Tougaloo professor, said.

Medgar admired the young activists, particularly those raised in the segregated South, who were willing to keep pushing even though they knew the risks of defying the calcified norms that kept white supremacy in place. He shared their belief that white supremacy could ultimately be defeated only through direct action. This surprised some of the young activists. "The students thought that he thought they were crazy," Reverend King said. "They thought he would echo the opinion of Roy Wilkins and people who for fifty years had said the last thing you should do is stir up the white police."

Far from it. Medgar used his Oldsmobile to ferry Tougaloo students to and from the mass meetings at the Masonic Temple, so they didn't have to ride in the back of Jackson's segregated buses.

Fred Douglas Moore Clark Sr. was a teenaged activist at the time, and president of a jazz club at all-Black Lanier High School. "I was always glad to be in [Medgar's] presence because he was the biggest name out there during those times," said Clark. "Every chance that I got, I would come to the meetings at Tougaloo's campus. The word would get around to me, where these meetings were and what time. Usually, James Meredith and Medgar Evers would be there, and I often got a ride [home] with him from Tougaloo campus."

Sometimes when Medgar gave a talk on the campus, Clark went there but didn't go inside. "I'd wait around his car," he said. "I always kept an eye on his car. So when he came out, I'd get a ride [home] with him." Clark admitted that Medgar's notoriety, particularly among the police, made him fearful at times, riding with Medgar. "Of course, I was always scared when I was around him. At the time they told us that we had white spies with us, and we had 'real niggers.' We had black people that would go back and tell the white man everything we had done." The Sovereignty Commission, he said, "had people at all these meetings."

Medgar, he said, had an "iron will. He had no fear. He was too bold. So right away, I saw that I got to be careful around this guy, in order to survive as a young man who was, in his words, 'skinny and black.'

"The last time I rode with [Medgar], I asked him, was he scared—cause I was: no street lights, pitch-black, and we were traveling from a hot campus meeting. He started talking to me about his spirituality, about God and his faith. Of course, I was halfway listening—looking at the window for the attacks."

Over time, Clark stopped taking those rides. "Every time I saw him, I wanted to be with him, but I was trying to survive, and I wanted to take forward what I was learning and be an activist. I didn't have to be with him all the time to pick up on what he's doing, or what he has done from other people."

The risks of "riding with Medgar," literally and figuratively ranged from the threat of violence to threats of losing what little normal high school life was available to young Black Mississippians.

For Amos Brown, now a senior at Jim Hill High School in Jackson, being the president of the NAACP's West Jackson Youth Council meant being stripped of his chance to be valedictorian, barred from senior prom, and threatened with expulsion, all because he used his NAACP platform to expose the truth about Mississippi's separate and deeply unequal schools. Chamberlain said, "He voiced concerns about the lack of resources, the dilapidated buildings, the secondhand textbooks they were receiving, [and] even the school food." When he traveled to the 1958 national NAACP conference in Cleveland, he told the *Plain Dealer* "exactly what was going on here in the state of Mississippi," she said.

That made Brown a target of the Sovereignty Commission as well, which labeled him a "full-fledged agitator. . . . I was just a kid," Brown said. "But this kid tagged along with Medgar Evers." According to Chamberlain, when the school threatened Brown with expulsion, "Medgar Evers stepped in and said that . . . if you do not allow this young man to be vocal about some of the issues that are impacting African American students in the city of Jackson, we will attempt to integrate the all-white high school"[38] in Jackson.

The Woolworth's sit-ins in Greensboro, North Carolina, in 1960 increased the desire of college and high school students across the South to go beyond court cases and petitions and take direct action against the recalcitrant segregation. With members of the Mississippi collegiate and youth NAACP chapters, Medgar crisscrossed the state tirelessly to set up similar protests. The desire for freedom spanned age. Eight months before the first lunch counter sit-in in Greensboro, Dr. Gilbert Mason Sr., a founding member of the NAACP chapter in Biloxi, Mississippi, had begun leading wade-ins to desegregate Gulf Port beaches. He later led the lawsuit against the Biloxi Municipal School district to desegregate its public schools.

Medgar's December 1960 field report highlighted the Montgomery-style consumer boycott he'd launched of Jackson's white merchants during the Easter season, when Black women flocked to downtown shops for new dresses and hats. The campaign urged Black Mississippians to wear what they already had instead of buying from segregated stores that failed to treat them with respect. He wrote, "More than 700 students combined and participated in a door-to-door canvas urging Negro citizens to cooperate in this 'Sacrifice for Human Dignity.' . . . Stores that do not recognize Negroes as Miss, Mrs. or Mr. do not deserve to have Negroes trade with them. Stores that do not employ Negroes are likewise not worthy of our patronage. We can, by this method, use the same items and clothes that we already have, as a step toward our contributions to Human Dignity, and create for the Negro a new respect and appreciation."[39]

The boycott was brief and ultimately faltered, in no small part because middle-class Black Jacksonians were wary of provoking white business leaders and the violent white supremacist organizations who backed them. Medgar was adamant that Mississippi needed to adopt the ferocity of what Dr. King was doing across the South, as well as the energy of youth-focused organizations like SNCC (Student Non-Violent Coordinating Committee) and CORE (Congress of Racial Equality) and the impatient young NAACP activists filling the Masonic Temple, his Lynch Street offices, and increasingly his home for training and planning meetings.

Medgar continued to catalog the latest outrages against individuals trying to register to vote, including another constitutional amendment approved by white voters, following a recommendation by the ACCM and Democratic governor Ross Barnett, which added the requirement that voters demonstrate "good moral character," to the registrar's satisfaction. This was directed squarely at the NAACP because segregationists regarded membership in the organization as a sign of moral decay. Another amendment eliminated the state's requirement that it provide free public schools, allowing Mississippi the option of having no public schools at all if it had to have even a single integrated one. A third amendment eliminated the requirement that jurors be registered voters, which was a way of getting around a Fifth Circuit Court decision finding that Black Mississippians were still being systematically excluded from juries.[40]

Medgar was working at a frenetic pace. His December 20, 1960, NAACP branch newsletter documented 2,871 pieces of outgoing mail, 40 branches visited, 2 new branches opened including a college NAACP chapter, and 16,295 fresh miles on his Oldsmobile,[41] sometimes speeding through the Delta at 100 miles per hour to elude Klansmen and anyone else who might try to run him off the road. A year later, he and the Jackson NAACP launched a Christmas boycott of Jackson merchants—his second try at peeling Black shoppers away from the retailers who disrespected them.

To keep his NAACP organizations off the radar of Citizens' Council spies and out of conflict with the direct-action-averse national NAACP, Medgar gave them varying names. In Jackson, he opened a North Jackson Youth Council *and* an NAACP Youth Council. Frank Figgers, who was born in segregated Jackson in 1950, graduated from Tougaloo and joined the NAACP as a teen, recalled, "Some days it would be the NAACP's Youth and College Division. Other days, it would be the North Jackson Youth Council or the North Jackson Community Council. That allowed him to do much more than a less creative person could have done."

Laura Terrell (later Figgers, when the two married) was a member of the North Jackson Youth Council. "She also was in the NAACP Youth Council," Figgers said. "On picket days when they were going to support the boycotts with pickets and passing out leaflets . . . the North Jackson Youth Council would do that work, because the NAACP may not want to get bogged down in using finances to get people out of jail. Medgar Evers was so creative and so strategic in his leadership . . . he made preparations for that. When people would go to jail or when they would have a picketing incident, he would already have raised money in the local community, among poor, low-wealth people for whatever eventuality would come up to get people out of jail, to help with bonds, to pay lawyers and that sort of thing."[42]

By the end of 1960, Bob Moses, the brainy, bespectacled New York math teacher and SNCC leader, was already in the state, working alongside Amzie Moore in Cleveland, Mississippi. Ella Josephine Baker, the human rights activist and organizer, had chosen Moses to be her man in Mississippi. Baker had left the national NAACP over differences in strategy—differences Medgar was painfully familiar with—and over the chauvinism she faced in the movement. She had returned to her alma mater, Shaw University, and served as counselor to the students who founded SNCC. "As they began to determine where to launch their program in what Bob Moses used to call the theater of the Movement," said Derrick Johnson, who eventually led the Mississippi and the national NAACP, "they looked at Albany, Georgia . . . they looked at a location in Arkansas, but she realized that Mississippi perhaps was the most fertile opportunity to launch a direct action program."[43] Baker assigned Moses to launch the SNCC operation in the state.

The Freedom Rides were set to arrive in Jackson the following March. Organized by CORE, they were designed to test a pair of Supreme Court rulings, made in 1946 and 1960, that ruled segregation in interstate transportation and public facilities such as bus terminals and restaurants that supported interstate travel illegal,[44] by sending interracial groups of riders from Washington, D.C., south to New Orleans.

By the time SNCC moved into the state in earnest in 1961, four major civil rights groups—SNCC, CORE, the Southern Christian Leadership Conference, and the NAACP—were operating in Mississippi, sometimes with competing priorities. Medgar, despite his frustration with the influx of outside groups, decided to make the best of it. On behalf of the Mississippi NAACP, he signed onto a compact whose mission was to coordinate the work of the various groups and to distribute funds from a national Voter Education Project. The Council of Federated Organizations (COFO) focused its activities on the rural Delta towns that had proven to be the hardest to crack when it came to voter registration, due to the ongoing state of Klan-led terror.

The network Medgar, Amzie Moore, and Aaron Henry (who was named COFO's president) had created provided crucial infrastructure and support to the other COFO leaders—Bob Moses and CORE's David Dennis—and to the young activists who were pouring into the state, hoping to coax terrified sharecroppers into putting their names on the rolls and force businesses and public facilities to accept integration as legal and constitutional.

Medgar was defying the New York leadership by pushing financial resources toward bail funds for the college students who were mounting protests, sit-ins, and marches in Jackson, Greenwood, and around the state, while trying to keep his voter registration numbers up enough to satisfy Wilkins and the home office. His priority was the Black Mississippi collegians and students from segregated high schools who were taking risks for their own freedom in the state where they would still be when the national activists went home. After all, many of the young activists gravitating to SNCC and the Freedom Rides had been NAACP Youth Council members first. He and they were determined to engage in direct action against segregation whether New York approved or not.

They most certainly did not approve.

Medgar's defiance was risky because he couldn't afford to lose his NAACP job—not with Myrlie and three little children to support. Myrlie had given up her job as Medgar's secretary when Van was born, and in addition to their mortgage, they now had two car notes to pay. The national office was constantly critical of Medgar's voter registration and membership numbers, and of the frequency and dollar amounts of his reimbursement requests for the mileage he was putting on his car and the expenses for gas as he traversed the state supporting the very militancy the national NAACP wanted shut down. Myrlie's concerns were more basic: she was concerned about her husband's safety, and that he didn't lose his mind.

To assuage New York and to prove that his strategies were working, Medgar needed a significant increase in Black voters on the books in America's most tenacious apartheid state, something he knew was unlikely, regardless of the determination of activists like Moses, or a major victory in court against the state of Mississippi.

A February 1961 phone call to the Lynch Street office provided the opportunity Medgar needed. James Meredith, a Black Air Force veteran and NAACP man who had seen service overseas, had applied to Ole Miss and been rejected via telegram a month later, after receiving no initial reply. He wanted the NAACP's help in filing a lawsuit to attempt to gain entry. For Medgar, it was as if the fates had called. Eight years after his own application to the University of Mississippi had been rejected, and with Clyde Kennard still wasting away at Parchman as punishment for seeking admission to a different "white" college, the opportunity to strike a historic blow against segregation in Mississippi was presenting itself again.

CHAPTER 5

Mississippi Freedom

You can't separate peace from freedom because no one can be at peace unless he has his freedom.

—Malcolm X

Medgar was a highly perceptive man," James Meredith said. "And he knew how to do things and how to get things done."[1] He recognized that these same qualities in Medgar would be important to him. Meredith was possessed with a confidence and bravado that whites in the South, especially Mississippi, considered unappealing in a Black man. After serving six years in the Air Force, Meredith had completed two years at Jackson State.

His determination to apply to Ole Miss had been reaffirmed by John F. Kennedy's 1961 inaugural address, in which the new president called for the nation to "pay any price, bear any burden, meet any hardship, support any friend, [and] oppose any foe to assure the survival and success of liberty." Meredith had served his country, had always done well in school, and was qualified by every reasonable measure. Why shouldn't he go to the state's top school? He wrote to the university requesting an admissions application the next day, on January 21, 1961.

Medgar had hoped to reapply to the law school at Ole Miss himself, to take his own stand for desegregation and to further his own ambitions. The New York office of the NAACP did not agree. Gloster Current wrote to Medgar in late March, saying that he had discussed the matter with Robert Carter, the NAACP's general counsel, who had been part of the team with Thurgood Marshall that successfully argued the *Brown* case: "It would appear that a combination study-work program is out of the question. Therefore, you may want to think this matter very carefully as to possible alternatives."[2] Myrlie was frankly relieved.

Medgar and James Meredith met at the Evers home. "He took me to his house to call Thurgood Marshall, who was the head of the NAACP Legal Defense Fund, and talk to him about my case," Meredith said. "Marshall said something I didn't like, and I hung up the phone."

Marshall had quizzed Meredith about his background and asked for documents to make sure he would be a strong plaintiff. Marshall knew anything negative the state of Mississippi found would be used to reject Meredith or worse.

Meredith was a hothead, like Charles, and Medgar talked him down after his conversation with Marshall. He also intervened with Marshall to make sure the NAACP would continue its legal support for the caustic applicant. "Medgar Evers took it upon himself to do whatever it was that needed to be done . . . without me knowing it," Meredith said. "And that's a smart man."

With tempers assuaged, Meredith submitted his application. It was formally rejected in February 1961, and Meredith, with his new NAACP attorneys, Constance Baker Motley and R. Jess Brown, filed suit against the University of Mississippi and prepared to head to court.

The first court date for James Meredith's appeal of Ole Miss's rejection of his law school application was scheduled for June 12, 1961. For the months until then, Medgar worked on preparing the brash young man to face the public and the media. "He took me to Atlanta, to the *New York Times* bureau," Meredith said.[3] "The only Southern bureau was in Atlanta. The head of it was Claude Sitton."

Sitton was a Navy World War II veteran and Atlantan. His great-grandfather had been a slave owner and a tax collector for the Confederacy. His father, a former railroad conductor, operated a Depression-era farm in rural Georgia, where Sitton worked the fields alongside Black sharecroppers during his high school years. After the war, he became a prolific reporter of civil rights events and leaders. He was on the bus out of Montgomery, covering the 250-mile trek to Jackson, Mississippi.

"He had been in the Navy in World War II," Meredith said. "He was the commander of Black troops, and he didn't like the way the Navy treated Blacks. He took it upon himself to teach me how to deal with the media. That is: 'Don't let them trap you, and don't let them get you to say stupid stuff. Understand [that] you don't ever know who your friends are or who your enemies are."

Indeed, when the suit was first filed, the white newspaper in Meredith's hometown of Kosciusko, the *Star-Herald*, obtained his name from the Sovereignty Commission.[4]

The first Mississippi sit-in demonstration to protest Meredith's application being denied occurred one month after he received the telegram. On March 27, nine undergraduates from the NAACP's Tougaloo college chapter—Joseph Jackson Jr., Albert Lassiter, Alfred Cook, Ethel Sawyer, Geraldine Edwards, Evelyn Pierce, Janice Jackson, James Bradford, and Meredith Anding Jr.[5]—attempted to desegregate the city's main library. Dressed in their Sunday best, the "Tougaloo Nine," as they became known, first visited the "colored" George Washington Library and then proceeded to the segregated Main Library in Jackson and began a "read-in," sitting down, books in hand. The librarian called the police, and they were quickly arrested. Medgar began sorting out NAACP legal help and money for bonds, which were set at $1,000 each. In his incident report, he wrote that the trial "was set for March 29, 1961 for 4 o'clock P.M. in the Jackson Municipal court building."[6]

On the night before the students' trial, Medgar organized a mass meeting and prayer vigil for the Tougaloo Nine, at College Hill Baptist Church. The crowd soon swelled to some eight hundred Jackson State students and supporters, "as well as a large contingent of Jackson city policemen."[7] The vigil was quickly dispersed after the Jackson State president, Jacob Reddix, called the police on his own students.[8]

The next day hundreds of Jackson State students boycotted classes. Fifty of them attempted to take over Reddix's office but were stopped by police. Medgar and local Jacksonians joined a second campus rally and marched to the courthouse on Eastland Street, whose principal feature was a sixty-by-eighty-foot mural, depicting contented Black slaves picking cotton while a judge advises a benevolent-looking family of white masters, titled "Pursuits of Life in Mississippi." "No one could get a fair trial standing in front of that mural," Rev. Ed King said.[9]

The Jackson city police surrounding the courthouse made it clear that few of those outside, Black or white, were getting inside. The marchers cheered and raised their fists as the Tougaloo Nine were brought in. Medgar wrote in his field secretary report on the incident that "hordes of policemen and two vicious police dogs converged on Negro citizens only and . . . began whipping us with night sticks as well as extending the leash on the dogs to the extent that Rev. S. Leon Whitney, pastor of Parish Street Baptist Church, was bitten on the arm."[10] W. B. Wren "was beaten so brutally by the police that his left arm was broken above the wrist," Evers reported. "The Field Secretary," he added, referring to himself, "was struck a number of times in the back by officers with Billy clubs and on the head with a pistol, by a man in plain clothes."[11]

Accused of "parading without a permit," all nine students were convicted of "breaching the peace." The *Clarion-Ledger* claimed the Tougaloo Nine had "apparently goaded police into placing them under arrest."[12] The *Jackson Daily News* accused the NAACP of providing propaganda for the Soviet Union.[13]

Medgar wanted NAACP executive secretary Roy Wilkins's support, and he wrote to the organization's national leader praising the Tougaloo Nine for having inspired a movement. "This act of bravery and concern on the part of these nine young people has seemed to electrify Negroes' desire for Freedom here in Mississippi," he said, without pointing to his own role. He asked the national office to make an "inspirational gesture" and invite the nine, who after all were NAACP collegiate members, to the National Convention in Philadelphia. There was no immediate reply.

On Guynes Street, Mrs. Young began noticing more Tougaloo students and other activists at the Evers house. When she went across the street to see Myrlie, she discovered that the frenetic pace and strains of the movement were wearing on the couple, and life in the Evers home was reaching a low point. Myrlie had made every accommodation for Medgar's civil rights mission. She was his cook, his unpaid secretary, and his speech editor, and her station wagon sometimes became a part-time shuttle, carrying not just schoolkids from the block but also NAACP officials from the airport to the house and back.

Six or seven days a week, she felt like a single mother, and she was the children's chauffeur, tutor, and piano teacher. She would curl up with the kids on the bed in her and Medgar's room to watch television on weekend nights. She picked up the pieces when Reena was too afraid to bathe after Medgar took her and Darrell, and three of the Wells kids, to the drive-in to see *Psycho*. She was frequently left to explain to Darrell why he had to come inside when strange cars were parked on the block, or that he must never touch the guns hidden in his parents' bedroom, or why she slammed down the phone when people called and hissed vulgar words about what they planned to do to her husband. Medgar was fighting for freedom for Black Mississippians, but it sometimes felt like a paralyzing confinement for his own family. Myrlie was increasingly resentful.

"As a matter of fact, it almost drove a wedge between us that I didn't think would ever heal,"[14] she said. "Those were very difficult times for us." They argued about him asking her to prepare yet another meal for an NAACP leader, or they quarreled about the latest important person's visit (like Lena Horne, the Staples Singers, or Dick Gregory). Segregation made these stars "unwelcome in restaurants or clubs. We had nowhere to host them except in our own homes," Myrlie wrote.[15]

She complained to Medgar that she didn't have enough money between her allowance and the allotment for paying their bills and feeding their children to feed more people. He, in turn, rebuked her for not managing money well enough.[16] That made her even angrier, and the silences between them were getting longer. "That was the first shutdown that we had in our marriage, where we barely communicated," she said. They were beginning to break their pledge of never leaving the house angry.

"One night, Medgar came home, and he said, 'This has lasted long enough. I can't take any more of this. I'm going to do my work.' I never shall forget. I told him, 'There's the door.' He said, 'I'll talk to you later' and left. I was heartbroken. I loved him so much. The children did. We needed him. But I do believe that he was that determined to take the path of civil rights and leave his family. I'll always believe that. It was a calling to him. I didn't have another woman to be jealous of," she said. "I had a cause."[17]

After one of these arguments, she snapped at him, "You know nothing about running a household. We're poor, and I'm stretching *our* money as far as I can." Medgar raised his hand, and she feared he would strike her. She grabbed a cast-iron skillet and sent the flat end careening into his temple. Medgar stood wide-eyed and stunned for what seemed like an eternity. "He had questioned my honesty and my abilities. I had questioned his authority," she later wrote. "Then, suddenly, Medgar retaliated, landing a large open palm on my left cheek. Every pin curl in my hair went flying." She stumbled backward, "more emotionally than physically" stunned.[18]

The two of them stood in horrified silence, before Medgar walked out and went back to work, with a large knot on the side of his head. Their children were not there to see their parents dissolve into frustrated violence. Myrlie had taken them to Vicksburg during a school break, and after shedding every tear inside her, she boarded a Greyhound bus and arrived at Aunt Myrlie and Mama's house at close to midnight.

The next day, Medgar knocked on Aunt Myrlie's door. He was with Clarence Mitchell Jr., the Washington bureau director of the NAACP and the national organization's longtime chief lobbyist in the capital. Mitchell, who had played a key role in the passage of the 1957 Civil Rights Act and who had come to be known as "the 101st Senator" for his constant presence on Capitol Hill, had a wisdom that made him a dear friend, counselor, and father figure to the couple. Mitchell took Myrlie aside and asked if she knew just how much her husband loved her and how important their marriage was to Medgar. She wondered aloud if that was enough. "Mr. Mitchell then called Medgar in," Myrlie wrote. And told them: "It would be criminal if you two fine people, who love each other as much as you do, let the stress of this job tear you apart."[19]

They returned home, and both agreed that things had to change. "I remember Medgar saying to me one evening, 'Myrlie, I cannot fight everyone out there and come home and fight with you.'" She held her breath waiting for what he would say next. "He said, 'If we can't make it, I will have to leave.' I remember saying to him, 'You love your work more than you do me or your children,' [and] he said, 'It is *because* of you and my children that I'm doing what I do.' I couldn't accept it . . . I didn't accept it. Not then. I did later. But not then.[20]

"The time came around to make a decision. You stay, or you leave. Darn it, love is such a funny thing. I chose love, and I stayed. Medgar told me to be sure that I knew what I was doing, because he knew what *he* was doing. . . . So, what do you do when you're in love? You stay. You learn to work along with that person. . . . For me, I had to learn the deep meaning of prayer, because when he left the house every day, I never knew whether I'd see him again."

Myrlie knew she would never pull Medgar away from his mission. "When you can't win, you join," she said. And they carried on. "The love, the respect, the marriage, lasted. And I became more supportive of him as he drove around the different counties of the Mississippi Delta. I didn't complain as much. I learned not to nag at him about what he was doing, but [instead] to pray with him and encourage him." Sometimes they just sat together silently on the living room sofa, or listened quietly to records, just to relax. Medgar seemed at times to crave an unattainable rest. "Quite honestly, our marriage improved tremendously after reaching that [low] point and crossing it," Myrlie recalled.

Some things, though, didn't change, and that included the threats. "My main mission was to keep our children from being hurt," Myrlie said. Meanwhile, Medgar's calling was increasingly at odds with the mission his bosses had given him. The NAACP's New York leadership had repeatedly made it clear they wanted their full-time field secretaries to focus on voter registration at the state level while NAACP lawyers battled segregation in the courts. According to Ed King, the national organization's message was "We don't use students. We protect students."

Roy Wilkins was a passionate defender of civil rights, but he and the NAACP board saw no point in wasting precious funds, which needed to be constantly raised from white, Northern donors, to bail hundreds of young activists out of jail when they were winning in the courts. He and other leaders of the major civil rights organizations, including Whitney Young Jr. of the National Urban League, hoped they would have an ally in the newly elected John F. Kennedy and his brother, Robert Kennedy, who had been named attorney general.

Burke Marshall was appointed head of the Justice Department's Civil Rights Division, and he assigned John Michael Doar, a young Princeton-educated assistant attorney general in the division, to the job "nobody wanted"[21]—investigating the widespread pattern of voting denial in Mississippi.

Two days after the police brutality in front of the Jackson courthouse, the FBI's New Orleans bureau interviewed Medgar and four other witnesses, including Willis Randall Wrenn, who was beaten there, and Rev. Sam Johnson, who had seen a Black photographer whose clothes were covered with blood. Doar and Marshall requested a summary of the interviews, indicating that the investigation into the actions of Jackson police on March 29 had reached the highest levels of the Justice Department.[22] That news soon made the papers.

It was not Medgar's only contact with the FBI. He repeatedly tried, to no avail, to report the apparent taps on his phone, and the threats and harassment he was receiving from local authorities.

In a March 31, 1961, FBI interview, Medgar described walking toward the building on Pascagoula Street that housed the Mississippi Municipal Court: "I heard three uniformed officers of the Jackson Police Dept, whom I cannot identify or describe, looking out a window at me and one of them remarked, 'There he is, we ought to kill him.'" Medgar told the FBI agents, "I smiled, did not reply, and joined my friends at the parking lot entrance."[23]

Not surprisingly, there was no federal action taken to protect Medgar or any other civil rights leader. J. Edgar Hoover was far more focused on what he believed was Communist influence over the civil rights movement and his fears that a Black "messiah" would rouse Black Americans into revolution.

Medgar was no messiah. But he certainly wanted revolution. And he was growing impatient with his bosses' opposition to the direct action he believed would bring it on in Mississippi.

On April 7, Medgar traveled with Aaron Henry to New York to appeal directly to Wilkins, Current, Hurley, and several NAACP attorneys and board members. The result was an urgent telegram dispatched to NAACP branches nationwide, launching "Operation Mississippi" and seeking to raise $40,000 for a legal defense of the nine Tougaloo students "arrested and fined for attempting to use [the] white library in Jackson, Mississippi, as they launched their appeals." It also said the NAACP "is mobilizing every possible strength to protect people from persecution by police and other authorities," and "this will include further challenges in all fields. Also [an] intensified voter registration campaign." Operation Mississippi was intended to "continue over the years" and would rally support from churches, labor unions, and other organizations.[24] What the NAACP telegram explicitly did not include were calls for more direct-action protests.

Some newspapers, including members of the Black newspaper the *Arizona Sun,* reprinted the telegram in full. The *Clarion-Ledger* ran only selected portions, leaving off the closing lines, in which Wilkins referred to Mississippi as "the snarling dog state," and saying it "must be the target henceforth of all decent Americans in an effort to erase the disgrace this state has brought upon our country in the eyes of all humanity." The anti-NAACP and Sovereignty Commission–allied *Jackson Advocate* damned the national organization with faint praise, declaring in an April 29, 1961, lead story: "The NAACP's 'Operation Mississippi' got off to a fast start in Jackson last week when four Negro students were arrested after sit-ins on a downtown bus."[25] An Associated Press report called the act of state violence that prompted the FBI investigation "the first major racial incident in the state"—overlooking the brutal lynching of Emmett Till.

President Kennedy had been anything but aggressive on civil rights thus far. His administration believed that integration should proceed gently, with each state going at its own pace without heavy-handed intervention from Washington. And as a Democrat, he didn't relish picking a fight with Southern Democratic governors and mayors from whom he would one day need help supporting legislation or seeking reelection. Particularly for a narrowly elected president, every state counted, and Southern states counted just as well in the Electoral College. With a reticent Democratic administration in Washington and far right segregationist Democrats in charge at home, civil rights activists like Medgar often felt like they were on their own.

Neither party in Washington seemed particularly interested in Black lives. Despite Abraham Lincoln's sacrifice and the promise of Ulysses Grant's administration, Republicans had ultimately betrayed Black Americans, cutting a deal with Southern Democrats to pull federal troops out of the South in 1877 in exchange for installing Republican Rutherford Hayes in the White House. This allowed Reconstruction to collapse under white robes, rifles, and ropes, and the planter class to come back from secession with renewed strength and ferocity. Now these former Confederate states were fighting modernity with every legal and violent trick they could dream up, while Washington was focused on the Cold War.

Still, the war on Southern streets would not be abated.

The attack by Jackson police had not produced the peace and quiet Jackson mayor Allen Thompson desired. On March 30, more than 1,500 people had packed into the Masonic Temple for an NAACP meeting, despite pouring rain and tornado warnings, braving not just the weather but also the five dozen Jackson police officers assembled outside, plus the FBI agents and local informants mingling among the crowd. Aaron Henry spoke, as did Clarence Mitchell Jr., who called for more federal civil rights laws to combat racist Southern police violence.[26]

With the Tougaloo Nine sentenced to $100 fines and thirty-day suspended sentences—conditioned, of course, on their promise not to participate in any further protests—and with appeals being filed and the outrage refusing to die down, Mayor Thompson took to the airwaves on April 7, with an address calling for "racial peace" in Jackson.[27]

Instead, sit-ins and demonstrations against segregation broke out all over Jackson, and soon young demonstrators were targeting the city's parks, buses, and swimming pools. In Medgar's April report, he wrote about four members of the NAACP intercollegiate chapter who sat in the whites section of a city bus. "They were arrested after refusing to move when ordered to do so," he wrote. As usual, the four were charged with "breach of the peace."[28]

Medgar wrote that he believed the brutality of Jackson police "brought on greater unity in the Negro community and projected the NAACP in a position of being the accepted spokesman for the Negro people."[29] In an April 20 speech at the Masonic Temple, Medgar quoted Thomas Paine's cry that "these are the times that try men's souls" and praised "these young people who have taken a giant step for freedom in the face of tremendous odds and impending crises."[30]

"Let it not be said of us when history records these momentous times," he told those who packed into the gaping auditorium, "that we slept while our rights were being taken away by those who would keep us in slavery and by those who say that we are doing all right." He laid down markers for what needed to be done: the hiring of Black police officers, firemen, typists, crossing guards, telephone operators, and other city employees, Black federal employment, including at the Veterans Administration and the Postal Service, the lifting of restrictions on Black voter registration, and "the unrestricted use of public facilities such as parks, libraries, etc., and the removal of segregation signs at the bus stations, train stations and city buses, as well as segregated seating arrangements for all passengers on the city bus lines."[31]

AS HE PUSHED THE ACCELERATOR, MEDGAR WORRIED THAT THE impending Freedom Rides closing in on the state would disrupt the hard-earned momentum the local efforts were gaining. On May 4, 1961, the day the first busload of Freedom Riders departed Washington, D.C., Medgar wrote to CORE's field director, Gordon Carey, to decline his request for assistance staging a mass meeting on May 16—a day before the annual NAACP commemoration of the May 17 anniversary of the *Brown* decision. Medgar said he believed "CORE's coming into Jackson at this time . . . will not have the effect intended and possibly hamper some of the efforts already in progress."[32] To Medgar, it was important that Mississippians stand up and fight for themselves, without relying on a movement traveling into their state. While he fully supported the goals of the Freedom Rides, he felt strongly that as had happened in Montgomery, the courage of Mississippians needed to be at the forefront of the movement in their state. His objections were ignored.

The first bus carried seven Black and six white Freedom Riders, led by CORE cofounder and national director James Farmer. The eclectic group, including SNCC cofounder John Lewis,[33] were bound for New Orleans to commemorate the anniversary of *Brown* and to test the 1960 Supreme Court decision in *Boynton v. Virginia* that declared the segregation of interstate buses and terminals to be unconstitutional.

The peaceful protests met with an immediate and vicious Klan response. The first group of Freedom Riders were dragged off their bus, beaten, and jailed in North Carolina and again in South Carolina. When a second group arrived in Anniston, Alabama, they endured a Klan firebombing of their Greyhound bus that rocketed the Freedom Rides to a worldwide news story. In Birmingham, Bull Connor, the fanatically racist public safety commissioner, encouraged KKK members to attack the riders and pulled police protection from the Greyhound and Trailways terminals, claiming sardonically that he did so because it was Mother's Day.

Freedom Rider Catherine Burks-Brooks recalled the riot on May 21 at the Montgomery Greyhound station, where a mob attacked a white fellow rider named Jim Zwerg. "Some men held him while white women clawed his face with their nails," she said. "And they held up their little children—children who couldn't have been more than a couple years old—to claw his face. I had to turn my head back because I just couldn't watch it."[34]

That night, a white mob three thousand strong menaced Freedom Riders and hundreds of their local supporters as they gathered inside the First Baptist Church to hear Dr. King and Rev. Ralph Abernathy, King's partner in creating the Southern Christian Leadership Conference. The mob became so frantic, they even threatened the federal marshals the Kennedy administration was forced to dispatch to protect the convoys. Bricks crashed through the windows, and those inside feared the sanctuary might be burned to the ground. King and Abernathy considered giving themselves up to the mob to save the 1,500 terrified people inside.[35]

Even as the administration sent federal marshals, they criticized the Freedom Riders, with Robert Kennedy saying the protests, and the violent rioting they triggered, had embarrassed the United States before the world. Abernathy, a World War II Army veteran born in 1926 in Linden, Alabama, and whose father had been the first Black man to qualify to vote in their rural county, tersely responded, asking: "Doesn't the Attorney General know we've been embarrassed all our lives?"[36]

Medgar had long believed that World War II had ripped open the great contradiction in America's claim to be a great nation, let alone the leader of the free world. In a 1959 speech, Medgar had stated that "a kind of national soul-searching began with World War II. While fighting a war against forces proclaiming a doctrine of racial superiority, it became increasingly difficult to justify racial discrimination at home. Since then," he continued, "the difficulty has mounted as questions about discrimination have been raised with each new court case, whether involving school desegregation or other efforts to obtain civic justice, each publicized case of violence against Negro citizens."[37]

King held a news conference on May 22 at Abernathy's home and announced that, with or without federal protection, the Freedom Rides would proceed to Mississippi and then on to New Orleans, after a pause to cleanse their spirits and participate in a nonviolence workshop with

Prof. James Lawson, an inspirational figure within the movement who had trained a number of SNCC leaders including Lewis, Bernard Lafayette, and Diane Nash.

Lafayette, a Freedom Rider and SNCC cofounder under the auspices of Ella Baker and the SCLC, and the college roommate of John Lewis, was inside First Baptist during the Montgomery siege. He, along with Nash, was a student leader of the Nashville movement, and he had been beaten at the Montgomery bus station. The next day, thirty-three movement leaders, including Lafayette and Nash, a battered Lewis (the back of his head covered in bandages from repeated blows with a milk crate at the station), Joseph Lowery, CORE cofounder James Farmer, and local activist James Bevel held a strategy meeting.

Lafayette recalled that even though King had asked Robert Kennedy for National Guard protection for the buses headed to Jackson, one young woman at the meeting "just insisted: if Martin Luther King would come with us, we would have protection." But, he explained, King was out on probation in Georgia from a previous arrest for civil rights activity, and if he'd been arrested, he "would have been [in jail] back in Georgia by himself."[38]

Mississippi governor Barnett had earlier announced that the state police would "escort" the buses through his state, which Abernathy at the King press conference called "a form of kidnapping."[39] Barnett was determined to prevent any Alabama-style scenes of burning buses or churches surrounded by violent mobs, but that didn't mean there wouldn't be arrests. There would be lots of them.

The first busload of Freedom Riders arrived in Jackson on May 24. They attempted to use the segregated restroom at the Greyhound Station on 219 N. Lamar Street and were promptly arrested for "breach of the peace." Before long, more Freedom Riders and protesters were pouring into the city—including a second Greyhound bus that day from Montgomery, and subsequent Greyhound and Trailways buses from Montgomery, Atlanta, Memphis, Nashville, New Orleans, and

St. Louis. Years later, Barnett boasted: "Well, we didn't have much trouble with the Freedom Riders. When they didn't obey the officials here in the City of Jackson in Hinds County, we just simply put them in jail, and when the jails were all filled and the mayor's chicken coops down on the fairground were all filled, there were thirty-two of them left, and it was my happy privilege to send all of them to the State Penitentiary at Parchman and put them in maximum security cells. We put them in maximum security cells so they would be protected, you see. You haven't heard of any more Freedom Riders in Mississippi."[40]

The Freedom Riders confined to Parchman's fetid cells—half of them Black, half of them white, a quarter of them women, and some as young as eighteen years old[41]—felt anything but protected. Nash, who was helping to guide the Riders through the South, wound up there, too, after being arrested for refusing to move to the "colored" side of the Jackson courthouse. She was nearly nine months pregnant and refused to bond out despite the pleas of other SNCC members, including Lafayette, saying, "Any Negro child born anywhere in Mississippi is born in jail"[42] anyway. Fred Douglas Moore Clark Sr., who had been recruited by Bevel and Nash, thought he would die in Parchman, as he struggled to breathe inside an overcrowded cell.[43]

Hezekiah Watkins, just thirteen years old, spent five terrifying days on Parchman's "death row." He had become fascinated with the Freedom Riders and with a friend named Troy, pretended to be too sick for church, and instead went downtown to the Jackson bus station to watch the Freedom Riders. By the time the boys arrived, the activists had all been arrested. So they staged their own small defiance by sipping from the "white" fountains outside the bus station. Watkins was arrested when his friend shoved him inside the station as a joke, then abandoned him, fleeing home. At Parchman, a terrified Watkins was locked up with adult inmates. "Those five days were like five months," he said.[44]

By year's end, with arrivals nearly every month, more than thirty-five busloads of Freedom Riders had come to Jackson and three to McComb, and there were at least ten desegregation actions at that Greyhound Station, more than in any other state.[45] Mississippi had replaced New Orleans as the terminus point and focus of the Freedom Rides.

Medgar noted in a June 21 memo to New York that "to date a total of one hundred thirty-one 'Freedom Riders' have been convicted for 'breach of the peace.' There have been a total of 43 released on bond; four have paid their fines, forty are in the penitentiary and forty remain in the jails here in Jackson."[46]

The New York headquarters of the NAACP was growing weary of writing bond checks for jailed activists, and they fundamentally disagreed that people who had been arrested ought to stay in jail to make a point. Better to bond out and fight it out in court. That forced some local creativity. When women incarcerated at Parchman lacked sanitary napkins, two Black women activists—A. M. E. Logan, who owned a Jackson cosmetic shop, and Thelma Sanders, who owned a millinery—formed Womanpower Unlimited to provide them.[47]

But the national organization was also frustrated with the Kennedy administration, which Wilkins viewed as too mild in its response to the civil rights upheavals around the country, and too slow to bring forth a legislative solution. If they wanted the protests to stop, governmental action was required. To that end, Wilkins wrote a terse April 5, 1961, letter to Harris Wofford, President Kennedy's special assistant on civil rights, saying: "It may be that the Kennedy Administration proceeded in other fields as it did in civil rights, but I would be inclined to doubt it. I will believe until shown otherwise that in any important field, labor, agriculture, industry, finance, housing, health, the leading figures were called in and told, in one way or another, what the Administration had in mind. Whether they cooperated on all phases or only in part of them, they at least knew where they stood. In civil rights, the information on what the Administration had in mind (I do not count the campaign utterances) . . . I may be in error, but at no time were the responsible Negro civil rights leaders called in and told formally what the Administration planned to do."[48]

Medgar was frustrated, too, and his frustrations reflected the mood of Mississippi's Black youth. As the Freedom Rides were seizing control of the national narrative, NAACP-backed youth protests continued. Even the Jackson Zoo was the site of sit-ins, on June 4 and again on June 14, launched by the NAACP Youth Council and the organization's college chapter.[49] Mayor Thompson wanted the protests to stop. Medgar and the Jackson NAACP requested to meet with him and presented a list of demands, including a reiteration of the demand that the city hire Black police officers, firefighters, and crossing guards, and that the state's impediments to Black voter registration and the implementation of the *Brown v. Board*–mandated school integration cease. Thompson seemed unwilling to budge, and on June 18, he received two calls from President Kennedy, who was placing calls to several Southern governors and mayors hoping to quell the violence rippling across newspapers around the world.

"Well, now let me ask you this, uh, what about these policemen?" Kennedy asked Thompson, regarding the NAACP demand for Black officers. "If these people all stop demonstrating and went home for a period, when do you think you could take the policemen [*sic*] and how many?"[50]

"Well, I just pick 'em as I get 'em ready. . . . Uh, I mean as I get them, when I think that they're qualified," the Jackson mayor said.

Kennedy asked how many Black Jacksonians were qualified to join the force.

"Well, I had two I was going to take on. I may even have to get a call from you to put 'em on."[51]

Kennedy, the ardent cold warrior, also wanted the demonstrations to stop, to alleviate the damage to America's reputation around the world, which the Soviets were fully exploiting. To make that happen, the civil rights leaders needed to win some concessions. "I'll tell you what," Kennedy said. "It seemed to me, that if I, if we could say to these fellows . . . that you were going to do something about the policemen, and . . . I mean that's not too tough."[52]

Thompson insisted to the president that the policeman must "be responsible to me and not to the NAACP." He also warned Kennedy that for his own politics, Thompson would need to denounce his fellow Democrat publicly.

"Well, listen," Kennedy laughed. "I give you full permission to denounce me in public as long as you don't in private."[53]

Throughout June, the Jackson Non-Violent Movement accelerated, as protesters who were released from Parchman were recruited by SNCC members from the Nashville Christian Leadership Conference, including Nash, Lafayette, Bevel, Marion Berry, and Charles Sherrod, and offered nonviolence workshops and movement training.[54] Medgar wrote that the workshops were intended "to recruit more Jackson residents into the Freedom Ride movement, which had not been advocated by the NAACP."[55] This revealed the tensions brewing between the direct action that young activists were insisting on and the national NAACP's courts-and-registration-first strategy. Medgar reported that young activists were targeting "various transportation facilities in the city of Jackson; also sit ins at the Walgreen's Drug Store and picketing of a meeting of members of the Southern Governors' Conference."[56]

Lafayette recalled that Governor Barnett "came out in the newspaper and congratulated the folks from Mississippi for not getting involved with the Freedom Rides." But Jim Bevel *was* from Mississippi. "He was from Itta Bena," Lafayette said. "He was already home for the summer. And I stayed with him because it was an insult to say that folks from Mississippi didn't get involved in the Freedom Rides. So that was the thing that motivated us to stay in Mississippi and recruit people. And that's . . . when we met Medgar Evers."

Medgar was skeptical of the Freedom Riders' tactics, which he felt didn't address the fundamental state of terror in the Delta, and their activities were competing with the sit-ins and protests the NAACP Youth Councils were conducting in Jackson and also increasing the pressure on him from New York as he frequently pushed for funds to help bail them out of jail. He also firmly believed that Mississippians had to fight for their own liberty. But he fundamentally supported young activists and understood that collaboration was the best path forward, given the enthusiasm the Freedom Rides were generating among young Mississippians. Medgar "was very supportive of the Freedom *Riders*" themselves, Lafayette said. "He got us an office . . . and he set up shop for us. And that's when we decided, that's Jim Bevel and I, that we would recruit folks *in* Mississippi."

The new SNCC office was located at 1104 Lynch Street, a few doors down from Medgar's NAACP office. Lynch Street, which would remain a center of the Black freedom movement throughout the 1960s, had been named, not for the terrifying Southern specialty in the public murders of Black people, but for John R. Lynch, the formerly enslaved man who became the Speaker of the Mississippi House during Reconstruction and then a member of Congress. Lynch was the first Black man to hold any such elected position in the United States.

Marian Wright Edelman, then a twenty-two-year-old first year law student at Yale, recalled traveling to Mississippi to reconnect with her friends from SNCC: Bob Moses and James Forman. Medgar's "was the first welcoming face I saw when I arrived," she wrote. "He picked me up at the Jackson airport, took me home to meet and have dinner with Myrlie and their children, and then drove me up to the Mississippi Delta where the SNCC headquarters in Greenwood was located, about 90 miles away. Our first news upon arrival was about a shooting which had terrorized the Black community that day."[57]

With direct action protests spreading across the American South, the White House responded to Roy Wilkins's appeal for a plan, two months after his letter to Mr. Wofford, with an invitation to the NAACP and representatives of several of its state chapters, including Medgar. They crowded into the Oval Office on July 12, 1961, with national board chairman Rev. Stephen G. Spottswood serving as the senior-most emissary for the civil rights organization. Kennedy presided over the meeting from a rocking chair in the center of the room. The meeting was intended as a demonstration of commitment by the Kennedy administration to do more to stem the tide of protest and recrimination that was spreading like wildfire. But the administration was searching for the right time and opening to offer a legislative agenda to match the promises of Jack Kennedy's presidential campaign. And they were reluctant to send a bill to Congress amid a state of siege.

As the heady summer of 1961 turned to fall, Medgar became increasingly distressed by the feeling that the Freedom Riders' blazing yet fleeting trail through Mississippi was leaving the NAACP, and terrified Black Mississippians, holding the bag. On October 12, he wrote to Wilkins, Current, and Hurley about the efforts by other groups to recruit students who were already active with NAACP youth organizations. Medgar noted that their efforts had been less than successful, and that CORE mass meetings featuring speakers as esteemed as James Farmer, and even Dr. King, had attracted thousands of attendees but raised little in donations. And those were the least of the problems.

He described a pilot registration and voting project set up by SNCC. "In charge of this operation was Mr. Robert Moses, a young man of Manhattan, New York City," Medgar wrote. He said they proclaimed to be SNCC and SCLC, and "they felt that the NAACP's name should not be brought in." Only after they landed in jail "did they ask for NAACP assistance publicly and cooperatively."[58]

Medgar noted the amount of money the NAACP was spending to bond out jailed SNCC activists, even though "the Voter Registration pilot project of this movement has not netted more than twenty registered voters in Pike County, [and] none in Walthall and Amite Counties. In the case of Amite County, one member of our Branch, a

Mr. Herbert Lee, was killed by a state representative (on Sept 25), allegedly because he was trying to attack him. However, it is generally believed he was killed because of his actions in trying to get Negroes registered to vote."[59]

The Herbert Lee killing was a low point for a movement that had created more headlines than registered voters and cost the life of a good man. All while putting Black Mississippians in greater fear and jeopardy, as anyone who set foot in a meeting—be it NAACP, CORE, or one of the "Freedom Workshops" conducted by Diane Nash, Bernard Lafayette, and other members of the Nashville movement—was added to the Sovereign Commission's files, spied on, harassed, or subjected to the White Citizens' Council's retribution.

When Bob Moses was released from jail in December 1961, he and Tom Gaither, CORE's field secretary, circulated a memo proposing an end to the rivalries among the various civil rights groups and the replacement of enmity with cooperation. Borrowing the name of an early effort to support the Freedom Riders—the Council of Federated Organizations—they found ready agreement from Aaron Henry, who had continued to sit on the national board of King's SCLC despite New York's opposition, as he was a founding member, and from fellow Mississippi activists like James Bevel. The idea was immediately opposed by the national leaders of CORE, SNCC, and the NAACP, who had no desire to see their hard-won resources doled out to other organizations.

Medgar was trying to nurture the young local activists he deeply respected while also assisting the rival national movements that now had operations dotting the state, and maintaining his relationship with the organization that paid his salary. COFO sounded like a way to make it all work.

On January 12, 1962, the NAACP filed a class action lawsuit regarding the arrest and conviction of the Tougaloo Nine,[60] plus subsequent arrests during sit-ins at the Jackson Zoo and those who had attempted to sit on public beaches since the Jackson melee. The suit demanded the desegregation of all public recreational facilities in the city. On February 1, at Gloster Current's request, Medgar sent a letter to Alfred Baker Lewis, a member of the NAACP board of directors, to explain why SNCC and CORE's much-publicized goal of registering voters in schools and clinics in McComb County had resulted in fewer than two dozen people registered. Medgar, exhausted by the rivalries and counterproductivity that had replaced what once felt like forward movement, explained that despite the NAACP's painstaking work to decrease the fear in the Delta, "the rash actions of some of the members of SNCC and the consequential shooting (to death) of Herbert Lee (a Negro) by a State Representative further embedded fear among Negroes that they should not try to register to vote."[61]

Myrlie recalled a few years later that "by the end of the summer of 1962, the other civil rights organizations had learned what Medgar had known all along. Negro voter registration was all but impossible in most parts of the state. For all the courage of the registration workers, for all the beatings and shootings connected with their work, progress was negligible. As Bob Moses put it that summer with an understatement typical of him, 'If you're really going to help the people all over the state and really make a change in this system down here, then there is going to have to be some additional help from the federal government.'"[62]

Despite his frustration, Medgar had concluded that unless the organizations cooperated, they would fail together. "Knowing Mississippi and its problems better than any of the others," Myrlie wrote a few years later, Medgar "felt he wanted the help the other organizations could bring. He felt strongly that he could protect the NAACP's reputation and assure it a fair share of publicity about Mississippi projects. But he felt just as strongly the need for help from the national office on a wider publicity front. After all, the NAACP was the oldest, best-established civil rights organization in the country."[63]

COFO was born out of necessity; an umbrella to coordinate the activities of the four major civil rights groups operating simultaneously in Mississippi and to keep them from running over each other. When

Medgar and Aaron Henry were in Los Angeles, where Medgar gave a speech, they observed how local Jewish groups worked together toward a common goal. Back in Jackson, the men met with Bob Moses, and a New Orleans activist named David Dennis. Aaron Henry, the state NAACP president, wholeheartedly agreed with the COFO concept, and he signed the compact, but he did so as the representative for the Southern Christian Leadership Conference. In August, Henry became the umbrella organization's president. Dennis signed for the Congress of Racial Equality, Bob Moses on behalf of SNCC, and Medgar for the NAACP.

Frank Figgers, who would join the NAACP Youth Council and years later become an NAACP leader in Mississippi, recalled the significance of these four national organizations "and seventy-plus indigenous organizations" coming together under a single umbrella. It felt like a revolutionary idea: to combine the moral capital of the fifty-plus-year-old civil rights organization with the energy of the newer, youth-driven groups. "Now, if that's not the height of creativity and strategy and strategic planning, who knows. And it didn't happen, no place else, but in Mississippi," Figgers said.[64]

By August 1, 1961, COFO existed, with Aaron Henry as its president, Rev. R. L. T. Smith as treasurer, and Bob Moses as the statewide project director. CORE was in charge of registering voters in Meridian and Canton, SNCC voter registration concentrated on the Delta region around Greenwood and McComb, SCLC continued to set up "Freedom Schools" around the state, helping to guide reluctant Black Mississippians into civic life, and the NAACP focused on the battle in the courts. COFO opened an office at 1017 Lynch Street, on "Cooper's Corner," in a building that housed WOKJ, a white-owned but Black-oriented radio station, and a pool hall. The building became a meeting and gathering place for the movement, local and national, in Jackson. It also became a target of the Citizens' Councils and the Sovereignty Commission.

"They doubled the number of spies," investigative journalist Jerry

Mitchell said of the Sovereignty Commission.[65] Rick Bowers added, "They enlisted private detective agencies with both white and Black investigators. There's 160,000 pages of spy reports talking about tracking Medgar Evers, talking about preparing for an arrival of Martin Luther King into the state of Mississippi, getting information in advance about what his route would be and what the strategy would be to undercut him."[66]

They soon had fresh reasons to target Medgar, and Myrlie had new threats to fear.

CHAPTER 6

Freedom from Fear

Freedom is never granted; it is won.

—A. Philip Randolph

The first victory for James Meredith in his fight for admission to the University of Mississippi came on June 25, 1962, when his New York NAACP attorneys, Constance Baker Motley and Jack Greenberg, along with his local attorney, R. Jess Brown of Vicksburg, won a two-to-one Fifth Circuit Court decision ordering the university to admit him. The *Mississippi Free Press* splashed the euphoric headline across its front page: "Ole Miss Will Integrate in July," announcing that Meredith would become the first Negro admitted to a white university in the state's history.

The judges had broken out laughing during the trial when the state's attorney declared that there is no segregation statute in Mississippi. In response, they said if that were so, "they would have to take judicial notice that segregation was nevertheless strictly practiced" in the state. The decision came down on Meredith's twenty-ninth birthday, but he said that day: "Now comes the real test."[1]

The state's appeals went all the way to the U.S. Supreme Court and dragged through September, ending any chance of Meredith enrolling that summer. Meredith saw the case as a mission from God, who often worked, when it came to Black Americans, in mysterious ways.

Medgar spent time with the Meredith's family, including his parents; his wife, Mary June; his young son; and his sister Hazel throughout the trials and appeals. He attended court hearings, and he and James traded news and advice as the case dragged on for more than a year. He became a frequent presence at the Meredith parents' house, said James's sister Hazel Meredith Hall, who at the time had just graduated from Mississippi Valley State College.

Medgar was concerned about Meredith's security and wanted an armed guard posted round-the-clock at Meredith's parents' home where he and his wife were staying. But Meredith wouldn't agree to it. He had a penchant for self-help that Medgar could certainly relate to. "During the worst of the Meredith mess, Medgar and Myrlie were barricaded in at home, couches piled up in front of their windows," Charles said, adding: "Medgar was nonviolent, but he had six guns in the kitchen and living room. He needed them."[2]

John Salter recalled going to the Evers home with his wife to check on Myrlie while Medgar was supposed to be in New Orleans, where the Fifth Circuit was deliberating Meredith's admissions case. They pulled into the driveway and knocked on the side door under the carpark. Medgar's dog was barking in the backyard and there was no answer. When Salter knocked again, the door swung open just a crack. "I could see a gun," he said. "I called my name and Medgar opened the door, instantly apologetic. He had come home to Jackson for the weekend. Inside the home, furniture was piled in front of all the windows. At least a half-dozen firearms were in the living room and kitchen."[3]

The couples sat around the dining table next to the kitchen visiting while the Evers children slept. Salter was struck by how calm Medgar and Myrlie were. He thought this was unusual, since other than Meredith, no one was a bigger target on the Mississippi Klan's hit list than Medgar Evers.[4]

Not long afterward, Charles came from Chicago to visit and to encourage his brother to take a break. But Medgar barely paused his work schedule to spend time with his brother. Myrlie admonished him that Charles didn't come around often enough to be ignored. Medgar reluctantly took the following day off.[5] As they spent time together, fishing at Medgar's favorite spot, Charles told his brother he was being foolish by working himself to death. Medgar shrugged it off. "It's what I want to do," he said. "I never thought I'd make a fortune at it."[6]

Before Charles headed back to Chicago, he handed Myrlie $50 as a gift and told the couple to use it to have some fun. "I want you to go someplace for a weekend and enjoy yourselves. Don't spend it on groceries or to pay bills."[7]

The next weekend Medgar and Myrlie drove to New Orleans with another couple, the Tates. "The first thing Medgar did when we walked into the motel room was pick up the telephone and call the local NAACP office," Myrlie said. "Fortunately, no one answered."[8] The moment they got home from their brief vacation, Medgar dove back into work.

On September 10, 1962, the U.S. Supreme Court ruled in Meredith's favor, ordering his admission to Ole Miss, yet Governor Barnett still refused to stand down. He named himself as the university registrar and twice physically blocked Meredith from entering the registration center, prompting fresh circuit court cases and federal fines that cost thousands of dollars per day. By September 28 the Fifth Circuit Court of Appeals had found Governor Barnett and his lieutenant governor, Paul Johnson, in contempt and ordered them to pay $10,000 and $5,000 per day until they complied with the court's orders to admit Meredith.

Instead, a defiant Barnett attended a Sunday afternoon Ole Miss football game on September 29 at Veterans Memorial Stadium and used the occasion to whip up a frenzy among the forty thousand white attendees, many waving Confederate flags and chanting "Never, Never!" as the governor declared: "I love Mississippi. . . . I love her people . . . her customs. . . . Never shall our emblem go from Colonel 'Reb' to 'Old Black Joe'!"[9]

In a tense phone call afterward with President Kennedy and Robert Kennedy, as hundreds of armed men converged on the Oxford campus, Barnett pleaded "Southern culture"—an indication that his segregationist bravado was largely a show to appease white Mississippi voters.

"I've taken an oath to abide by the laws of this state and our state constitution and the Constitution of the United States," Barnett said. "How can I violate my oath of office? How can I do that and live with the people of Mississippi? You know, they expecting [*sic*] me to keep my word. That's what I'm up against."[10] President Kennedy made it clear that federal troops were being deployed to see the rulings of the courts accomplished and urged Barnett to find a way to comply. Barnett then cut a secret deal. He would make a public pretense of standing firm while being "overwhelmed" by federal marshals.[11] Meredith was allowed entry that evening, to be in a dormitory overnight before a final attempt to register on Monday, October 1. The governor's concession failed to prevent two thousand or more enraged segregationists from swarming the campus. For more than eight hours, they amassed to block Meredith from entering, not realizing that he'd already been taken inside by U.S. Marshals.[12] The ruse didn't prevent a riot.

U.S. Army troops were pelted with bricks and rocks, which were also hurled at passing vehicles, while other cars were set on fire. The old Greek Revival Lyceum, with its red brick façade and towering columns, was bathed in tear gas smoke. White infantrymen faced cries of "Yankee go home!" while Black infantryman "stood gritting their teeth while the hecklers taunted them with shouts of 'Nigger, why don't you go back to New Jersey!'"[13] Shots were fired from the frenzied crowd, killing Paul Guihard, a photographer for Agence France-Presse, and a local jukebox repairman who was part of the insurrection, while more than two hundred marshals and National Guard troops were injured. Police arrested another two hundred. In the end, President Kennedy ordered the Army to deploy twenty thousand National Guard troops from Tennessee, and hundreds more from Memphis.

After spending the night in a lonely dorm, James Meredith walked into the admissions office on October 1, flanked by his U.S. Marshal escorts and Assistant Attorney General John Doar, and registered for classes. What struck him, even after the violence of the previous night, was that the Army units protecting him had been segregated, just as they had been overseas. According to Meredith, the Kennedy Justice Department begged him not to release a statement about that at the time, because, according to journalist Tom Dent, "they felt that once he was in safely, he should be happy and keep his mouth shut."[14]

Meredith suddenly became a Black cultural hero. Letters and telegrams poured in, from Rosa Parks, Langston Hughes, and Josephine Baker.[15] But for the two years he attended Ole Miss, he never had an easy day. He needed armed federal guards protecting him daily, and he was shunned by most of his fellow students, making him, as he called it, "the most segregated Negro in America."[16] He was nearly run off Highway 93 in his hometown of Kosciusko once, only to be saved by an elderly Black man who sped to the other side of the attacking vehicle, and aimed a rifle out of his window.[17] In December, he was arrested in Kosciusko, and told reporters he was called a "nigger" and "ordered to remove his hat, shoved and jostled and mishandled," which the local cops, who claimed they didn't realize who he was, denied. The arrest, for an alleged traffic violation, made national news.[18]

Meredith's family felt the fallout, as well. "I could not get a job, I could not keep a job," James's sister Hazel said. "I was pulled over by the police. They pulled a gun on me. They shot in our house. They called and said, 'We're going to come down and shoot in your house.' They did all kinds of things to us. But you expected those things to happen." James's father and mother saw some of their neighbors keep their distance, fearful of the Klan backlash for associating with them.[19] But as they tended to do, the Merediths made do.

Medgar was affected, too. "When Meredith reached Ole Miss," Charles Evers said, "whites asked, 'Who cooked up this stunt: Medgar Evers, the Communists, John Kennedy?'"[20]

Dorothy Gilliam, the first Black female writer for the *Washington Post,*[21] captured the mood among other Black Mississippians after the Meredith triumph, reporting on October 14, 1962, that "the hope is that Meredith signals the coming of the light for all of them. The fear is that the inevitable changes will bring further death, destruction, and repercussion." Gilliam quoted Medgar as saying Ole Miss was just the beginning. "Petitions are pending to desegregate local schools in Jackson and Leake County. And we're going to make it known to high school and college students that Meredith's suit was designed to break down barriers in all institutions of higher learning." But, he added, "we don't expect to win without a fight."

IN AUGUST, MEDGAR TOLD MYRLIE HE WISHED TO ADD DARRELL'S and Reena's names to a petition headed to the Jackson School Board of Trustees and the school superintendent demanding the integration of Jackson public schools.

"I looked at him and said, 'Not my children,'" Myrlie said. The tension was thick between them. Darrell was preparing to enter fourth grade, and Reena was going into third. "Medgar was determined to go ahead," she recalled. "And I was determined to protect my children."[22]

Medgar dug in his heels. He couldn't ask other parents to take risks he wasn't willing to take himself, with his own children. Myrlie saw little choice but to concede. As Medgar's wife, and thus a core part of the movement, she knew that she had little choice but to sign on to the petition, though she did so reluctantly.

Medgar gently explained to Darrell and Reena why they needed to integrate the schools; why it was so important. It was the same way he would explain why they couldn't go to the local swimming pool or enter a movie theater or a restaurant through the front door, or walk freely into the zoo like any child would, or use whichever water fountain they wanted to. Medgar fought for the space for his kids to be kids, but he didn't shield them from the truth of what it meant to be Black in Mississippi. He would explain to them how Africans were brought to America as slaves and that some died on the way. He would explain the horrors of slavery: the families who were separated and the horrors of the slave markets. And he would explain lies white men told themselves about Black inferiority and their own superiority. And he emphasized that these *were* lies. He wanted his children to fully understand that racism and discrimination were wrong and that they had as much right to grow up to achieve their dreams, to vote, and to live and be what they wanted to as any white child in Mississippi. But they needed to know that evil existed, and he told them it did.[23]

Medgar always made it clear to his children that they were inherently equal—and that he was working hard to make sure they were treated that way. Myrlie maintained her fears and occasional doubts about the path Medgar had them on, but she adored her husband and still believed he was brilliant and fascinating as much as she had when she was a seventeen-year-old college girl. He was a gentle and patient father. And his children so admired him.

Darrell later recalled the times he spent with his father as full of "quality time and quality love." Medgar taught his eldest son how to protect himself, how to fight if he had to, and how to protect his younger siblings. He imparted to Darrell the same lessons "Crazy Jim" had taught him: be strong, don't let anyone put you down, and don't let anyone take away your rights.[24]

Putting their children's names on that petition shook the delicate balance the Everses had achieved on Guynes Street and raised the wariness of even their activist neighbors. Still, Medgar remained adamant. "He had a heart of steel, I'll put it like that," Myrlie said. "He tried to be persuasive. . . . We held meetings at our home until people were afraid to visit."

Myrlie understood her neighbors' fears. The people who had moved to Guynes Street didn't do so as activists. They didn't sign up to have their homes firebombed or shot into. They didn't want to lose their jobs or their mortgages to Citizens' Council retribution on behalf of Medgar's cause. Some of them began to keep their distance from Medgar and even from Myrlie. The Everses lost some friends, though her closest friends on the block hung in, and she continued to play at normalcy at the block's garden club. Some neighbors, she said, began to speak to them only "in the dark of night, and by phone," while others "waved behind curtains as we walked or drove by."

Medgar was undeterred and relentless, pressing their Guynes Street neighbors to support the Jackson schools desegregation efforts as important for all of their children. This was a version of the gentle but firm persuasion he employed in the Delta, where the punishment for registering to vote or taking an NAACP membership could easily be lynching. Medgar sometimes expressed an emotion that ran somewhere between frustration and disgust that so many Jackson teachers, who enjoyed a more comfortable life than that of the terrified sharecroppers in rural Mississippi, seemed to show less courage in many cases than their own collegiate or high school children. Those frustrations occasionally spilled into his monthly reports, but even more often in his conversations with Myrlie. It was why he placed so much emphasis and hope in direct youth action. That was where the courage was.

"A few close friends said, 'Please stop. Don't pursue this anymore,'" Myrlie said. "Medgar's answer was, 'I'm in this until they—meaning white authorities—stop me.' That broke my heart, because I knew that he meant every word he was saying, and he intended to put the children that I had given birth to . . . in danger. I learned that Medgar Evers would do as his heart, his soul, his mind persuaded him to do." And come what may, "our children, Darrell and Reena, were going to be [among] those first students integrating those schools."

It was yet another difficult stretch for the Everses' marriage. Myrlie was at loggerheads with herself. She couldn't bear to leave the man she loved and didn't have the heart to take his children from him. But staying meant accepting that the danger she and he lived with every day would now be shared by a nine-year-old and a seven-year-old. Still, Myrlie could do little but give way. "Needless to say, love won," she said. "I loved my husband. I respected him terribly."

The petition, which cited the *Brown* decision, was submitted on August 17, 1962, and it contained the names of nine parents and fifteen children, demanding that they "and other similarly situated Negro children, be admitted to the so-called 'white school' nearest their residence or within their proper district."[25] Medgar told the *Mississippi Free Press*, "This is not just a demonstration. We are deeply concerned about having our children receive a good education. We will stay with this until they do."[26] The signers' names would be in the local newspapers, meaning they could be fired from their jobs in the white community.

The risks, though, brought the signers together. There was a strength and community that grew out of the shared plunge into the deep water of challenging "the Mississippi way." The families would gather at one of their homes, quite often Medgar and Myrlie's, to fuss or to laugh, to listen to music together and share a meal, and just to convene as fellow travelers heading into what they hoped would be a new era in Mississippi and America.

THE MEREDITHS ALSO CONTINUED TO LIVE UNDER CONSTANT threat. Medgar and Aaron Henry were among the few Black men who regularly dared to drive to Oxford to look in on Meredith, who eventually moved out of the dorms where he faced constant harassment, to an apartment with his wife and son. One time after visiting Meredith, Medgar's Oldsmobile broke down outside Ruleville, and he and Henry were forced to leave the vehicle overnight with a white mechanic who refused all of Medgar's attempts at friendly charm. When they picked up the car the next morning, after staying overnight with some NAACP members, they were certain the mechanic had rigged the car to explode. Myrlie marveled at her husband's fearlessness. He laughed when he told her, but she failed to see the humor in it.[27]

Myrlie also began to doubt how concerned the national office was about Medgar's safety. "The only times the national office wanted Medgar to be careful," she wrote, "were times when a member of the New York staff was with him. They came in, did their work, and got out, sometimes within a few hours. I wondered, resentfully, if they really cared about Medgar's life as much as they obviously cared about his work."[28]

Medgar, Salter, and Tougaloo student activists wanted to build on the momentum from the Meredith victory and opted to repeat their 1961 boycott[29] of the State Fair for Colored People, which took place each October for two days following the official Mississippi State Fair. As Ed King described it: for the first five days of the fair, white farmers advertised and showed off their "white chickens," while their children enjoyed the rides, food, and amenities at the segregated Jackson fairgrounds. Then for the final two days, Black patrons were admitted, and Black farmers were allowed to show off their "Black chickens"; the amenities were sparse, having been largely dismantled. Medgar saw an opportunity. Unlike filing a desegregation petition, marching in a protest, or even signing up for an NAACP membership, boycotting was something anyone could do, risk free. Not every Black Mississippian was willing to risk their lives or economic well-being by walking into a courthouse to try to register to vote, but if they simply refused to buy a new dress or a new pair of shoes from the segregated shops in downtown Jackson, they would be taking a small but meaningful "psychological step towards becoming freedom fighters."

The fair boycott was a success. Just 3 percent of Black Jacksonians attended the fair,[30] matching the participation rates of the prior year's action. A fresh boycott of downtown Jackson businesses followed, with Tougaloo College NAACP and North Jackson Youth Council members, alongside SNCC and CORE activists, leafletting Black neighborhoods and calling on Black citizens not to do their Christmas shopping in downtown stores. This time, more Black Jacksonians got on board. The flyers carried the Jackson Movement label and proved that COFO could bring together the various civil rights organizations. The activists who picketed outside of Jackson businesses, including John Salter, his wife, Eldri Johanson, and other Tougaloo faculty members and students, were arrested for "obstructing the sidewalks" and released from the Jackson jail on $500 bond, setting off the now-familiar dance between city authorities and the NAACP attorneys.

Medgar embarked on a speaking and media tour, and he was interviewed about the Meredith case and the ongoing push for desegregation in Mississippi. On November 10, just as the Kennedy administration was putting a quarantine on Cuba, Medgar told the *Los Angeles Times*, "It is just as important to put a quarantine on Alabama and Mississippi and make it possible for Negroes to be able to register and vote."[31]

During the tour, he wrote letters to Myrlie and the children on hotel stationary. On November 27, 1962, he began:

> *My darling wife and children, I love you dearly and miss you terribly! I am now aboard TWA'S #54 For Idlewild Airport N.Y. City and the time is 12:50 PM Eastern Standard time or 11:50 your time. It is a beautiful day with a slight overcast and bright sun coming through my cabin window. Honey, tell the children daddy will be returning soon and that when Xmas comes, if it is in the Lord's will, we are all going to enjoy Santa Claus and a good Xmas. You be sweet and take care of yourself. Be assured this trip can't end too soon. Love, Medgar.*[32]

New Year's Day 1963 was the start of James Baldwin's Southern lecture tour for CORE. His novels *Go Tell It on the Mountain*, *Giovanni's Room*, and *Another Country* had made him a star to rival Richard Wright. Like most prominent Blacks who set foot in Jackson, Baldwin, who first met Martin Luther King Jr. in 1957, stopped by Guynes

Street, where he visited the Evers house and that of fellow writer Margaret Walker Alexander.

Baldwin didn't just chat with Medgar and Myrlie at home. He tagged along in the Oldsmobile and headed into the Delta with Medgar, accompanying him as he investigated the murder of a Black man, allegedly at the hands of a shopkeeper. He learned firsthand what it was like to speed down back roads at one hundred miles per hour to avoid the Klan, and to look into the eyes of terrified sharecroppers who had faced disrespect and threats, or who had lost a loved one to the common racial violence of white Mississippians' cherished "way of life."

"Many people talked to Medgar that night, in dark cabins, with their lights out, in whispers," Baldwin wrote in the foreword to his 1964 play *Blues for Mister Charlie*. "And we had been followed for many miles out of Jackson, Mississippi, not by a lunatic with a gun, but by state troopers. I will never forget that night."[33] Medgar drove Baldwin to the airport the following day, and they promised to see one another again.

Those who rode with Medgar consistently noted how disciplined and unflappable he was even while being followed by one or more patrol cars that waited for him to exceed the speed limit or some other infraction so they could pull him over. He got so used to the tap on his phone he sometimes ended calls by announcing into the receiver: "And I hope the white folks are listening!"[34] That January, Medgar also investigated the case of Sylvester Maxwell, a Black man whose mutilated body was found by his brother-in-law less than five hundred yards from the home of a white family in Madison County. "While the body bore markings of that of a person having been lynched (including castration)," Medgar wrote in his report, "a Negro is being held in connection with the killing. We are in serious doubt that this act was committed by the Negro in question."[35]

MEDGAR WAS PARTICULARLY HAUNTED BY THE CASE OF CLYDE Kennard, who remained imprisoned on trumped-up charges of theft to punish him for attempting to register at all-white Mississippi Southern College. At Parchman, Kennard was forced to do daily hard labor on the prison planation even while he was dying from colon cancer. The *Mississippi Free Press* reported on January 26, 1963, that he was made to work "although he is so weak that he has collapsed several times during the 2 or 3 mile walk to work."[36] Kennard's plight stung Medgar even more after Meredith successfully enrolled at Ole Miss. Myrlie later recalled an NAACP Freedom Fund banquet a year after Kennard's conviction.

After Medgar and Aaron Henry gave out awards, Medgar spoke about a recent conversation with Kennard's mother. He began his speech but soon had to stop, as he was overcome by emotion. Myrlie recalled praying quietly herself because she knew Medgar didn't approve of public displays of emotion, let alone tears. "Men don't cry," he often told Darrell. He expected public strength in others, but even more so of himself.

Myrlie said Medgar regained control, only to stop again. "It happened three more times. Finally, tears streamed down his face as he spoke, and he just gave way. He stood there in front of hundreds of people and cried as though his heart would break. Hundreds of us cried with him."[37]

For Medgar, James Meredith was the dream and Clyde Kennard was the nightmare. Meredith faced constant harassment, but he was a free man and defiantly so. Kennard had been no less brave at war or valorous in fighting for his civil rights at home—yet he was barely living, and on borrowed time. Medgar had kept Kennard's name alive, in interviews and lectures, hoping to shame the State of Mississippi into ending his unjust incarceration. The headline of a November 1962 essay in *The New Republic* paired the two men: "James Meredith Goes to College—Another Negro Went to Prison."[38]

When Kennard's mother told Medgar and Attorney Brown that the thirty-six-year-old former Army paratrooper needed help from fellow inmates to dress himself, they saw an opening. Brown filed an emergency petition for Kennard to be transferred for treatment at the University Medical Center in Jackson, pointing to the medical neglect during his two-plus years of confinement—with some five years remaining in his sentence.[39] Medgar and Brown went to see Kennard on January 23 and vowed to do everything they could to get him released.

That decision lay with Governor Barnett, who believed that Black life was valuable only as menial labor. Medgar and Brown pressed their case with the governor, but also with local Black newspapers and national media, such as *Ebony* and *Jet*, which lamented on its pages that Kennard had become a forgotten man, even as Meredith had emerged as a hero. This caught the attention of Dick Gregory, a St. Louis–born Army draftee who honed his skills doing stand-up comedy during the war, winning awards at Army talent shows and working in Black nightclubs when he came home. By the 1960s he was a crossover star even while he laid bare the mistreatment of African Americans, selling out concert halls of white audiences and performing at Hugh Hefner's Playboy Club.

Gregory had emerged as a civil rights activist, and he was periodically a dinner guest at the Evers home. And Medgar, who treasured the small kitchen blender in which he whipped up homemade fruit shakes and talked constantly about healthy eating and fresh food, had an influence on Gregory, down to his diet. Reena recalled being six, seven, and eight years old and not knowing who these famous adults were, as her parents closed the pocket door between the living room and kitchen while they had their meetings. Even without knowing who was being entertained on the other side of that door, she and Darrell and Van got to eat shrimp creole, scalloped potatoes, and other treats they didn't normally have for dinner, and if they stuck to Mama's side in the kitchen, they could be her tasters as the delectable smells filled the house.

When Gregory heard the news of Kennard's condition, he contacted Medgar about new treatments available in Chicago. Under public pressure, Barnett finally relented, and Kennard was transferred to the colored wing of Jackson's University Medical Center, and then granted executive clemency on January 28.[40] By then, Kennard had been given just a one-in-five chance of surviving for another five years.[41]

News reports of the governor's order illustrated the difference between the white and Black press in America. The *Mississippi Free Press* reported that Kennard planned to return to his chicken farm to care for the land and his mother, and that he still hoped "to earn a degree in constitutional law and work for the rights of Negroes in Mississippi."[42] White newspapers referred to Kennard as the "Negro convict . . . apparently dying of cancer" and praised Barnett, about whom Kennard supposedly said: "Whatever happens in the future I will always regard it as a tremendous favor."[43] The white Southern press typically presented Black life as a constant exercise in gratitude at the undeserved blessings of white beneficence.

Even though Kennard was now a free man and soon being flown at Gregory's expense to Chicago for treatment, he was deeply in debt. His sentence included a $10,000 fine, and he still owed more than $4,800 on the FHA mortgage on his farm. Medgar set up a Clyde Kennard Fund to assist Kennard's sixty-nine-year-old mother and his sister.[44]

Medgar went to the hospital on the morning of Kennard's release with Thomas Covington "Tom" Dent, a New Orleans–born Morehouse graduate, writer, and poet who at the time was working as a press assistant for the NAACP Legal Defense Fund in New York. Dent later wrote, "The segregatory devices had apparently been designed by a psychotic with a fascination for labyrinthine geometries." As Medgar stood inside the medical center in the endlessly long "colored" line to fill a prescription for Kennard, Dent and Kennard sat in Medgar's Oldsmobile, waiting and talking about the newly freed man's experience. Kennard, who by then weighed little more than ninety pounds, described Parchman as a "modernized slave-labor camp"—where white prisoners got the better accommodations and the easier work details, while Black prisoners were fed the leftovers from the white prisoners' meals and worked sunup to sundown on the penitentiary's multiple farms.

Kennard also didn't praise Barnett for any "favor," as the white papers claimed. Instead, he told Dent, "The way Mississippi is going now, it's going to fall very hard." Kennard had been stripped of his freedom, his health, and his right to an education, but not of his militancy. He told Dent: "Let's sue the prisons, too."[45]

Two days after the Kennard clemency announcement, Medgar and Meredith held a press conference at the Masonic Temple. The expectation was that Meredith would concede his place at Ole Miss due to the endless taunts, threats, and misery. The Temple was jammed with thousands of Black supporters, including James Baldwin, and the scene that played out was purely cinematic.

The two men sat at a table facing the claque of about fifty mainly white reporters and around one hundred and fifty Black spectators. The hall fell silent as Meredith began reading his statement slowly and deliberately. "After listening to all arguments, evaluations and positions, and weighing all this against my personal possibilities and circumstances," he read, pausing for dramatic effect, "I have concluded that *'the 'Negro'* will not return . . ."[46]

At that moment, according to Dent, a handful of white newsmen rushed out of the room to phone in the good news to their newsrooms: Ole Miss would be rid of its bombastic Black interloper. But Meredith had only begun what would be his greatest performance. He drew an extended pause, waiting for the white reporters to disappear through the doors. Only then did he deliver his dramatic crescendo: "but I, J. H. Meredith, *will* register for the second semester at the University of Mississippi."[47] The room, now almost exclusively Black, exploded in cheers and adulation. Baldwin and Dent exchanged a glance filled with the innate, mutual *knowing* that characterizes Black existence in America. Meredith had exposed the lie of the "contented Negro" with a dramatic flourish and made fools of the racist Mississippi press. Meredith and Medgar continued the press conference, but for all intents and purposes it was over. "That was it," Dent wrote. "We were all limp."[48]

The *Mississippi Free Press* blared two big headlines: "Meredith Will

Return to Ole Miss" and "Kennard is Free."[49] These triumphs led Black Mississippians to push hard against the boundaries of segregation. A second Black man, Dewey Greene, went to court seeking to follow Meredith in integrating Ole Miss. Parents in Clarksdale filed a petition seeking to integrate the schools there, and a boycott was launched against segregated businesses downtown, and Black would-be voter registrants in Rankin County were beaten, prompting a federal investigation. And that was just in February.[50]

ON MARCH 4, 1963, MEDGAR AND MYRLIE EVERS, AND FIVE OTHER families officially filed suit in federal court demanding the desegregation of Jackson schools. "We don't care for all the flamboyancy," Medgar said in a press statement, days before the filing. "But we want equal school opportunities for our children."[51] To avoid and prevent desegregation, Mississippi officials had built new Negro schools they claimed were equal, in the hope that Black leaders would voluntarily agree to maintain the status quo. But the facilities were still inadequate. Science classrooms had Bunsen burners not even connected to gas pipes, and no beakers or microscopes. The textbooks were out-of-date, often used, and without a word about Black contributions to the country. Black parents often had to buy playground equipment. Mississippi was clear it had no intention of educating Black children, who were still seen as worthy of nothing more than being farmhands a few months a year or household domestics for white families.

The fight for her children's education brought out a fire in Myrlie she scarcely knew was there. She had told a friend her name had to be on the Jackson desegregation petition because she was Medgar's wife. (He replied, so they both could hear, that *his* name was on the petition because he *wanted* it to be.)[52] Now she was to be a full partner in seeing the petition succeed. "I'm most thankful for the love that Medgar and I had and being able to finally reconcile," she said. "And I would stand by his side all the way. All the way to the end, I was not afraid [anymore], beyond the fear that I already had: that my husband . . . who was leading the cause, who was doing all of the organizing . . . that his outcome would not be a good one."

Myrlie recalled the continuing harassment of the phone calls and said that "threatening" cars and trucks "drove around in our neighborhoods." White Mississippians were sending a clear message: "No desegregation, segregation stands." The intimidation "went on and on and on and on," she said. "People in my community were . . . hesitant to be upfront to speak out, and wanted to see the process go on without any conflict. That was not to be, and it took a few strong people, particularly in the city of Jackson, Mississippi, to say, 'No. We pay taxes. Our children will go to those schools too, whatever it takes.'"

Meredith said that after he desegregated Ole Miss, the Klan created a list with thirteen names on it. "Number one was James Meredith," he said. "I don't know what number Medgar was, but he was on it [too]. Everybody likes to pretend like Clyde Kennard was a fluke. I mean, they eliminated him by putting him in prison. They eliminated the other fellow from Alcorn"—Clennon King, an eccentric man who tried to integrate the graduate school at Ole Miss in 1958 but who also allegedly cooperated with the Sovereignty Commission—"by taking him to the crazy house. Mississippi got rid of potential threats to their way of life, and everybody knows that . . . I'm sure that Medgar knew that. He not only lived in Jackson, he worked in the Mississippi Delta. . . . So, there wasn't nothing about Mississippi that I think Medgar Evers didn't know."

Rev. Ed King said his name was on the Klan's death list, too, which also included Tougaloo student activists. He said the Klan distributed a "Wanted" poster at one point. Tougaloo student activist "Anne Moody's name was on that poster," King said. Moody grew up with her family of sharecroppers on a plantation in Canton, Mississippi. When she was fourteen years old and working as a maid in the home of "the meanest white lady in town," she overheard this Mrs. Burke and her friends refer to Emmett Till not as a child, but as a Northern Negro who didn't know his place and got what he deserved. This drew Moody to the movement, and she made the Klan's list for setting up a "freedom house" in rural Canton and helping her fellow activists in SNCC, CORE, and the NAACP to register Black Mississippians to vote.[53]

Despite the fear and hardships, Myrlie recalled the sense of togetherness and courage her neighbors got from acting:

> For those who gathered, who supported each other, who went to churches, who went to homes and had private prayer meetings to support each other, it was a blessing . . . and a joy, because it meant that in that particular community, whether it was in Jackson, Mississippi or some other place, [Black Mississippians] had finally come together with a strength that said, this is something that must be done, and we will pay the price. . . .
>
> When you have people or an individual who feels that way, and those who are opponents . . . realize how strong that feeling is, [including] the willingness to lose your job, to lose your home, to possibly lose your life, that was one of the strongest statements that could be made. And it helped to bring other people on. And it certainly helped to bring a younger generation into that part of it, even though they could not do everything that they wanted to do. . . .
>
> I was definitely afraid for Medgar, afraid for our children, afraid for my community, but [there] was something about us gathering together in each other's homes over corn cakes and tea and prayer, that [took us] forward. And I am so thankful that I was a part of that. . . . We had to be able to break down those barriers of segregation and open up the schools for all of our children.

MEDGAR THREW HIMSELF INTO THE ESCALATING FLURRY OF ACTIVITY. On May 12, he and the Jackson NAACP sent letters to Mayor

Thompson and local white business organizations, demanding that they end segregation in the city or face demonstrations. The move was designed to trigger federal support for civil rights legislation that could address racial discrimination across the South.

Ed King said the goal was "to get the white [power] structure to set up a biracial committee, to look at changes in Jackson." But, he added, Thompson "said, 'there are no changes needed because our Black people . . . our colored,' in his word . . . are satisfied and want no change." According to King, "Medgar had suggested . . . 10 or 12 changes, from opening golf courses to Blacks, to public school desegregation. He never said what should be first. And the white powers realized if they said anything should start, Medgar had a long list of what might be next, and that ultimate freedom for Black people was his goal; and ending Jim Crow and desegregation."

Thompson, backed by the Jackson Chamber of Commerce, the Junior Chamber of Commerce, and the White Citizens' Council,[54] refused to back down, and Medgar concluded that demonstrations had to start.

Three days later, on the nine-year anniversary of the *Brown v. Board* decision, Medgar took the stage at the Masonic Temple. After Clarence Mitchell Jr. addressed how little had changed in Mississippi despite the Supreme Court's ruling and Meredith's admittance to Ole Miss, Evers announced a boycott of three products popular in Black households made by companies that had contributed financially to the White Citizens' Councils: Barq's soft drinks, Hart's bread, and McRae's department store. Myrlie later wrote that "it was a success from the beginning," and it was quickly "widened to include virtually all the white shops on Capitol Street, the main downtown shopping area.[55] Student-led sit-ins, and pickets quickly spread across the city and to the parks, train and bus station waiting rooms, downtown Jackson department stores, and restaurants.[56]

This was the Montgomery-style mass boycott campaign that Medgar had long dreamed of.

High school students were surging into the movement. The mass meetings at the Masonic Temple and nearby churches were filling to capacity with younger and younger activists. Students from all-Black Lanier, Brinkley, and Holy Ghost high schools were ordered by their principals to cease their protest activity and responded by walking out of class.[57] Medgar advised a group of high schoolers to get better organized before marching; after failing to take his advice, they were violently arrested. Once the NAACP bailed them out, the organization offered them training and flew in the national youth field secretary, Willie Ludden, to help give some order to the quickly spreading demonstrations. Myrlie recalled that the young protesters soon "knew how to drop to the ground and protect themselves"[58] from police baton blows.

"The students were more ready than any of us thought," Ed King said. "And as negotiations with the city broke down, the white moderates turned back to silence. We had gotten a few of them saying that Medgar's demands were reasonable and trying to put behind-the-scenes pressure on the city."[59] As the protest widened, that backing cooled.

Myrlie later wrote that the first round of student demonstrations "was prepared like a military campaign." Picket signs were painted and assigned. March lines and assembly points were designated. When the students finally arrived to march to Capitol Street, "there was nothing to be seen but an enormous mass of humanity, flooding the street, spilling over the sidewalks."[60]

More than five hundred Black junior high and senior high students marched downtown, according to Ed King, and they were quickly arrested. "Another thousand tried to march at different schools," he said. Their schools were surrounded by police who blocked them from joining the main demonstration. Students were piled into the filthy beds of garbage trucks and taken to a makeshift prison camp at the city fairgrounds. "Bull Connor in Birmingham took [protesters] on school buses," King said. "We used garbage trucks [in Jackson]. In theory, they were supposed to have been cleaned, but it was an example that things were worse here even than in Alabama."

Thompson's fairgrounds jail was surrounded by a chain-link fence and was so packed and fetid that it came to be nicknamed "Mississippi's concentration camp."[61] The stockades quickly filled with high school students who were forced to stand for hours in the hot sun, with little food and few provisions. "Food was often thrown on the ground, and they were told, 'Eat, dogs, eat,'" Salter later wrote. "Police sometimes urinated in the drinking water buckets. Physical brutality was commonplace. Medical assistance was nil."[62] There were few sanitary facilities: no toothbrushes or combs. The students were determined to remain there and refused the bail Medgar was hurriedly raising and frantic parents were scrambling to put together. The city wanted the students to sign pledges not to protest again if they were released, but the students refused. Medgar was caught between parents and their activist children. Finally, New York sent $200,000 in bond money to Jackson.

On the night the students were to be released, victorious in not having signed the pledges, their parents and supporters first waited for them inside the Masonic Temple. But Jackson police required parents to pick up each child individually, making the process as miserable as possible to the very end. When the students finally arrived at the Temple, they were greeted as heroes with cheers and applause by the gathered adults, many of whom were embarrassed by their own reticence compared to their own children's valor. Myrlie wrote that "one young boy, describing the lack of facilities [in the jail] for brushing his teeth," ended his time on the Temple stage "by crying out, 'Look Mom! Cavities for Freedom!' The audience screamed its approval."[63]

Freeing the students didn't end the crisis. Police fanned out across downtown Jackson, arresting anyone who tried to march or picket, or for any reason they could concoct. Their vans with barking dogs circled Black businesses and stalked Lynch Street, with officers writing down the license plate numbers of anyone who went inside the Masonic Temple. High school students threw rocks at the officers posted downtown, prompting more violent arrests. White citizens organized to pack and deliver box lunches to the police officers.

As the month of May continued, the drumbeat of arrests and police brutality grew daily. State police and Jackson police seemed to merge with gangs of Klansmen and the whole, violent mass converged on Jackson. The growing violence and the repeated arrests only increased the alarm in New York. The youth leaders in Jackson, along with local leaders like Salter and Ed King, wanted to continue the marches and sit-ins, to force the leaders of Jackson to relent on their demands for immediate desegregation. Medgar agreed with them, and young Jacksonians clearly did, too. But the national NAACP objected, as did conservative local clergy. They firmly favored a less confrontational course that focused on voter registration and NAACP membership appeals, in the hopes that more registered Black voters would yield more moderate government officials, while taking the fight against segregation to Congress and the courts. But this strategy presumed that the local officials who decided who could register and who could not, would ever relent and allow significant Black additions to the voter rolls, and it required a faith in Washington that the militant young activists did not share.

Medgar was caught in the middle, and Myrlie saw less and less of him as he zigzagged between his office, the picket lines downtown, and the fairgrounds jail, bail money in hand, and his office, where negotiations with New York were increasingly tense. The hate-filled phone calls to the Evers house were constant. Myrlie sometimes just left the receiver off the hook, but she couldn't always do so because of other calls for help, for bond money, for Medgar's presence at a rally or a planning meeting. They got an unlisted number, but Medgar gave it out to so many people, it quickly became known, too.

Driven back on his heels, Mayor Thompson gave a local television address to assure Jacksonians that the protests were being perpetrated by outside agitators and that the "good Negroes of Jackson" were quiet and content. Medgar demanded equal time in a letter not just to Thompson, but to President Kennedy, Attorney General Robert Kennedy, the Jackson Chamber of Commerce and the Junior Chamber of Commerce, the Mississippi Economic Council, and the Mississippi Bankers Association.[64] The matter landed quickly in court, and to everyone's surprise, not least Myrlie's, Medgar was given twenty minutes to deliver a televised response to the mayor.

News of the impending speech brought so many fresh threats that Medgar was forced to tape it in secret, far from the local television studio. Myrlie knew that once the broadcast aired, the white Mississippians who up to that time had despised Medgar as a faceless troublemaker would now know exactly what he looked like. The danger of that was incalculable. When the speech was over, he could be recognized everywhere: at a stoplight in the city, on a lonely road in the Delta, in the light from the fuel pump at a gas station."[65] She listened to him as he practiced, and he tested lines on her and wrote and rewrote what would be the most important speech of his life.

Medgar met the moment. On May 20, the night his speech was televised, he spoke the truth of what it meant to be Black in Mississippi—which left a man, woman, or child with the constant burden of contempt, of not being able to receive a decent education, to travel without humiliation, or to attend the best schools in the state of your birth, to be employed where you might achieve your fullest potential, or simply to live without fear and the constant threat of violence or death.

"I speak as a native Mississippian," Medgar told the television audience, including an untold number of white folk. "I was educated in Mississippi schools and served overseas in our nation's armed forces in the war against Hitlerism and fascism."[66] He said the wider world was visible to Black people.

> Tonight, the Negro knows from his radio and television what happened today all over the world. . . . He knows about

> the new free nations in Africa and knows that a Congo native can be a locomotive engineer, but in Jackson he cannot even drive a garbage truck. . . . Then he looks about his home community and what does he see, to quote our mayor: in this "progressive, beautiful, friendly, prosperous city with an exciting future"? He sees a city where Negro citizens are refused admittance to the city auditorium and the coliseum; his children refused a ticket to a good movie in a downtown theater; his wife and children refused service at a lunch counter in a downtown store where they trade; students refused the use of the main public libraries, parks, playgrounds, and other tax-supported recreational facilities. He sees Negro lawyers, physicians, dentists, teachers, and other professionals prevented from attending meetings of professional organizations.
>
> He sees a city of over 150,000 of which 40 percent is Negro, in which there is not a single Negro policeman or policewoman, school crossing guard, fireman, clerk, stenographer, or supervisor employed in any city department or the mayor's office . . . except those employed in segregated facilities. He sees local hospitals which segregate Negro patients and deny staff privileges to Negro family physicians. The mayor spoke of the twenty-four-hour police protection we have. . . . There are questions in the minds of many Negroes whether we have twenty-four hours of protection, or twenty-four hours of harassment.[67]

Medgar said Black Mississippians wanted the end of segregation and the right to register and vote without "special impediments imposed on him alone," jobs above the menial level, and to be treated with respect in the places where they spend their money. "Jackson can change if it wills to do so," he said. "If there should be resistance, how much better to have turbulence to effect improvement rather than turbulence to maintain a stand-pat policy. We believe there are white

Mississippians who want to go forward on the race question. Their religion tells them there is something wrong with the old system. Their sense of justice and fair play sends them the same message."[68]

Medgar concluded by saying the Negro "has been in America since 1619, a total of 344 years. He is not going anywhere else; this country is his home. He wants to do his part to make his city, state, and nation a better place for everyone regardless of color or race." A victory for democracy in the State of Mississippi, he said, would be a victory for democracy everywhere.[69]

Myrlie had never been so proud of her husband. She later wrote that "it was the speech of an intelligent, thoughtful Negro; a Negro who stood without fear or subservience and spoke with self-assurance as an equal to the white man."[70]

It was a speech that marked Medgar Evers for certain death.

CHAPTER 7

Countdown

A knowledge of how to live was a knowledge of how to die.

—RICHARD WRIGHT

The day after Medgar's television speech, Mayor Thompson met with a group of his selection: fourteen prominent Black opponents of the NAACP, including Percy Greene, the status quo–supporting, Sovereignty Commission–paid editor of the *Jackson Advocate*. In response, a group of fifty Jackson ministers, businessmen, professionals, and workers formed a Jackson Citizens Committee and repudiated Thompson's group of "false Black leaders" and reaffirmed their support for the Jackson NAACP's desegregation demands.[1] A week later, Thompson met with the Jackson Citizens Committee, and at first agreed to hire Black police officers and crossing guards, as he had promised President Kennedy. But he quickly reneged on the deal, claiming that Medgar and the other council members had misunderstood if they thought he would allow any changes to Jackson's "way of life." The demonstrations resumed.[2]

On May 20, 1963, the Supreme Court ruled in *Lombard v. Louisiana* that states enforcing segregation in restaurants were in violation of the Equal Protection Clause of the Fourteenth Amendment. Eight days later, on May 28, Medgar was working with John Salter and others to arrange rides for a group of Tougaloo students to conduct a sit-in at the Woolworth's on Capitol Street downtown. The plan was for a picket line to form outside the store to divert police attention while three Black Tougaloo students—Anne Moody, Pearlina Lewis, and Memphis Norman—sat down at the counter and asked to be served. The students arrived at 11 A.M. and entered through the rear "Colored" entrance. They were ignored at first, but once a waitress approached them and told them they could only be served in the back, to which Moody replied that they wished to be served where they were, the situation deteriorated quickly. The waitress cut the lights behind the counter and she and the other waitresses abandoned their posts as white men began to fill the store. Outside, the picketers had been swiftly arrested, eliminating the intended decoy, and news of the protest had been spread by local radio hosts, who urged all available white men to go to the store, punctuating their appeals by playing "Dixie." The first group to respond to the call came from a local all-white high school. They immediately began hurling racial epithets and chants of "Communist!" at the students, who sat stoically at the counter. Memphis, Moody would later recall, suggested that they pray. As they bowed their heads, the violence began.

Memphis Norman was dragged off his seat and thrown to the floor, as a former police officer named Benny Oliver kicked him in the head and torso until blood trickled from his ears. The attack only ended when a policeman pushed into the store and arrested both men.[3] Pearlina was knocked off her seat as well. Moody was slapped and shoved into the counter, but she managed to get back in the seat. Moody said someone grabbed a rope that had been strung across the counter area to prevent others from sitting down and tried to tie it around the women's necks.[4] As the noon lunch hour approached, the crowds grew larger, and wilder.

Joan Trumpauer, a white activist and Freedom Rider who spent two months in Parchman before becoming the first white student to attend Tougaloo, had traveled to the Woolworth's with Lois Chafee, a Tougaloo house mother, Ed King, and John Salter, to serve as "spotters" outside the Woolworth's. From a public telephone outside, they periodically called Medgar at the Jackson NAACP office to report what was going on. Once the picket line outside was broken up and most of the people on it arrested, they decided to go inside the Woolworth's to join the sit-in. Salter, Chafee, and Trumpauer pushed through the crowd, as young white men clutched at their hair and tried to drag them back outside, and they sat down beside Moody and Pearlina.

A tall white man immediately approached the interracial quartet at the counter and demanded to know Salter's name. His answer touched off a fusillade of violence. As a very public activist, and one of the few who presented as white, Salter had become both well known and, for Mississippi segregationists, a prime target. Once the tall man shouted that this was "John Salter" seated at the counter with Black and white women, the crowd's unmitigated fury was unleashed. Salter was beaten with bare hands and with brass knuckles; his face was sliced open and the back of his head cut with a glass sugar container someone had smashed into a weapon. The blood pouring down his face and head was soon mixed with whatever food and drink and sludge that the crowd could find to pour over the activists' heads. They were doused with ketchup, mustard, sugar, vinegar, and even the remains of the pies that had been placed on the counter for the lunchtime rush. Pepper was thrown into Salter's eyes, and the group were burned with cigarettes. Salter later described it as "a lavish display of unbridled hatred."[5]

Medgar asked King, when he called in to report, if they should call it off. It was far too late for that.

After more than two hours, as the mob began throwing furniture and all but tearing the store apart, Tougaloo president Dr. Adam D. Beittel, arrived to plead with police, more than ninety of whom were assembled outside—some peering into the five-and-dime and watching the mayhem—to calm the crowd and to get the activists safely out of harm's way. Once the group was finally liberated from the Woolworth's they retreated to Medgar's office, where Myrlie was also headed, after picking up Darrell, Reena, and two of the neighbors' children from school. News of the protest was spreading fast among Black families and civil rights organizations. Myrlie sent the children inside to get their father, where they got a firsthand lesson in civil rights activism, as the students, some injured, others just shaking off the shock of their experience, were milling around inside. When Darrell saw them, the ten-year-old was amazed and confused.

"They had sugar, ketchup, syrup . . . whatever you can think of that would be in a cafeteria—on the top of their heads, their shoulders, their whole body," he later recalled. "As a young kid, I couldn't understand. My father took me aside and he said, 'Darrell, I want to tell you that these people are standing for their rights. They want to be served where . . . only white people are allowed to eat, and they would like to have the respect . . . of any other human being.' It was a little confusing for me at that time because I couldn't understand why someone would submit themselves to that sort of treatment and why someone would not want to fight back. But that was one of my father's main goals and objectives, a nonviolent action. That had more power than anything else. And he tried to explain that to me the best way possible. . . . It was a very practical lesson for me at that point."[6]

Myrlie went inside the office and found Reena and Darrell excited over having met the student activists. Despite the anxiety, and with the demonstrators safely out of the Woolworth's, Medgar quickly understood that the sit-in had given the Jackson campaign momentum and potential leverage against the recalcitrant mayor.

At a packed mass meeting that night at Pearl Street AME Church, Willie Ludden, the NAACP national youth field secretary, Gloster

Current, Medgar, David Dennis from CORE, and leaders of the Youth Councils spoke to a capacity crowd, as did Salter, who still wore the clothes covered in ketchup, mustard, and blood from the protest earlier that day. There was a determined feeling in the air, and Medgar hoped that what was happening in Jackson, through its fearless young activists, would match what Dr. King and others had sparked in Montgomery and then in Birmingham. He used his time at the podium to call for a "massive offensive against segregation."[7]

The story of the Woolworth's protest rocketed through Black Jackson neighborhoods and hardened people's resolve. It was the most violent reaction to a sit-in the country had yet seen. The local TV news in Jackson barely covered it on the night it happened. But by the following morning, an Associated Press photo of the "Mustard Man" and his two female "accomplices" were splashed across the front pages of newspapers around the world.

The NAACP also scored some victories. The May 29 *Clarion-Ledger* reported that twenty-one-year-old Cleve McDowell, a former Jackson State student from rural Drew, Mississippi, had successfully sued for admission to the Ole Miss law school.[8] It was a second victory for the NAACP Legal Defense Fund's Constance Baker Motley, yet with the federal troops gone, McDowell would be forced to face the angry, spitting crowds alone on his first day of class in June. He would do so with a gun concealed in his belt.[9]

The night of May 29 wasn't all victorious news. Myrlie was in the bedroom drifting off when she heard one, then another car pass, followed by the sound of shattering glass, with a "whoosh of muffled explosion" that caused their dog Heidi to bark frantically. She ran into the living room and saw flames licking up outside in the carport. She ran outside to grab the garden hose and douse the flames, as Jean Wells threw open her door and joined her on the lawn to help. As the flames receded, the women could see that the source of the blaze had been a twisted rag that had been doused in kerosene, lit on fire, and tossed from one of the passing cars.

Myrlie panicked, thinking the assailant might still be out there, waiting to shoot her as she tried to put out the flames. By the time Mr. Wells and Mr. Young came running over as well, the flames were out and the police had arrived. Somehow the children never woke. The police officers, rather than taking note of the crime, began to question Myrlie. They held out a gas can they discovered next to the house and asked, "Is this yours?"—implying that perhaps Myrlie had started the fire. Growing angry, Myrlie told them the can was used to fill up the lawn mower. After more insulting questions, the officers told her it was likely just a prank.

When Medgar arrived, he leapt out of the car and scooped Myrlie up in his arms, asking if she and the children were okay. Assured that they were, he talked with the officers. The conversation grew tense. Later, when everything had calmed down and the neighbors had gone home, Medgar and Myrlie walked quietly down the hall to check on the children, gently opening and closing their bedroom doors. Medgar, who was walking in front, said, "The police told me you cursed them."

Darned right she did, she told him, and she wanted to do more. When she turned to look at him, Medgar was grinning. "But Myrlie Mae, you don't curse," he said, a full smile now spread across his face. He just couldn't resist teasing her, even at a time like this. Medgar always told her she was stronger than she thought she was. This incident proved it, but a cold dread set in once they fully processed what could have happened. That night, "Medgar took me in his arms and held me and rocked me back and forth," Myrlie wrote. "'I don't know what I'd do if anything ever happened to you or the children because of what I'm doing,' he said softly."[10]

Burying her head in his chest, Myrlie reminded him that whoever tossed that Molotov cocktail wasn't trying to kill *her,* they were trying to kill *him*. "And if anything happened to you," she told Medgar, "I don't think I could live."[11]

The next morning, they told the older children what happened. "I will say this," Myrlie said. "Medgar was wonderful in training those young people," noting that Darrell and Reena were just ten and eight years old. "He had sessions with them. You hear a certain noise, what do you do? You fall to the floor. You get your three-year-old brother, you drag him along with you. Where is the safest place in the house?" The children would yell that it was the bathroom tub, with proud delight. It was low to the ground and at the back of the house. "He took them through drills."

They learned to crawl on their stomachs the way the infantrymen had in Europe. "To me it was . . . Army and combat," Darrell said years later. "A self-protection game." His father would say, "Okay, we're going to pretend . . . if someone approached you what would you do? And I said well, I guess I'd run. And he said, no." The answer was to fight. "If you heard a loud noise or you heard a menacing sound, I think the best thing we should do is fall on the floor and get under cover, get under a table, or get under a bed . . . so that we're not hit or hurt," To Darrell, it was all just a game, and a way to play at combat like his father had seen overseas. Seeing it this way was less frightening, perhaps, than having to confront, at ten years old, that something violent might happen to his father, his sister, his little brother, or him.

A similar attack happened to Aaron Henry on April 12 in Clarksdale, only the Molotov cocktail had gone through a window of his house. Mississippi was in the throes of a terror campaign against anyone involved in the struggle for integration and civil rights. The NAACP had officially appealed to the Justice Department, asking for federal protection for Medgar and Henry, but according to Charles Evers, "the Justice Department hardly lifted a finger."[12]

Myrlie watched as Medgar's impatience, frustration, and exhaustion grew and his talk became more fatalistic. He told her one morning, after she'd spent the previous afternoon washing and ironing a full load of fresh shirts for him, that while he appreciated her efforts, he probably wasn't going to need them.

Other times, he came home and collapsed on the living room sofa, and she had to shake him and get him to move to the bedroom for a proper sleep. On the nights she couldn't get him off the couch, she sat down beside him and eased his head into her lap. "I could feel the tension and bruises of the day slip away from him as I stroked his hair and rubbed his temples," she recalled. "In a few minutes he would drop off to sleep, and I would sit there looking down at him, so tired, so much like a little boy who had pushed himself beyond all endurance."[13] His six-day workweeks were stretching to seven days—with no time for the fishing and hunting trips that had provided such a pleasing distraction for him. He had less time to toss the football with Darrell and the other boys on the block or to balance Reena on his knees while he did his Jack LaLanne morning workouts.

Their family time together was at breakfast when Medgar talked to the children about his work. Once, Myrlie recalled, Darrell declared, "I hate white people," and Medgar told him, "You're wrong. You're only hurting yourself . . . hating people is no way to live." Another time, three-year-old Van made the whole table laugh, when he broke into a civil rights anthem, belting: "Let nobody turn you around!" Invariably Reena, whom Myrlie called the house's mini-mom, told her father he worked too much and needed to take some time off.[14] Those moments of joy were far too fleeting.[15]

THOMPSON AND THE CITY OF JACKSON, ALONG WITH THE WHITE Citizens' Councils, weren't prepared to back down. After the Woolworth's incident, the mayor obtained an injunction, naming Medgar, Salter, Ed King, the president and trustees of Tougaloo College, Dick Gregory, Gloster Current, the NAACP, CORE, and about a dozen others, enjoining them from "engaging in, sponsoring, inciting or encouraging mass street parades or mass processions or like demonstrations without a permit." The activists were barred from "unlawful blocking of the streets or sidewalks, trespassing on private property after being warned to leave the premises or . . . congregating on the streets or public places as mobs, and unlawfully picketing business establishments or public buildings in the City of Jackson."[16] Thompson made it clear he intended to enforce the injunction.

"They wanted things stopped and controlled," Ed King said. "The injunction told us to stop lunch counter sit-ins, marches, demonstrations.... We appealed . . . and we got to the federal judge in Jackson for this district in Mississippi, who said that it was a very serious issue of the right to demonstrate and march.... You couldn't even hand out literature.... We appealed to the Fifth Circuit in New Orleans, which upheld the local federal judge, as did the Supreme Court. [But] Medgar said, 'You have to defy the court system, even if it's been upheld by federal courts, even if we might win in the Supreme Court a year from now, the movement is destroyed.'" Medgar believed the boycotts and demonstrations needed to continue until Thompson backed down.

And they did. While the NAACP general counsel Robert Carter added to the flurry of lawsuits by filing yet another—seeking to end segregation in all public accommodations in the state, activists held a sit-in at Primo's Restaurant downtown, while a separate group successfully, if briefly, integrated the city golf course. Another group of more than two dozen knelt in prayer in front of the downtown Post Office and were hauled away by police.[17] With city jails full to bursting, the stockading of activists in the fairground detention camp continued, too.

On June 1, with more than 550 protesters—many of them children—packed into the prison camp, Medgar sent an urgent telegram to President Kennedy: "Please, mistreatment of Negro children and their parents reported behind hog wire confines of Jackson Concentration Camp. City, county, and State Law officers involved. Medical attention being denied. Injured in some cases. Urge immediate investigation by Department of Justice agents of these denials of constitutional rights to peaceful demonstrators and protests."[18]

Roy Wilkins arrived in Jackson that same day and joined Medgar on the picket line in front of the downtown Woolworth's—the same one where, less than a week before, violence and mayhem had met the small group of Tougaloo sit-in protesters. Medgar wore a handmade sign over his suit jacket and tie that read "End Brutality in Jackson." He and Wilkins were quickly arrested by helmeted police brandishing cattle prods as press photographers captured images that would rocket around national newsrooms. Also arrested was Thelton Henderson, the first Black lawyer to serve in the U.S. Justice Department, who had merely been observing the demonstration, and Helen Wilcher, who had succeeded Aaron Henry as state NAACP president at Medgar's urging when Henry stepped down. Henderson was quickly released. Wilkins, Wilcher, and Medgar were booked on charges of restraint of trade and released on $1,000 bonds.

Hours later, young activists staged a march downtown that attracted the now-standard response from police and led to the arrest and detention of forty additional activists.[19] Even with this dismal conclusion of the march, Thompson finally relented, agreeing to hire Black police officers and crossing guards and to "upgrade Negro city employees." He said the negotiations for other demands, including school and public facilities desegregation, were "ongoing." He also announced that Jackson voters would be asked to approve a $500,000 to $1 million bond to add more stockades to the detention camp.[20]

At the mass meeting that night, Wilkins took to the stage and spoke passionately, in terms Medgar had used before. "In Birmingham," he said, "the authorities turned the dogs and fire hoses loose on peaceable demonstrators. Jackson has added another touch to this expression of the Nazi spirit with the setting up of hog-wired concentration camps. This is pure Nazism and Hitlerism. The only thing missing is an oven."[21]

Outwardly, Wilkins's presence at the protest and his fiery speech at the Masonic Temple were a show of national NAACP support for Medgar's headlong dive into grassroots protest. But behind the scenes, tensions were rising to a boil.

Medgar had deliberately taken Wilkins to that Woolworth's because with the injunction in place, he knew what would happen, and he hoped the high-profile arrests of himself and the national leader of the NAACP would get Washington's attention and force the mayor's hand. King said he was told that Wilkins believed otherwise: that despite the injunction they wouldn't be arrested "just for picketing." Still, Ed King had come away from Wilkins's willingness to march with Medgar and particularly his speech at the mass meeting impressed and hopeful that perhaps the NAACP's attitude toward Medgar's activism was changing.

King said he was quickly disabused of that hope during the NAACP strategy meeting upstairs at the Masonic Temple the very next night. Medgar's allies at the meeting, including Houston Wells and his brother James, known as "J.G.," reiterated their appeal for the national office to pay for full-time security for Medgar and for the Evers home, citing the firebombing attempt just days before, which could have injured or killed Myrlie and the children. But Gloster Current, who was in Jackson at New York's behest, and who considered Medgar a friend, told the men the national organization had "more important things to do with its money" than to look after Medgar.[22] King was stunned. But there was more to come.

After the meeting, during which the national office's priorities—voter registration and NAACP membership sign-ups—were reiterated yet again, Wilkins asked to speak with Medgar alone. Medgar motioned to Ed King to come with him anyway, and King said he felt that Medgar wanted someone to stand witness. Wilkins consented to King coming along. The Tougaloo chaplain had become one of Medgar's closest aides and confidants. He said Wilkins must have presumed that, as a white Southerner and a college chaplain, King understood that this student militancy and insistence on continuing the cycle of protests and arrests, and drawing violent responses from authorities, was the wrong approach.

The three men went into Medgar's office and closed the door, at which point Wilkins unloaded on Medgar for getting himself and

Wilkins arrested. As King described it, an angry Wilkins practically yelled at Medgar: "Who do you think you are? Another Martin Luther King? There's too much Martin Luther King in this country now.'"

The Kennedy administration, which had been a reluctant player in the desegregation events unfolding across the South, didn't want "a second Birmingham anywhere in America." "And Wilkins told Medgar, 'If you work with Dr. King, and if you do not stop these demonstrations, you will be fired,'" King recalled. Medgar was diplomatic in the moment, and according to King, he told Wilkins he understood.

After Wilkins left, Reverend King said Medgar told him that this was not the first time Wilkins had threatened to fire him. He said Roy Wilkins made the same threat a year before, over his support for James Meredith's bid to enter Ole Miss. According to King, the administration wanted to quiet the violent opposition to integration until after Kennedy was reelected in 1964, and to keep the peace with the Southern, overwhelmingly Democratic, states. With the Birmingham upheavals finally cooled on May 10, Kennedy wanted a respite from the image of continual uprising in the American South. For that to happen, the civil rights movement needed to "get off the newspapers, get out of the streets," as Ed King put it. The violent Woolworth's sit-in had achieved the opposite result, and Wilkins was just as frustrated by Medgar's insistence on backing the militancy of Mississippi youth as Kennedy was. Ed King, for whom militancy was the only course, even accused Wilkins of "carrying out the orders of Washington" in seeking to slow Medgar down.

Thurgood Marshall and the other lawyers at the national NAACP had nonetheless backed Meredith's bid; a sign that Wilkins's opinions weren't universally shared in the national office. But national had pointedly dissuaded Medgar from applying to Ole Miss Law School himself.

Whatever Medgar and Wilkins's past exchanges had been, this new rebuke stung Medgar, King said. He knew the NAACP was tired of bailing out protesters, whose tactics they opposed. He knew they opposed the sit-ins and marches, and that NAACP headquarters in New York had lost patience with him. The actions taken by Medgar's Youth Councils and high school and college activists clearly defied New York and their mandate to concentrate on voter registration. But he also deeply believed that only direct action, from and by Black Mississippians, would turn the segregationist tide in the state.

Medgar left the meeting feeling defeated. Myrlie wrote that "Medgar was more despondent that night than I had ever seen him. He had aged ten years in the preceding months. As he related what happened at the meeting, tears trickled down his cheeks."[23] And then there were the ongoing security concerns. Houston Wells and other friends of Medgar had begun pressing the national office to provide Medgar with security protection, in the form of bodyguards or, at least, armed patrols at the Evers home. The requests were repeatedly declined. "I was livid that the NAACP put so little value on Medgar's life," Myrlie wrote. When she told Medgar as much, he replied: "It's okay. When my time comes, I'm going to go regardless of the protections I have. Besides, I don't want anyone to get hurt trying to save me."[24]

No one who knew Medgar believed he had a martyr complex. Far from it. His friends insisted vigorously that he wanted to live, for Myrlie and for their children. Since Van was born, they had even talked about having another child, as he had always wanted four. Myrlie had recently given Medgar the blessed news that she was pregnant again, which she'd discovered not long before the firebombing. They'd barely had time or space to absorb, let alone make plans, as they each felt their daily mission was to fight for their lives.[25] On the night of Wilkins's rebuke, as they lay holding each other after much tossing and turning, Medgar for the first time expressed doubts about bringing another child into the world,[26] particularly in the state considered the most violent and segregated in the nation.[27]

Ed King said, "Medgar went through hell the next week or so. The National Office sent people down here to really control him." NAACP headquarters was straining under the weight of $64,000 in bond debts,[28] and Medgar, Salter, King, and others were in open defiance of New York.

On June 7, Lena Horne arrived to support the Jackson Movement by appearing at an NAACP rally at the Masonic Temple that night. Medgar picked her up from the airport and brought her to their home for lunch. Myrlie was thrilled to have the actress and singer visiting them. She attended the mass meeting that night, and her heart swelled with pride as Ms. Horne talked about how blessed Mississippians were to have a leader like Medgar, who had allayed her every fear as they sped through the streets of Jackson in his Oldsmobile. The hall, jammed with more than three thousand people to see Horne and Dick Gregory, too, was captivated.

"The battle . . . being fought here in Jackson, as elsewhere in the south, is our nation's primary crisis," Ms. Horne said. "Let it be understood that the courage and grim determination of the Negro people in these cities of the South have challenged the moral integrity of the entire nation."[29]

Myrlie recalled that police "ringed the building and patrolled the halls and doorways inside. The press was out in force, and the words of freedom songs swelled and echoed and burst through the open windows to flood the air for blocks around. It was a night of tears and laughter, of high emotions, of unity and determination and brotherhood. When the words of 'We Shall Overcome' rang from thousands of throats, we *were* overcome, and elderly Negro men wept along with high school girls."[30]

"Freedom has never been free," Medgar told the crowd that night. "I love my children," he said to a hushed room. "And I love my wife with all my heart. And I would die and die gladly, if that would make a better life for them."[31]

For all the pride and joy she felt in that moment, in her heart, Myrlie knew with an aching certainty that she *would* lose him. There was not even a question in her mind anymore. She felt incredibly lonely. It was unfair. She felt scandalously robbed before anything had yet been taken from her.

At a small, private party after the mass meeting for the out-of-town guests that night, a Friday, Medgar and Myrlie shared a rare evening of much-needed laughs. When a group of friends began debating the wisdom of "young marriages," Medgar joked that even though he had "robbed the cradle," it had worked out quite nicely. Then he set Myrlie blushing by declaring to the room, rare for him in public, how much he loved her. They left the party separately: she took some friends home in her station wagon so she could pick up the children from the babysitter, and Medgar went to drop off some NAACP workers at their homes.

Myrlie expected to be home first, but she was surprised when Medgar sped into the driveway just behind her. Once the children were in bed, he explained that he and several others had noticed three white men they didn't recognize in the Masonic Temple that night. One of them was smoking a cigarette. His secretary saw this man had wandered upstairs to the floor where Medgar's office was; he'd said he was just looking around and then left. One of the NAACP workers Medgar drove home said they thought they'd seen those same three men in a car, possibly following them after the party, meaning that maybe they'd followed them to the party as well.[32] This news alarmed him enough that Medgar didn't want Myrlie going into a dark house that night alone.

They already lived with safety plans—never sit or stand by a window; always exit the car on the front passenger side, to be closer to the house's front door; and avoid the large, wooded lot adjacent to the Youngs' home. Medgar had walked that lot area during the day and had decided it was not safe. He discouraged the children from exploring and playing there. The woods formed the point of a triangle of streets where Missouri Street, which stretched behind the Youngs' home, and Guynes Street ran into Delta Drive, where the businesses were white-owned. There was a cleaners, a small nightclub, a small restaurant called Dog and Suds, Joe's Drive-In Theater, where Medgar had taken the kids to see *Psycho*, and Pittman's Handy Andy Grocery.

The following day, Saturday, June 8, Medgar spent all day at his office, intermittently driving down to Capitol Street to see that the boycott was holding up and how empty the streets were. He had begun periodically calling home to speak to each of the children, and on one of the calls that day, Medgar seemed shaken. He was being followed every day, by one or two police cars, but that day, he told Myrlie, as he was stepping out of his car, one of them had jammed "into reverse" and tried to back into him.

"I jumped away just in time," he told her. "I have witnesses . . . several other people saw it. It was no mistake." This incident seemed to genuinely rattle Medgar, who didn't frighten easily.[33]

THE NEWS FROM THE NAACP NATIONAL OFFICE AT THE STRATEGY meeting that day was not good. New York had begun "to cut off the bail bond money to end all large demonstrations," Salter later wrote. They also packed the local strategy committee with conservative clergy, he added. Medgar, already under intense pressure from national headquarters, was "functionally immobilized. Knowing Medgar," Salter added, "we felt his heart and mind were with the struggle in the field. He made no effort to bridge the quickly deepening gap, and his involvement from that point on was minimal. The national office was choking the Jackson Movement to death. It waned into almost nothing [by] the second week in June."[34]

Medgar and Myrlie were awakened Sunday morning by the phone, and Myrlie had had enough. She snatched the receiver off the hook and put it right back down, insisting that Medgar get even a bit more rest. When the phone rang again as she was serving him breakfast, Myrlie lost her composure. She grabbed the receiver and told the person on the line, who was calling from the NAACP office and asking where Medgar was, that he would get there when he got there.[35]

Medgar was leading groups of Black protesters that day to white churches to attempt to enter the sanctuaries. It is an idea that Ed King said had come from Martin Luther King Jr., who favored challenging clergy to live up to their faith when it came to opposing racism and segregation. Unsurprisingly, the activists were all turned away. "Medgar made himself very visible, taking some Black people to First Baptist Church where Gov. Ross Barnett was a Sunday school teacher," Ed King said. "Medgar could understand and [even] laugh about the media angle," he added. "Wouldn't it be wonderful if Ross Barnett had let some Black people come into his church? Anyway, they were turned away, too." Medgar was not arrested, as he had expected to be. "Maybe the white powers backed off it for a little," King said.

Medgar returned home before dinnertime and collapsed on the sofa, Myrlie remembered. She asked if she could do anything for him. "'No,' he said. 'Just love me.'" Myrlie laughed and told him that wasn't a hard thing to do. And then she took the phone off the hook for the rest of the evening.[36] He was still asleep on the sofa when Myrlie and the children returned from evening church services, where she often played the piano for the choir.

When he finally stirred, after the children had already gone to bed, Myrlie was sitting opposite him, just watching him sleep. It felt like a blessing seeing him rest. She told him that several church members had told her they were praying for him, and with his eyes still closed, he responded that he would surely need it. When he opened them and saw where she was sitting, on a chair facing the sofa and the front window, he gave a hard look. "Girl, if you don't get up from there. You're gonna get your head blown off," he said to her, sitting up.

Myrlie, who always had a comeback, quoted one of the things he would say to her. "My philosophy," she told him, "is that I'm not going until my time comes."

He still insisted that she move out of sight of the window. "There's no use courting it," he said.[37]

She asked him where he expected her to sit, with his big self sprawled across the sofa, then squeezed in beside him, his head in her lap. He seemed relaxed, but he wouldn't stop talking about their life insurance policy, vowing to find the money to pay the premium. For the first time, he expressed genuine fear that something might happen to him, and he made her promise that if anything did, she would take good care of their children.[38]

"I told him I couldn't live without him," Myrlie said. "Medgar was shedding tears at the same time. And he told me, 'Myrlie, you are stronger than you think you are. You take care of my children.' I'll never forget that, never forget that. He trusted me. He felt that I had a strength that I knew I didn't have. But he knew that I was a fierce protector, not only of him, but of our children as well. I'll never forget that."

They lay on the sofa together that night and wept in each other's arms.

The following day, Monday, June 10, the family had breakfast, and Medgar spent much of the morning in the backyard with Van, tossing a tiny football while Myrlie took the older kids to school. When she returned, he asked Myrlie to take Van inside, so he could spend time on his own admiring the plum tree he'd planted there. Myrlie felt that something had shifted in Medgar. He was settled, and no longer afraid, but also palpably despondent.

"Myrlie, I think we're going to have our best year ever for plums,"[39] he said, with a kind of empty optimism that made her feel more sad than hopeful.

MEDGAR RELEASED A DEFIANT STATEMENT IN RESPONSE TO THE city's latest injunction against demonstrations. In it, he slammed Jackson officials' "unique capacity for speaking from two sides of their mouths . . . why spank a tottering infant? Why enjoin a 'faltering' movement, as they describe it? White leaders in Jackson gave the world the answer today. Their injunction proceedings have proven that our movement is sharp, vital, and inclusive. They are hurting inside. This is their outcry."[40] Despite his bravado, Medgar was discouraged, and with the relentless obstruction of Black conservative clergy, paid operatives of the Sovereign Commission including press outlets like the *Jackson Advocate*, community resolve was indeed buckling.

Medgar got home that night and read to the children before they went to bed. Once they were asleep, he and Myrlie talked in a way that left her more afraid than ever. "If I go tonight, if I go next week, if I go next year, I feel I'm ready to go," he said, in a voice as calm as could be.

Myrlie told him not to talk that way, and he told her she shouldn't be afraid of death. "I know it's hard not to be," he said. "But it's something that comes to everyone someday."[41]

He hadn't told Myrlie that earlier that day, he'd been called by Felix Dunn, who headed the NAACP branch in Gulfport, Mississippi. Dunn said a local white attorney who was privately sympathetic to the movement had told him to warn Medgar that he should "be careful to have someone see him home each night and to arrange for guards around the house." The attorney had it on good authority that "an attempt was going to be made on Medgar's life."[42]

On Tuesday, June 11, Medgar was up early, and after breakfast, Myrlie noticed he kissed each child on the forehead repeatedly. He held her close and lingered in the hug. He called home several times that afternoon. "What's the matter, haven't you got anything to do?" she remembered chiding him after the third call.

"I just wanted to hear your voice," he told her. "My love to you and the kids. I'll see you tonight."[43]

At his office, Medgar met with Aaron Henry to discuss their plan to travel to Washington, D.C., the following day to testify on behalf of the Mississippi NAACP before the House Judiciary Committee in support of civil rights legislation, and to coordinate their testimony.[44] Salter recalled that he "saw Medgar late . . . [that] afternoon. He was dead tired and really discouraged—sick at what was happening to the Jackson Movement, but still too much an organizational staff man to openly challenge it. Back in January . . . he had openly pushed the national office, telling New York to speed up the Jackson school desegregation suit—in which two of his own children were plaintiffs—and hinted if they didn't, he might resign his job. The national office had speeded it up—a little. But in this situation, he didn't buck the national office. We had a long talk and, despite the internal divisions, an extremely cordial one, much like old times. He was more disheartened than I had ever known him to be."[45]

The situation for the Jackson Movement was bleak indeed. After 650 arrests, and with so many still being held in the hell of the fairground stockades, there was still no biracial commission, and few concrete gains, other than Thompson's vague promise to add a couple of Negro police officers. Voter registration remained anemic in the Mississippi Delta, and the Voter Education Project had growing doubts about the efficacy of the COFO coalition in the state. There were the persistent threats and police harassment. Medgar mused to a friend, "I'm looking to be shot, any time I step out of a car."[46]

In Alabama that afternoon, Gov. George Wallace, channeling Governor Barnett, made himself a hero to white nationalists by defying a federal court order that allowed Vivian Malone and James Hood admittance to the University of Alabama. Wallace made his stand in front of Foster Auditorium before Alabama National Guard troops, federalized by the Kennedy administration, ensured that Malone and Hood would integrate the university as Meredith had done in Mississippi.

Medgar and his team watched this unfold on television from the office. It was a welcome uplift. And then at 8:00 P.M. Eastern time, President Kennedy's television and radio address began. The notes he sounded were not unlike those in Medgar's televised speech.

"Today we are committed to a worldwide struggle to promote and protect the rights of all who wish to be free," Kennedy said. "And when Americans are sent to Vietnam or West Berlin, we do not ask for whites only. It ought to be possible, therefore, for American students of any color to attend any public institution they select without having to be backed up by troops. It ought to be possible for American consumers of any color to receive equal service in places of public accommodation, such as hotels and restaurants and theaters and retail stores, without being forced to resort to demonstrations in the street, and it ought to be possible for American citizens of any color to register to vote in a free election without interference or fear of reprisal. It ought to be possible, in short, for every American to enjoy the privileges of being American without regard to his race or his color. In short, every American ought to have the right to be treated as he would wish to be treated, as one would wish his children to be treated. But this is not the case."[47]

No president had ever put into words meant for a national audience such expressions of racial equanimity. Kennedy, who had not begun as a civil rights man, was speaking as much to the humanity of Black lives as Medgar did every day. He spoke from the same source of moral authority—the role of international moral warrior America had inherited in World War II. He presented to Americans the fundamental moral crisis that had plagued the nation from its very founding.

And he was making an announcement.

"Next week," he said. "I shall ask the Congress of the United States to act, to make a commitment it has not fully made in this century to the proposition that race has no place in American life or law." Kennedy touted the forward advances the Supreme Court had authorized and the executive branch's modern commitments to hiring without regard to race. He also said there were things only the legislative branch could do. "I am, therefore, asking the Congress to enact legislation giving all Americans the right to be served in facilities which are open to the public—hotels, restaurants, theaters, retail stores, and similar establishments."

Kennedy went on to announce that with the pace of integration moving anemically, despite progress in "seventy-five cities" over the prior two weeks, the legislation he planned to send to Congress would "authorize the Federal Government to participate more fully in lawsuits designed to end segregation in public education," and seek greater protection for the right to vote. It was a full-scale war on the Southern way of life, and an embrace, from the White House, of the "first-class citizenship" Medgar had been touting.

"This is one country," Kennedy said. "It has become one country because all of us and all the people who came here had an equal chance to develop their talents. We cannot say to 10 percent of the population that you can't have that right; that your children cannot have the chance to develop whatever talents they have; that the only way that they are going to get their rights is to go into the streets and demonstrate. I think we owe them and we owe ourselves a better country than that."

Kennedy spoke for just fourteen minutes, but his words echoed into history. The speech was thrilling for Medgar and his fellow activists. It was the culmination of all their cajoling and demands of the White House. It was also a triumph for the NAACP, which the summer before had gathered at the White House to meet with Kennedy. For white Southerners, including the Klan and White Citizens' Councils in Mississippi, it was a declaration of war. Kennedy's bill called for the federally sanctioned desegregation not just of schools and colleges, but hotels, restaurants, shops, beaches, and other public accommodations—the very things activists were conducting sit-ins and marches to achieve.

MYRLIE HAD ALLOWED THE KIDS TO STAY UP AND WATCH KENNEDY'S speech. She and Van had curled up on the bed in her and Medgar's room, while Darrell and Reena sat on the floor to watch. It felt like a singular triumph: the president of the United States echoing Medgar's call for dignity, decency, and first-class citizenship for the millions of Black Americans whose grandfathers' and grandmothers' hands built this country and more than one million of whom had, like Medgar, gone to war for its ideals. Kennedy was a fellow World War II veteran, and it was striking that it fell to these veterans to take up the fight against racial tyranny at home that they had abroad. Myrlie felt prouder than ever that her husband had played a part in Kennedy's transformation from reluctance to eloquence and action on the matter of segregation. She thought of her own father, whose bitter disappointment after serving his country had been so unshakable. Perhaps other Black men, sometime soon, would not have to carry that burden around. She drifted off, thinking how thrilled she would be to congratulate Medgar when he got home, and how she and the children would pepper him with questions until he begged them to let him get some sleep. After all, tomorrow was a workday.

A MASS MEETING WAS HELD AFTER KENNEDY'S ADDRESS, AT NEW Jerusalem church—a venue the Jackson Movement hadn't used before. It was quite a comedown from the inspiration of the president's speech, and a far cry from the packed auditorium that had gathered at the Masonic Temple for Lena Horne and Dick Gregory less than a week before. "The mass meetings had [quickly] collapsed to just token pretty participation," Ed King said. The Jackson Movement, King said, "had been destroyed because of the interventions of Washington putting pressure on the National NAACP."

The meeting lacked some of the basics of logistics and security that had become standard at the Masonic Temple. Instead, organizers tapped a group of teenagers, including then fifteen-year-old Hezekiah Watkins, whom they'd used in the past to pass out literature and leaflets outside prior mass meetings, to patrol the church grounds and watch for anyone who seemed out of place. After his nightmarish stint in Parchman, Watkins been drawn into the movement by Medgar and participated in the Jackson protests. He had gone from being an angry teenager whose little gang was spoiling for a fight with white Mississippi, to an activist who had spent time in the fairgrounds gulag the governor had built. He was enthusiastic about his assignment that night.

"We were given guns because it had been stated that there was a plot . . . on [Medgar Evers's] life." The teens rode up and down the block on their bicycles before and during the meeting. "We were told if you see anything suspicious to come back and let us know, but if anybody tries to jump on you, you defend yourself. And we were all for it, to be honest with you," he said. His only regret was that he wouldn't be able to hear Medgar's speech.

He wouldn't have missed much if he had been searching for inspiration.

Salter recalled the meeting as tense. National NAACP staffers used the event to formally announce that the focus of the Jackson Movement would now officially be voter registration and that while the boycott could continue, there would be no more demonstrations of any kind. "NAACP T-Shirts were being sold by Medgar who had no enthusiasm at all," Salter said. "He said virtually nothing at the meeting [and] looked, indeed, as though he was ready to die."[48]

Ed King recalled a time when James Meredith and Medgar had tried to explain to him the constant tension between activists on the ground and the national NAACP. Medgar, he said, asked: "Ed, do you think the NAACP exists by having fish fries and donations out of the poverty of Black people in America?" He reminded King that "there's no Black middle class big enough" to fund a massive national organization. "The NAACP exists because of foundation money and rich whites and money from Wall Street. And the NAACP is controlled by the white House, the Justice Department, and no donations will go, that Washington does not approve of. And Washington does not want Dr. King and Medgar Evers working together."

Ed King had been schooled in the multiracial collaborative haven at Tougaloo, and it didn't make sense to him that factionalism could exist in a movement that supposedly shared a single goal. Besides, he said, it was already too late.

King believed that by June 11, 1963, Medgar had decided to shake off that sense of defeat and to trust his own instincts about how best to force a change in Mississippi. "Medgar called me aside and to a small room right at the entrance to the church," King said, "and we talked.

Medgar Evers's senior photo.
Courtesy of the Evers family

Myrlie Beasley's graduation photo from Magnolia High School in 1950.
Courtesy of the Evers family

Myrlie Beasley (*second from left*) and the Chansonettes. Music would remain central in Myrlie's life.
Courtesy of the Mississippi Department of Archives and History

Medgar posing in his Army uniform in Cherbourg, France. © *John Storey/Getty Images*

Medgar and Myrlie Evers on their wedding day on December 24, 1951. *Courtesy of the Evers family*

The Evers's wedding party. *Courtesy of the Evers family*

Medgar and Myrlie in the early 1950s.
Courtesy of the Evers family

Medgar with his children, Darrell Kenyatta and Reena. *Courtesy of the Evers family*

Myrlie and Reena. *Courtesy of the Evers family*

Medgar and Reena. *Courtesy of the Evers family*

Roy Wilkins and Medgar Evers being arrested for picketing outside a Woolworth's department store in Jackson, Mississippi, in 1963.
© *Bettmann/Getty Images*

Medgar Evers and James Meredith at a press conference announcing Meredith's decision to return to the University of Mississippi on January 30, 1963.
© *Bettmann/Getty Images*

James Baldwin and Medgar Evers in Mississippi in 1963.

Martin Luther King Jr. (*bottom left*) leads the procession of mourners on their way to Medgar Evers's funeral in Jackson, Mississippi, on June 15, 1963.

Myrlie at Medgar's funeral.

EVERS
DIED for
YOU-
Join N.A.A.C.P.
FOR HIM!
THE
"Club 5
Stop
Jim Crow
Stop
Jim Crow
JOIN
N.A.A.C.P.
UNITE
FOR
FREEDOM

ONE WAY
NO RIGHT TURN
NO HALF-WAY HOUSE TO FREEDOM
CONGRESS
NOW
EVERS
Join N.A.A.C.P. FOR HIM!
FIGHT
FREEDOM
JOIN N.A.A.C.P.
EVERS DIED for YOU-
Join N.A.A.C.P. FOR HIM!
UAW Supports
NAACP
CORE
URBAN LEAGUE
IN FIGHT FOR FREEDOM
EVERS

MARCH ON WASHINGTON FOR JOBS AND FREEDOM

AUGUST 28, 1963

LINCOLN MEMORIAL PROGRAM

1. The National Anthem	*Led by* Marian Anderson.
2. Invocation	The Very Rev. Patrick O'Boyle, *Archbishop of Washington.*
3. Opening Remarks	A. Philip Randolph, *Director March on Washington for Jobs and Freedom.*
4. Remarks	Dr. Eugene Carson Blake, *Stated Clerk, United Presbyterian Church of the U.S.A.; Vice Chairman, Commission on Race Relations of the National Council of Churches of Christ in America.*
5. Tribute to Negro Women Fighters for Freedom Daisy Bates Diane Nash Bevel Mrs. Medgar Evers Mrs. Herbert Lee Rosa Parks Gloria Richardson	Mrs. Medgar Evers
6. Remarks	John Lewis, *National Chairman, Student Nonviolent Coordinating Committee.*
7. Remarks	Walter Reuther, *President, United Automobile, Aerospace and Agricultural Implement Wokers of America, AFL-CIO; Chairman, Industrial Union Department, AFL-CIO.*
8. Remarks	James Farmer, *National Director, Congress of Racial Equality.*
9. Selection	Eva Jessye *Choir*
10. Prayer	Rabbi Uri Miller, *President Synagogue Council of America.*
11. Remarks	Whitney M. Young, Jr., *Executive Director, National Urban League.*
12. Remarks	Mathew Ahmann, *Executive Director, National Catholic Conference for Interracial Justice.*
13. Remarks	Roy Wilkins, *Executive Secretary, National Association for the Advancement of Colored People.*
14. Selection	Miss Mahalia Jackson
15. Remarks	Rabbi Joachim Prinz, *President American Jewish Congress.*
16. Remarks	The Rev. Dr. Martin Luther King, Jr., *President, Southern Christian Leadership Conference.*
17. The Pledge	A Philip Randolph
18. Benediction	Dr. Benjamin E. Mays, *President, Morehouse College.*

"WE SHALL OVERCOME"

The program for the historic 1963 March on Washington touting that "Mrs. Medgar Evers" was scheduled to address the crowd, though Myrlie was unable to attend.

The march almost didn't include any female speakers; only after pressure from Anna Arnold Hedgeman, the only woman on the planning committee, was a "Tribute to Negro Women Fighters for Freedom" added to the program.
© Heritage Images/Getty Images

Myrlie addresses an NAACP Freedom Rally at Howard University on August 25, 1963. To her left is her son Darrell.
© *Bettmann/Getty Images*

Myrlie and her children with then attorney general Robert F. Kennedy during an NAACP protest outside the Justice Department.
© *Bettmann/Getty Images*

Demonstrators hold images of Medgar at a rally to protect Section 5 of the Voting Rights Act in front of the U.S. Supreme Court on February 27, 2013.
© *Chip Somodevilla/Getty Images*

Myrlie delivers the invocation at President Barack Obama's second inaugural on January 21, 2013.
© *Justin Sullivan/Getty Images*

Myrlie and family at Medgar's grave in Arlington National Cemetery on the fiftieth anniversary of his assassination. © *The Washington Post/Getty Images*

And it was like a religious experience. He had made up his mind. He was a liberated person. He said, 'I am going to invite Martin Luther King to come to Jackson, to work with SNCC and CORE.' And I said, 'There have been these threats.' And he said, 'Yes, I will be fired from my job with the NAACP tomorrow or Thursday.'" Medgar said he expected his firing to make the news, maybe even nationally, not that it mattered. "I've made up my mind. And I think I'm doing what I have to do." King said the conversation lasted ten or fifteen minutes, "and in a religious context that I don't talk to many people about. . . .

"I wasn't his pastor, but I was close to him," King said. "He knew I would understand everything he was talking about. . . . He was no longer the indecisive person who might be crying at his desk. He had mentioned to me at one point that he had trouble paying his life insurance and did not have enough . . . that was very heavy" on his mind. He knew what he wanted to do, and he intended to see it done.

Charles Evers later recalled that "until '63, Medgar mostly did what Roy Wilkins asked, but in '63 Medgar began stepping out on his own. If Wilkins had fired Medgar that year, I wouldn't have been a bit surprised."[49]

After the meeting, followed by dinner at a friend's home, Medgar dropped Gloster Current off at attorney Jack Young's home, where he was staying in Jackson. It was nearly midnight, and Medgar seemed weary. He told Current, "Everywhere I go lately, somebody has been following me," and so Current invited him to come inside. He felt certain Young would let Medgar stay until morning, so he could drive home at sunup.

Medgar declined. "I'm tired," he said. "I want to go home to my family." They briefly revisited Medgar getting a bodyguard, which Current had rejected days before on the organization's behalf. Medgar could never have afforded protection without the NAACP's help, but regardless, he was too exhausted to discuss it further. Current recalled that as they parted, Medgar "just held my hand and held it and held it."[50]

He got into his car, backed out of the driveway, and started for home. It was now just after midnight, June 12.

Darrell and Reena had begged to stay up after the president's speech and the news to watch *The Untouchables*, and Myrlie consented. It was summertime, so there was no school the following day, a Wednesday. She cuddled a sleeping Van on the bed and drifted off herself as Reena and Darrell sprawled out on the floor, elbows down, heads in hands, staring into the TV screen. They were lost in their escape to 1930s Chicago, where Elliot Ness and his band of FBI do-gooders battled organized crime, when they heard their father's car pull into the driveway, at nearly half past midnight.

For the two elder Evers children, that sound meant precious "dad time" and little gifts or sweets and time to play or cuddle before finally giving in and going to sleep. They sat up with a bolt of excitement. "Daddy's home!" However, their joy quickly turned to shock, as the low hum of Robert Stack and Walter Winchell was shattered by a single loud bang. It sounded almost like an explosion.

The sound startled Myrlie and Van out of their sleep and she sat straight up on the bed, knowing instinctively what that awful sound was. The children reacted quickly, too, out of instinct and the instruction that Medgar had provided. Darrell grabbed little Van in his arms and cradled him. They went flat on the floor. Everyone was terrified. The bang was followed by a crash that made it clear something had come through the living room window.

Myrlie told the children to stay down as she walked gingerly down the hallway toward the front door. Standing in the dark, she pulled the door open, to find her worst nightmare had finally become real.

She screamed. It was loud and guttural and deep. She screamed and screamed, and she dropped to her knees.

Medgar was lying facedown in a pool of blood, his torso on the low steps just outside the door. There was a long, semicircular pool of gore stretching from the porch, around the front of Myrlie's station wagon, and toward the carpark where Medgar had parked behind Myrlie's car. He was moving just a little, and his hand was outstretched, clutching his keys in his right hand.

Myrlie was screaming so loudly and with so much shock and agony that Darrell and Reena forgot their training. They leapt up from the bedroom floor and sprinted down the hallway, Van tottering behind them. Soon, all three were beside their mother on the stoop, and everyone was crying.

"Daddy, get up. Get up, Daddy. Get up!" Now the children were screaming, too.

Myrlie was clutching at Medgar and trying to somehow pull him inside. She was yelling his name, and desperately praying. Scattered on the ground in front of him were the T-shirts and posters he was carrying from the meeting earlier that night. They read "Jim Crow Must Go." Medgar had been shot in the back, with the bullet exploding out of his chest and crashing through the living room window. The bullet had knocked Medgar down, but he had used all his strength to drag himself halfway up the driveway and around the front of Myrlie's station wagon toward the door. He clearly tried desperately to drag himself into the house, where his family, but also his guns, were. He seemed to be trying to talk, but no sound was coming out.

A second shot rang out. This one was even closer. Myrlie thought for certain the whole house was about to be under siege. The children were in a complete panic, begging their father to *please* get up. This was the strong man who could do anything. He had to be able to do *this*, too.

Across the street, Johnnie Pearl Young, who had been up, unable to sleep, heard the gunshots clear as day. "I was sitting up in my kitchen, sewing," she said. "And all of a sudden, I heard those shots: boom, boom."

The second shot had been fired by Houston Wells, Jean's husband, who when he heard the gunfire ran out from next door and fired into the air to try to frighten the assassin (or assassins) away. He was still in his underwear and T-shirt; after firing, he ran back inside to get dressed. He quickly ran back outside and across the gory carpark while Jean stood on her front porch in shock and tears, aching for her friend.

"All of us were on the patio then," Myrlie said. "Too late. That was it. My life, my love, was gone. There were three little children standing there."

"He must have been awfully tired," Myrlie later recalled. "Because he got out on the driver's side, and we had determined that that was not the thing to do. You get out on the other side, which was closest to the door, and there was less of a chance of being a target. But he got out on the driver's side that night, and he was the perfect target."[51]

For Mrs. Young, the night was full of shocks. Hearing Myrlie's screams was just so unusual—not something you'd expect from the couple—and her first thought was to walk over and admonish Myrlie for hollering so loudly. "I got across the street," she said, "And there was Medgar down on the [ground] just pumping blood like water. It scared me so bad I forgot what I even went over there to tell her. I turned around and ran straight back to my house."

Young's husband had managed to remain asleep through the gunshots and screams, but she shook him awake, yelling, "Get up, get up. Something has happened to Medgar! When I said that, he [pulled] a pair of pants on and forgot his shirt, and he passed me and ran back over there across to Myrlie's house."

By the time the Youngs got to the Evers house, Houston Wells and another neighbor had already pulled the twin mattress off Reena's bed and carried it outside to use as a gurney. Two police officers had arrived, responding to multiple calls. One of them later said there was so much blood, it looked like someone had butchered a hog.[52]

It was the summer before her tenth-grade year, and Carolyn Wells (later Carolyn Wells Gee) was taking advantage of the chance to stay up late. Her younger sister was close friends with Reena, and Carolyn had once spent a nervous night in the Evers home babysitting the Evers kids. Her parents didn't allow their children—including Carolyn's younger brother Terry, who was best friends with Frank Figgers—to participate in marches or protests, but the children knew that their parents were NAACP members, and their phone sometimes rang with death threats from white racists. When she heard the gunshot and screams, Carolyn and her younger sister peered out their bedroom window, which was standing height and directly faced the Evers carport.

"I went to my window because I heard crying and screaming," she said. "I saw [Mr. Evers]. He was laying halfway across the steps on the porch, and Myrlie and the children were standing over him crying and screaming. Police came out but the ambulance never came.[53]

Mrs. Young and Jean Wells were soon guiding Myrlie and her sobbing children back inside the house. Mrs. Young recalled saying, "Let the men take care of it, Myrlie. I don't want you out there listening. And I don't want you looking at your husband. You know he's been shot. . . . And I don't want you to keep on hollering and screaming. You are going to upset these children [even more]."

Medgar's friends rolled him onto his back and placed him on the mattress. With the officers' help, they placed the makeshift gurney into the back of Wells's station wagon. Medgar had been shot through his back. The bullet had cracked his ribs and tore through a lung.[54] His eyes were open, and he was breathing rapidly. The men covered him with a blanket, and as Jean and Johnnie Pearl kept Myrlie from going back outside and climbing into that station wagon with Medgar, the car sped off to University Hospital.

Medgar was still trying to speak but managed to get out just two short sentences that he half whispered as the car barreled down the road and blood gurgled from his lips: "Sit me up," he said, and then, "Turn me loose."[55]

Two doors down from the Everses, Dr. Britton took a frantic call from Myrlie and dashed out his front door. He hopped into his car and followed Wells's car to the hospital. Britton was the Everses' personal physician, and he had delivered Van and often treated the family free of charge. He hoped that as a member of the Federal Civil Rights Commission, he could get the segregated hospital to take urgent action to save Medgar's life.

When they arrived there, Medgar had been wheeled into the Negro wing. Britton yelled to the all-too-passive white physicians, "Do you know who this man is? This is Medgar Evers, field secretary of the NAACP." That caused them to take action,[56] but there was no saving him.

BACK INSIDE HER HOME WITH HER CHILDREN, MYRLIE COLLAPSED in prayer and tears. She sobbed and sobbed that she could accept God's will. She knew in her heart that Medgar was gone. She snatched up the telephone again and called Jack Young's home, and he handed Gloster Current the phone in time to hear Myrlie scream: "They've killed my husband! They've killed my husband!"[57]

Mrs. Young took the children across the street to her house for the night, while Jean Wells tried to comfort Myrlie as she furiously began packing Medgar's toothbrush and pajamas for a hospital stay her heart knew would never happen. She became obsessed with figuring out how many pajama pants he might need.

Jean answered a call from Dr. Britton, who said Medgar had regained consciousness. Then another friend, Harriet Tate, came into her bedroom, and Myrlie could tell by the look on her face that it was over. Medgar was pronounced dead at 1:14 A.M. on June 12, 1963.[58]

Myrlie needed to see her children, to hold them and comfort them. She staggered across the street to Johnnie Pearl's house, past a smattering of neighbors and white bystanders from the neighboring street who had begun to gather in front of the house. "My mission now was to protect them," she said of her three young children. It was what she promised Medgar. She just didn't know where to begin, because she had never had any intention of living without him.

When she got to the children, they were silent. They seemed stunned. She held them and told them everything was going to be all right. Neither she nor they seemed to actually believe that, though. She told them they'd be spending the night at Auntie Jo's house and that she would come back for them in the morning. Then she somehow managed to get back across the street to her house, which the police, who had now grown in number, were now scouring.

"They were standing in my yard, stooping over the blood in the carport, everywhere," she recalled. "And I saw them and recognized them as the men who had followed Medgar everywhere for months; the men who had tried to run him down a few days before, the men who had asked me if I had used the gasoline can recently, and they looked at me and I screamed at them, 'Get off my property!'"

Myrlie's shock and grief now turned into a cold rage. "I clenched my fists and wanted a machine gun to mow them down, knowing and not caring that I, too, would be cut down as Medgar had been. For the first time in my life, I felt a hatred so deep and malignant I could have killed every one of them."[59]

She screamed at these empty white faces, demanding to know if a Negro's blood looked any different to them, or if they thought that by killing Medgar, they could kill the movement he was leading. One of her friends calmed her enough to answer whatever questions she could. Myrlie reached down at one point and touched Medgar's blood, then looked at the blood on her hand. It was warm, and she just looked at it and looked at it.

That blood, she believed, was on the hands of every police officer there and every police officer in Jackson. It was smeared all over Mayor Allen Thompson, who would soon express "shock" on behalf his bloodstained city. Medgar's blood rained like a monsoon over Gov.

Ross Barnett and Ole Miss and over the White Citizens' Council and the Klan and the Sovereign Commission. Medgar's blood stained every segregated part of Mississippi.

At some point in those painful, and still dark, early hours, Myrlie made what would be the hardest calls. She called Aunt Myrlie in Vicksburg, to tell her the awful news. She could barely summon the words: "Medgar is gone." Aunt Myrlie immediately offered to come to Jackson, and she was relieved. Her final call was to Charles's wife, Nan. She had been reluctant to call her. She and Nan were close in age and in temperament, and that gave them a bond.

Myrlie knew it would be easier telling Nan than telling Charles directly. He and Medgar were so tight; the proverbial "two peas." She knew Charles was going to take this hard, and that he would be bent on revenge. She would let Nan tell him. When the two women hung up, sobbing and spent, she padded into her room and sank onto her bed. The house was empty, and there was no one left to call. She buried her head in her hands, and let the tears fall.

"And then," she said, "everything became a blur."[60]

Charles got the bad news from Nan when he came home from the club he ran in Chicago, a few hours before sunrise. "They shot Medgar tonight," she told him. Charles first thought his brother had been injured, and being a solutions man, he started talking through what he needed to do: to pack a bag and head to Jackson to help Myrlie take care of Medgar at the hospital and navigate the issues around his being a Black patient in a white hospital. He was hearing what he wanted to hear. After all, it wasn't easy to kill an Evers. Crazy Jim had taught his boys that. Nan took his hands and held him still.

"No Charles," she said. "He's dead."

With that, Charles's world seemed to collapse, all at once. Every emotion from grief to rage to guilt surged through him at the same time. And disbelief, even as Nan explained the few details she knew from her heartbreaking call with Myrlie. Medgar had just come home from an NAACP mass meeting . . . Someone shot him as he got out of his car . . . He never made it inside. It really couldn't be, could it?

Charles couldn't help but think that had he been there, it wouldn't have been so bad. Had he been with Medgar, they surely would have been together at that meeting and driven home together, and Charles would have been well armed and able to protect his brother from harm. None of this made sense. He stormed into his room and snatched a suitcase out of the closet and began to throw clothes and shoes inside. Before he snapped it closed, he added three more items: a rapid-fire carbine shotgun and two .38-caliber pistols.[61] His heart was drowning in grief, but his mind was full of vengeful rage.

CHAPTER 8

How to Be a Civil Rights Widow

This is the decisive battleground for America. Nowhere in the world is the idea of white supremacy more firmly entrenched, or more cancerous, than in Mississippi.

—Michael Schwerner, twenty-four-year-old civil rights activist murdered by members of the KKK, along with Andrew Goodman and James Chaney, both twenty-one, in Mississippi in 1964

When you are the wife of a civil rights martyr, everyone wants to take your picture. You make the covers of *Ebony* and *Jet*—and even *Life*. The photographers prefer that you appear demure and serious, befitting your tragedy, but you must neither smile nor cry, nor should your children, because it would ruin the photograph. You and the children must always be neatly and tastefully dressed, and you must never yell or scream, because that would be undignified. Your face must always remain perfectly composed, with enough powder and lipstick to make you pretty but not so much that you appear gaudy.

The newspapers will print your home address, and the curious will find your street, stand in front of your house, and point. The home of the martyr is a public attraction, and people will knock on your door and pose your children on the lawn or even on the carport where their father's blood still casts a shadow that all the scrubbing bubbles and bleach you could muster could not remove. When you speak, you must talk of grace and forgiveness, and say something profound about faith in God and his unchangeable will.

Myrlie Evers had to learn these rules because one wrong move, one errant word or flash of public anger, could ruin the legacy of the man she loved. Medgar Evers, who would have turned thirty-eight years old in less than a month on July 2—twenty years after he enlisted in the United States Army to fight the Nazis for his country in World War II, only to find himself fighting Nazism in America when he came home—had been gunned down and stolen from her and their three young children just feet from his own front door, leaving Myrlie alone to tell his story.

She had to be a quick study, without a tutor. Betty Shabazz and Coretta Scott King still had their husbands, Malcolm and Martin, and were not yet experiencing the torture Myrlie was enduring. Freedom Summer was still a year away and Michael Schwerner's wife, Rita, could still hold him in her arms and pursue their dream of helping to change Mississippi and America together. He had not yet climbed into that station wagon with James Chaney and Andrew Goodman and sped away from the Neshoba County jail with a convoy of Klansmen in pursuit. Jackie and Ethel Kennedy still watched their young husbands leave their bedsides every morning to wield the awesome power of the federal government. It was Myrlie Louise Evers, just three months over thirty years old, who was the first of the national civil rights widows.

Eight years earlier, Mamie Till-Mobley had preceded her in public mourning, not as a widow but as a grieving mother. Medgar had aided Mrs. Till in Mound Bayou, but Myrlie had never thought to study her, as she had no intention of following her into love martyrdom. There was no one to call, or to send a telegram to, and ask how this should be done. She had only the fastidious social training she had received in the homes of Mama and Aunt Myrlie to prepare her for her new role.

She woke up alone at 5:00 A.M. on June 12, in the house Medgar had designed for his family's security, in the bed where so often she had buried herself in the strong arms that hadn't changed since her husband's days as a halfback at Alcorn College. Medgar had always been so proud of his physique. He worked at keeping his body fit. How easily an assassin had shattered it.

She reached across the bed and was somehow surprised to find his side empty. She still felt the haze of the sedative Dr. Britton finally injected into her forearm, forcing her to get some sleep. Where were the children? *Ah, right!* They were across the street with Jo. *Why were they there and not in their beds?* Oh, yes, their father was murdered just feet from the comfort and serenity of his living room, while she and they watched him lie a pool of his own blood, gripping his house key and reaching for the door. Perhaps if she stayed in bed long enough, God would somehow find the mercy he lacked just hours before and take her to where Medgar was.

Myrlie needed to get up. She had to go through the motions. The house was full of people—friends milling around, cooking, helping. She could hear the soft, faint murmur of their voices, whispering, she supposed, because they thought she was still asleep. Or maybe she still *was*. Perhaps it was all just an awful nightmare, and now she could wake up.

Someone clicked on the television in the living room. She climbed out of bed and padded down the hallway. When she looked to the right, she could see that a big chunk of the wall by the kitchen had been torn away. As she looked left toward the living room, she could see there was a hole in the front window and the venetian blinds were broken and bent. That was the path the bullet had taken when it entered the house after going through Medgar.

Lena Horne and Roy Wilkins were on the *Today* show. She could see their mouths were moving, and they must have been talking about Medgar, but she couldn't make out what they were saying. Her ears must have been clogged by grief.

Someone took her into the kitchen and showed her where the bullet smashed into the tile wall, and the dent in the refrigerator where the ricocheting projectile hit next, before shattering a coffee pot and landing on the opposite counter beneath a watermelon she had bought as a treat for the kids.

She fixated on what the white policemen must have said to each other when they saw that watermelon, and how the *Clarion-Ledger* and the other racist white newspapers would run wild with disdainful stereotypes because of it. She was thinking just like her media-savvy husband. And that made her angry—at the lying white media that set the table for Medgar's assassination and at the white policemen who followed Medgar everywhere but were completely useless in his moment of need.

Back in the living room, she remembered Medgar saying to her just two days before, "Girl, if you don't move from in front of that window, you're gonna get your head blown off." He was so right. Had she been standing there last night—or warming up food for Medgar in the kitchen, or washing the dishes, the same bullet that took Medgar would have taken her, too. Part of her wished it had.

"I felt that my life was gone, over, without reason or meaning," she later wrote. "Then I remembered the children that were all I had left of Medgar, and I walked out of the house straight into the lens of a television camera."[1] Myrlie neither smiled nor frowned. She gathered herself and calmly gave the press the statement they wanted. Then she walked through the phalanx of media and onlookers across the street to collect her children.

Mrs. Young was in tears. She hadn't been able to bring herself to tell the children that their father was gone, and she had kept the television off so they wouldn't hear the news. It was down to Myrlie to say the words that would devastate them.

"I went to them," Myrlie wrote, "took them into a room by ourselves and told them their father wouldn't be coming home anymore. 'Is he dead, Mommy?' Reena, just eight years old asked. And I died a little as I told her that he was."

The Evers children were dazed, as she took them home to pack a few things to take to another friend's house to stay for a couple of days. Van didn't want to go. And he didn't understand. "He kept running to me everywhere I went, asking, 'Daddy's gone? Daddy's gone?'" she wrote. "It tore me apart. When the time came for them to leave, he said, 'Mommy's going, too!' I took him in my arms and said I'd be here when he got back."[2] Reena and Darrell were sullen and drained. They didn't cry, and for a long time, Darrell couldn't. He seemed completely lost.

THE *MISSISSIPPI FREE PRESS*, ON JUNE 15, DESCRIBED THE MOOD among Black Jacksonians as "one of deep horror and anger. Many Negroes were reported to be carrying guns. The chief of police has made an appeal for people to leave the situation in the hands of police." The paper also reported that the NAACP youth leaders who visited Myrlie told her "they planned to have everyone wear NAACP T-shirts like those Evers was carrying when he was killed"—the ones that read "Jim Crow Must Go!" In Harlem, Garveyite activist James R. Lawson, the president of the United African Nationalist Movement, expressed shock and sadness about Evers's death, but in a statement said, "It points up the futility of Dr. Martin Luther King's philosophy of nonviolence."[3]

By 11:25 A.M., all over Jackson, protesters were pouring into the streets. Thirteen ministers conducted a silent march toward city hall and were stopped by Jackson police and arrested. The *Times* reported that soon after that "approximately 200 Negro teenagers marched out of the Masonic Temple Building on Lynch Street, site of Mr. Evers's office. Some 100 city policemen, Hinds County deputy sheriffs and state highway patrolmen, armed with riot guns and automatic rifles, halted them a block away. A total of 145 demonstrators, including 74 aged 17 and under, were then arrested. One girl was struck in the face by a club, deputies wrested a middle-aged woman spectator to the sidewalk and other Negroes were shoved back roughly."

John Salter observed the bitter irony that "[Medgar's] death was the resurrection of the Jackson Movement. . . . Within hours, we had organized huge demonstrations that poured out onto the streets; the national office had no alternative, under the circumstances, but to accept this. Police brutality and terror mounted steadily—it was in a much grimmer dimension than it had ever been."[4] Protests broke out from Los Angeles to New York to Virginia, often sparking violent reactions from police in those cities, too.

Salter had driven to Ed King's house in the middle of the night to tell him and his wife, Jeanette, that Medgar had been killed. King wondered for a long time what might have happened had he tried to go home with Medgar that night. Or had someone followed him home to provide security. King observed that the assassin had chosen to act when "the movement had been so destroyed in Jackson." He noted, "When people are really down and out that the white racists here in Mississippi think they can get away with the most." He added that it was widely believed the conspiracy to assassinate Medgar was bigger "than just one person."

Aunt Myrlie arrived by late morning, and that was a relief. Together, they showed the cameramen and press people out of the house, which had become like a beehive. Myrlie was frenetic, pacing, talking about Medgar and trying to remember little things he'd said before they faded from her mind. "I talked and talked, and I don't know what I said," she wrote.[5] Finally, she asked if a mass meeting would be held that night, and insisted, over many objections, that she wanted to go. In the early evening, Ms. Hurley and a group of friends drove her in her station wagon to Pearl Street Baptist Church.[6]

Rev. Bennett W. Smith, who had served in the Air Force and taught in the Chicago public schools before joining the ministry and working with Dr. King in the Southern Christian Leadership Conference, was speaking when Myrlie walked into the sanctuary. There was an immediate hush. Myrlie was familiar with this place. She sometimes left the children with a babysitter and went with Medgar to meetings, particularly if they were held in churches. She sometimes played the organ or piano after the benediction, before the main proceedings began.

Myrlie was no stranger to public performance. She had sung on stage as a member of a Vicksburg Black girls' singing group called the Chansonettes and played the piano at her church. As a child, playing piano to entertain the family of that white woman Big Mama worked for, she'd dreamed of someday playing for real at Carnegie Hall. She knew how to stand before this crowd, one that loved Medgar and supported her. The performance of her life was required. Medgar always said she was more than the wife of a civil rights leader. She was now the torch bearer representing everything he ever did or tried to do. As she walked down that aisle toward the stage, she remembered him telling her, "Bury the fear and do what you have to do." That evening, her fear was buried deep in a cold rage.

"I found that I was a wall of fire," she said. "I never saw myself that way, but I'm glad that I eventually did because I intended to survive . . . after Medgar was killed, because we had three children. I could not afford to be weak. I could not afford to give up, not only because of those children, [but] because of all the other children, regardless of the color."

Claude Sitton of the *New York Times* recounted the events of that June 12 event. "Mrs. Evers spoke tonight to some 500 persons at a mass meeting at the Pearl Street church. Dressed in a pale green dress, she appeared tired but composed. Many women in the audience wept openly."[7]

"I come to you tonight with a broken heart," Myrlie said as she faced the hushed crowd. "I am left without my husband, and my children without a father, but I am left with the strong determination to try to take up where he left off. And I come to make a plea that all of you here and those who are not here will, by his death, be able to draw some of his strength, some of his courage, and some of his determination to finish this fight. Nothing can bring Medgar back, but the cause can live on. . . . We cannot let his death be in vain."[8]

"Referring to her husband's death," the *Times* continued, she said, "'it was his wish that this [Jackson] movement would be one of the most successful that this nation has ever known.' Mrs. Evers, who had requested that she be given the opportunity to speak, said her husband had spoken of death last Sunday and said that he was ready to go."[9] In the months before his death, Medgar had told the *Times*, "If I die, it will be in a good cause," and separately, he told the *Times:* "I've been fighting for America just as much as the soldiers in Vietnam."[10]

When Myrlie finished speaking, the sanctuary erupted in applause and shouts. Then, just as quietly as she had entered, she walked down the aisle toward the door. She could see people weeping and she could hear voices singing. She didn't know what they were singing, and she didn't care. She got in her car to leave because if she stayed in that church one second longer, she feared the rage inside her would set her alight.[11]

WHAT HAPPENED NEXT WAS AS PREDICTABLE AS SPRING RAIN. Official white Mississippi, from the segregationist governor to the segregationist mayor to the segregationist, NAACP-hating newspaper editors issued high-minded statements decrying the dastardly murder, with some even offering rewards leading to the killer.[12] Many of the editorials that ran in the days after the murder were pointed in laying the blame for Medgar's murder on Black activists themselves, whose insistence on protesting segregation had, in their view, created the anger that ultimately and inevitably brought Medgar down. The Jackson mayor, who had so pointedly sparred with Medgar and the Jackson Movement joined in the double-speak, embellishing his feigned outrage at the assassination by offering two $5,000 rewards: one for information leading to Evers's killer, and a matching sum for information leading to the arrest and conviction of a "sniper who shot a white youth who was in a car on Lynch Street." That youth, unlike Medgar Evers, was alive and well.[13]

The assassin's rifle was quickly found, in a thatch of honeysuckle bushes in the empty lot across the street, adjacent to the Youngs' house. The attached scope had allowed the killer to take the fatal shot as he viewed Medgar in silhouette from 150 yards away.

A Jackson police officer told the *Jackson Daily News* that Medgar's killer "destroyed in one minute everything we've been trying to do here," then admitted, "We're scared to death. That's the truth." Rumors were spreading that Black Jacksonians were arming themselves, and that white residents were worried they might take revenge.

A northern newspaper reporting from Jackson quoted a white man in a local bar who perhaps summed up the sentiment of Mississippi segregationists: "Maybe this will slow the niggers down."[14]

The *New York Times* reported that "the Rev. Dr. Martin Luther King Jr. mourned Mr. Evers as a 'pure patriot.'"[15] He told reporters on June 12 that "the brutal murder of Medgar Evers came as shocking and tragic news to all people of good will"[16] and speculated that whoever was responsible might have feared the renewed determination, righteous indignation, and urgency that President Kennedy's June 11 televised address would arouse in Black Americans. Kennedy's speech, King said, "was a very passionate plea for justice and freedom and it was a firm statement. And I'm sure there are many in the country, and the South in particular, who responded negatively to that statement; and it may well be that those who engaged in this tragic act were trying to retaliate for what they had heard the president say, and they could see within his statement a determination now within the federal government to do something about these conditions."[17]

If King was sorrowful but diplomatic, Roy Wilkins was spitting fire. His public statement said Medgar's death "demonstrates anew the blind and murderous hatred which obsesses too many Mississippians. In their ignorance, they believe that by killing a brave, dedicated, and resourceful leader of the civil rights struggle, they can kill the movement for human rights. . . . Every Negro citizen has lost a valiant leader in the death of Medgar Evers. The entire nation has lost a man who believed in America and died defending its principles."[18]

The national NAACP offered a $10,000 reward for information leading to the killer. Gloster Current, who had spent the past month trying to steer Medgar's efforts back to what the national office wanted, and who was the last person to see Medgar alive, angrily challenged Jackson officials "to match our reward offer," adding, "The cowardly ambush murder of Medgar W. Evers . . . should awaken all Americans to the plight of Negroes in Mississippi." One can only speculate on the pangs of guilt he felt at having been the one to tell his friend that the organization had better things to do with its money than to protect him. And some of Medgar's friends quietly blamed NAACP headquarters and the Kennedy administration as surely as they blamed the shooter, the Klan, and racist Mississippi for Medgar's demise.

Clarence Mitchell Jr.'s son Michael was a seventeen-year-old high school senior when he learned of Medgar's death. "The call came from the vice president of the branch in Jackson, Mississippi, that they had murdered Medgar," he said. "My father was on the phone, and he just was in a rage . . . a quiet rage because he had spent so much time with Medgar. . . . after a while, we finally tried to get Myrlie on the phone and . . . we could hear that she was inconsolable. And my father then immediately called the FBI."[19]

The protests continued into Thursday, when "Jackson police charged the porch of a Negro home and clubbed a group of youngsters and adults into submission after they had chanted and jeered at them" and then into Friday, June 14—Flag Day—when thirty-seven young marchers were arrested for walking two by two, "some carrying tiny American flags."[20]

"We had demonstrations defying the injunction [against public demonstrations] each day, leading up to the funeral," Ed King said. The funeral was scheduled for Saturday. And the state's Supreme Court the day before had received an urgent appeal by leaders of the Jackson Movement, protesting the injunction and "the misuse of power by state officers to deprive Negroes of their citizenship rights."[21] Medgar had signed the petition, along with Ed King, John Salter, and Dick Gregory.

"The NAACP did not try to stop us, because obviously, the people were going to do something," King said. There was pressure building in the community that needed to be released.

THE DAYS AFTER MEDGAR'S ASSASSINATION WERE A CONFUSING morass of distraught parents, personal fear, and deep trauma for the children of Guynes Street. The Sweet children were away with their mother at Southern University in Baton Rouge, Louisiana, where she had gone to graduate school because she was unable to obtain such a degree in segregated Mississippi. "I remember my mama hitting the floor screaming when my dad called," Dennis Sweet III, who was seven years old then, said. "She said, 'They killed him!' I remember she was on her knees crying."

Frank Figgers was thirteen years old and attending the last week at a segregated Boy Scout camp with Terry Wells, when they heard the news. "Terry said these words that really just pierced me," Figgers recalled. "He said [of Medgar Evers], 'He didn't bother nobody. He tried to help everybody.' As we were going to our evening meal, those words just kind of lingered with me. I knew that a great man, a great person that was doing God's will, had been assassinated."[22]

"It was a traumatic experience," Dennis Sweet III said. "I don't think people understand what a terrorist act that was in that community. You have a community where you have kids . . . This guy comes in here and just kills the guy everybody loves . . . [that] the kids love. . . . It just traumatized everybody, all the kids."[23]

Mrs. Sweet Owens recalled how much things changed. The fences between the homes on Guynes Street, when they existed at all, were low and chain-linked, so she would frequently see her mom or dad chatting with Medgar across the backyards. "They would be . . . talking about what needed to be done, voting, the boycotts . . ." Sweet said that after Medgar was gone, "Mom would never go downtown to shop. Literally . . . all my clothes came from [the] Spiegel catalog. When I would go to school, people would say, 'Where did you get that?' I said, "From Spiegel catalog.' I said, 'Mom, are we ever going to shop in a store?' She said, 'I promised Medgar I'd never go downtown and shop.' After that, I always wore catalog clothes proudly."

Hezekiah Watkins heard the news of Medgar's murder on June 12. "I was sad," he said. "The first thing we tried to do was to get on our bicycles and ride to his home, but we could only get so close because the police officers had it all blocked off." Instead, he and a growing group of neighbors and onlookers gathered about a block away. "And we stayed there for quite some time, just . . . just sad."

Carolyn Wells remembers "NAACP people" including Gloster Current coming to their house and to the Everses' next door the day after the shooting, and the adults including her father and uncle huddling in her living room. Her uncle had seen something strange on the block adjoining Guynes Street: stacks of tin cans stacked in rows stretched across Missouri Street, which was the route Mr. Evers often used to come home. She could hear the men speculating that the cans were placed there so that Evers's car would run into them, and he would have to exit his car so the killer could get a clear shot at him, but Medgar, for whatever reason, or perhaps because he saw them, had gone another way. She could no more forget those chilling conversations than she could get the image of Mr. Evers lying on the ground in a pool of blood out of her mind. Or the sound of Myrlie and the children screaming. Nor would her younger sister, who was soon sent off to an aunt's house to get away from the block for the rest of the summer, while Carolyn was told to go on to band camp as planned, and to try to get back to normal. That was, of course, impossible.

FOR THE EVERS CHILDREN, THE TRAUMA CLEARLY RAN DEEPER. When they returned to the house and attempted to resume something like a normal life, it eluded them. "The children, after a traumatic experience like that, they were having nightmares," Myrlie said. Particularly Darrell, who would wake up screaming in the night, or disappear into his room during the day, silent and distant.

Darrell Kenyatta Evers. His father had given him the name of an African warrior against colonialism during a time when much of the continent was in an uprising to throw off its European colonial masters, even as African descendants in America was doing the same. He had been the first to follow Myrlie to the door and to see his father dying.

"I remember . . . being in the house . . . the day after the death of my father and this overwhelming grief that was in the house," Darrell Evers later recalled. "A number of people had come by to comfort my mother and to comfort our family, and there was just . . . a lot of grief, because so many people loved Medgar, and . . . he was so respected . . . throughout the country, and especially . . . in Mississippi. And it was a little bit too much for a ten-year-old at that time. . . . My father, I felt, was in peace and I felt that he was finally resting."[24]

Whatever sense of peace Darrell felt that day didn't last.

Myrlie recalled a day, not long after Medgar died, when Darrell was out in front of the house playing baseball with some of the boys on the block, as she watched him out of her bedroom window. "He hit the ball as it was pitched to him," she wrote. "And a boy ran to catch it, and Darrell stood there a moment, and he broke into sobs, and he ran from the street around the house to the back yard and the plum tree. I ran to meet him, and he cried as though his heart would break standing there under the tree that Medgar had planted. It was the first time he had cried."[25]

Another time, Darrell went to Myrlie saying, "Mom, I'm going to go shopping with you."

"Okay. What do you want?" Myrlie asked.

"I want a gun," Darrell said.

"What kind of gun?" she asked him.

His answer was straightforward and deadly serious.

"'I want a rifle,' he told me," Myrlie recalled. "And I said, 'Why do you want a rifle?' 'I'm going to kill whoever killed my dad,' he said. He was fixated on that. We finally went to a department store and bought a toy gun. He went to sleep every night with that gun next to him for the longest time."

Myrlie said Reena was a "motherly soul," who took care of her brothers and in many ways mothered her mom as well. Myrlie felt pangs of guilt for how much she often leaned on little Reena for comfort. Reena, just nine years old, was sometimes afraid to sleep in her room—knowing that it was on her mattress that her father's bleeding body had been carried away. On those nights she would snuggle with her mom in her parents' room, which was a comfort to both of them.

"Little [Van] was so young, but it affected him," Myrlie said. "Look at pictures of him then. You could see [the] strain and sadness written all over that three-year-old boy's face." He would ask for his father insistently, not understanding why he was gone, and follow Myrlie around the house.

The Evers home felt like a way station for family, friends, detectives, reporters, and *Life* magazine photographers. While Myrlie was forcing herself to plan a funeral—recalling that Medgar always said that when he died, he wanted to be buried quickly—she also had to deal with the investigation. Thompson had asked the FBI to get involved, and an endless stream of detectives, local and federal, were in and out of the house. Myrlie had been around Medgar too long to believe that any investigation, especially one by local police, would result in justice. She had to restrain herself from cursing the police who repeatedly asked her if she knew any Blacks who might want to kill her husband.

Myrlie was grateful when Medgar's sisters arrived. They and Dr. Britton began planning a Saturday funeral, while she continued to respond to the endless requests for interviews from the police and the press. Charles arrived soon after. He felt a deep urge to take out some white Mississippians—Klan or not—as retribution for his brother's murder, but he managed to channel his rage, for now, into a focused determination to help Myrlie. It was Charles who gently coaxed Myrlie to make the painful choice of what clothes Medgar would be buried in. And he soon took over the job of dealing with the press. The presence of Medgar's brother in her home was both comforting and torturous. He was a physical reminder of what she had lost, but she needed someone to lean on and she knew that the children did, too.

More than anything, she wanted all of the many white faces to leave her home. "Everyone," she wrote, "was always white—the cameramen, the interviewers, everyone—and a white skin had come to have a meaning I didn't want to explore."[26]

At one point, Charles threw a polite but persistent young television reporter, Dan Rather, out of the home. "He said he'd be happy to leave the house," Charles wrote. "But this was a big story, and he was going to be filing reports to CBS News in New York from out on the street." Right then, Charles understood how important Medgar had become, and after that, he allowed Rather to follow him around, even confiding to Rather his murderous thoughts toward white people, to which Rather, in his Texas twang, replied, "You can't let yourself do the same thing they did . . . not every white man is like the men who killed Medgar."

The reaction to Medgar's assassination was quick and reached the highest levels of political and social power.

President Kennedy sent a typewritten condolence letter that referred to "the cause for which your husband gave his life," and he handwrote at the bottom, "Mrs. Kennedy joins me in extending her deepest sympathy."[27] Bill Russell, the great Boston Celtics champion called Charles and offered his help. Lena Horne, who heard the news as she prepared for her *Today* appearance, vowed never to return to Mississippi, declaring her heart thoroughly broken. A distraught James Baldwin declared that in Medgar's honor he would complete the play he'd begun as a tribute to Emmett Till, *Blues for Mister Charlie*. Fannie Lou Hamer, who was from Sunflower County, Mississippi, not far from where Till was murdered, was in jail when Medgar was assassinated, being beaten unconscious for trying to register to vote. When she emerged from jail, she cried out, "Something's got to break!" And the paper that Medgar and Charles had tried to become paperboys for, so long ago, the *Chicago Defender,* made Medgar's murder their top story for two weeks straight.[28]

MYRLIE TOOK DARRELL AND REENA TO COLLINS FUNERAL HOME and asked the funeral director to give her and the children a few minutes alone with the body. It was the first time they were seeing their father since they watched him bleeding and dying on their carport, and it was important to Myrlie that they be allowed to do so in peace. "The children left after a moment," she wrote. "I stayed. The tired lines were gone from his face, and I had a terrible urge to hold his head and stroke his temples and say that everything would be all right."[29]

To her dismay, though, she soon realized she wasn't alone; the *Life* magazine photographer had lingered. When she glared at him, she realized his eyes were filled with tears. And in that moment, she said, the hatred that Medgar's murder left her feeling at the sight of white skin vanished, never to return.[30]

The days leading to the Saturday funeral were a blur of meals cooked by loving friends and family, comfort at Aunt Myrlie's side or lying in her lap. Myrlie bristled when Ruby Hurley insisted that they purchase a new dress for her to wear, but she put up with it all—if only to get it all over with.[31]

Salter recalled that "between 5,000 and 6,000 people, from all over Mississippi—from places into which no civil rights worker had set foot—came to Jackson for Medgar's funeral. A number of nationally prominent people were there."[32] Dr. Martin Luther King Jr., Ralph Abernathy, Roy Wilkins, and his top aide and public relations director joined the mourners, along with Gloster Current, Clarence Mitchell Jr., and the other leading New York NAACP staff. Dr. Ralph Bunche was also in attendance. He had served as an advisor to FDR as part of his "Black cabinet," later declining the position of assistant secretary of state under Harry Truman due to the segregated housing conditions in Washington, D.C.; at the time of the funeral he was the assistant secretary general of the United Nations. James Meredith and his wife were there, as were Representative Charles Diggs, who in 1954 had been elected the first Black U.S. congressman from Michigan; Dick Gregory; and Dr. T. R. M. Howard, who had come to pay tribute to his former young charge and coconspirator for the upliftment of Black sharecroppers in and around Mound Bayou. Amos Brown, who had learned of the assassination while at Morehouse, sat near Dr. King at the service. And of course, Medgar and Myrlie's friends from Guynes Street.

Dr. Howard drew "Amens" from the sweltering crowd as he railed at the white supremacy that ultimately took Medgar's life. "The NAACP was feared and *is* feared and hated by the white people of this God-forsaken state," he said. "And Medgar knew he was hated." He spoke Black Mississippians' and Black Americans' rage and their exhaustion. "For one hundred years, we have turned one cheek and then the other," he said. "And they hit us on both cheeks. Now the neck is getting tired." And with that, he urged those in attendance to "keep on marching."[33]

Myrlie knew how much Medgar would have hated the whole production, but he would have been pleased by Dr. King's presence. Medgar deeply respected King, and one of his goals had been to bring Dr. King to Jackson and to work with him to replicate the movement he was building in places like Alabama. King had recently agreed to come, even though Medgar knew the national NAACP did not approve of a King-Evers collaboration.

Salter had called King and asked if he could come to Jackson for Medgar's funeral. "King readily agreed," Salter recalled, "and I picked up him and several of his staff at the airport." King, it was clear, had no formal role at the funeral, but he wanted to be there.

The service was at the Masonic Temple, where more than four

thousand people were packed inside the gaping auditorium and thousands more were overflowing into the hallways and onto the streets in the steaming Mississippi summer heat, which reached an unusually high 103 degrees that day. It was a fitting venue. Medgar's office lay untouched upstairs. The typewriter where he composed his reports and letters, the desk piled high with papers related to voter registration, boycott flyers, letters, and more, were all still there, as if awaiting their owner's return.

Mama and Big Mama came to Jackson for the funeral, too, joining Aunt Myrlie and Myrlie's aunt Francis from Chicago, whom she'd stayed with when she and Medgar took the summer trip that preceded their engagement. Myrlie was annoyed when she later learned that the crowds made it difficult for her grandmothers to get seats. In the moment, all she could do was find hers, and settle Reena and Darrell beside her. She wasn't sure if it was the heat or the crowd that aggravated her. Or the open casket, which she had definitively asked to have closed.

Myrlie wanted something different for Medgar's going home. She wanted what he would have wanted. He had told her once that he preferred his funeral to be short. "When I'm gone, I'm gone, and I won't know anything about it,"[34] he said. She wished she could call off this whole affair, send everyone home and along with just her loved ones bury her husband in the quiet family plot she and Medgar had purchased in a Black cemetery ten minutes from their house. She had let other people take over the details of Medgar's funeral to relieve her anxieties, but that assured that it quickly got away from her. Not just the open casket, and the lack of assigned seating for her family, but also the seemingly endless eulogies that went on for nearly two hours in the blazing heat.

Roy Wilkins gave the main eulogy, in which he condemned "the Southern political system" that put Medgar's killer up to his evil task. "In faraway Washington," Wilkins said bitterly, "the Southern system has its outpost in the Congress of the United States. They helped put the man behind the deadly rifle. The killer must have thought that he had, if not immunity, then certainly a protection for whatever he chose to do."[35]

Charles, who sat beside Myrlie and the children, was too distraught to speak. After the busy week of funeral planning subsided, all he was left with was grief.

Salter wrote that at the funeral, "much less was said about Medgar the man—and much more was said about his career at the NAACP."[36] Rev. Ed King sat with Dr. King, who was not allowed to speak at the funeral. "He sat with visiting clergy from the National Council of Churches," Ed King said.

"Several denominations sent clergy to represent them at Medgar's funeral,"[37] Ed King added. Adam D. Beittel, the president of Tougaloo, spoke, and Salter wrote that he "was the closest to a movement representative to speak. But the NAACP was in charge."[38]

The Evers children seemed to be barely holding up under the pressure of sadness and exhaustion. Reena wept and wept throughout the speeches, and Darrell, who later said that when he saw his father lying on the ground that horrible night, with all the blood around him, he'd felt the spirit of God around his father's body and a strange kind of peace, fidgeted in his suit, because he hated dressing up.[39] He spent the service just staring at the open casket until in a sudden rush, all of his tears seemed to come at once.

Myrlie recalled that other than the day he cried under that plum tree, Darrell had not cried again. "He would disappear into his room and sit there alone, not speaking, not playing, and it was hard for me to imagine what was going on in his mind. Now, sitting beside me at the funeral, I saw him stare at the open casket, and I felt what he must be thinking. There would be no more telephone calls from his father. No more basketball and football with him, no riding bicycles with him in front of the house, no fishing. The promise, so often deferred, to take Darrell hunting would never be fulfilled. The nights when Medgar came home with boxes of Cracker Jack for each child—they, too, were over. Darrell sat there and stared at the casket, his head slightly bowed, and then suddenly he sobbed and sobbed until I guess no more tears would come."[40]

Myrlie knew she needed to remain composed for her children's sake (she had left Van behind with a sitter; his little heart was spared the funeral ordeal). She succeeded throughout much of the service, buckling only as the procession began to carry Medgar's now-closed coffin out of the building.

Charles had been her rock in the days leading up to the funeral. He turned to her at this moment and said, "Don't break down now, sis,"[41] even as his own heart was broken, with his best friend and eternal co-conspirator gone. "Medgar's death left me all alone,"[42] he later wrote. There would be no more hunting trips, or phone calls, or opportunities to needle his younger brother for working too much.

Myrlie realized this was the last time Medgar would be inside this building. Tom Dent, who also flew down for the funeral, had the same feeling: the Masonic Temple was the location just five months earlier of the triumphant press conference for James Meredith. There were so many ironies to Medgar's final hour of life. "He had been taken to the emergency room of the same hospital where he had been made to wait hours for Clyde Kennard's pills," Dent wrote. "But it was too late, they could not make him wait any longer."[43]

Student organizer Diane Nash, who was married to James Bevel (the child she was carrying while locked up in Parchman was theirs), had asked Myrlie if the young Jackson activists Medgar had supported could march after the funeral. Myrlie had agreed, as long as it was done with a dignity that would make Medgar proud.[44] Rev. Allen Johnson, Rev. Robert Stevens, and Rev. L. L. Wilkins had even obtained a permit from the city, bypassing the injunction on the grounds that the march would be a "silent, mournful procession."[45]

"We had a mass march—but didn't call it that—of . . . several thousand people walking behind the casket as we left the building," Rev. Ed King said. Sitting in the lead car, as the marchers followed on foot,

Myrlie had all but forgotten Nash's request. She was surprised at the expanse of the crowds appearing as they rolled down Lynch Street toward Collins Funeral Home, where Medgar's body would be placed on a train bound for Washington, D.C.

The Kennedy administration offered to have Medgar interned in Arlington National Cemetery, a nod to his service in Europe and in Mississippi. The decision by the president to honor a fellow World War II veteran who had died in the cause of liberty at home drew an onslaught of hateful letters to the White House from segregationists objecting to the burial of a Black man with such honors.

Myrlie objected for other reasons. She wanted him buried in the little family plot they had purchased close to home, where she and the children could go and sit with him from time to time. But she reluctantly agreed to the Washington plan because she understood that Medgar's burial needed to play a part in his legacy.

As the car cruised slowly down the seventeen blocks from the Masonic Temple, Myrlie began to confront the distance growing, with every second, between her and the body of the man she loved.

Aaron Henry, who considered Medgar to have been one of his best friends, sat beside Myrlie in the back of the limousine. He and Medgar had fought together since they were opening NAACP offices in the Delta region and bonded further at that inaugural SCLC organizational meeting. Now, as the car turned onto Farish Street, he said to Myrlie: "Look behind you."

The massive procession was a human ocean, filling every inch of space. Many of the mourners carried American flags. Most were young, but many were old, and bore the visible signs and drawn looks of a life lived under segregation. A handful, maybe a dozen, were white: mostly clergy and Tougaloo professors like Ed King. And some of the white (and partly white, in the case of John Salter) men and women had been Medgar's allies and endured beatings and death threats for championing desegregation.

Helmeted white police officers lined the side of the road, and mounted police escorted the parade of mourners, which stretched for nine full blocks. As the hearse drove by, with Medgar's flag-draped coffin, some of the officers removed their headgear and stood at attention. Myrlie didn't know if the gesture was genuine or required, but she knew Medgar would have marveled at it.[46] Black men, women, and children stood on porches and hung out of doors, and as the procession passed a white restaurant where a jukebox was blaring, a group of young Black men stormed in and unplugged it. The white patrons and workers didn't do or say a thing.[47]

Despite his angry rejection of his Mississippi field secretary's tactics, Roy Wilkins was "destroyed" by his assassination, Charles wrote. "Roy had no kids of his own and knew few young folks well. He didn't know how to treat the younger generation. . . . If Roy Wilkins ever hated whites, it was the day a white man murdered Medgar in cold blood."[48]

Dr. King made his presence known as the funeral spilled out onto the main street. He walked at the front of the procession with Ralph Abernathy, Wilkins, and the other national civil rights leaders. "Medgar's killing shocked Martin Luther King and his family," Charles later wrote. And Coretta Scott King believed the assassination was a grim premonition of her own husband's fate.[49] Jackie Robinson wrote a lengthy telegram to the White House denouncing the assassination and imploring the Kennedy administration to use all available means to protect King during the funeral, lest another assassination lead to a national uprising.

"Should harm come to Dr. King to add to the misery which decent Americans of both races experienced with the murder of Mr. Evers," Robinson's telegram read, "the restraint of many people all over this nation might burst its bonds and bring about a bloody holocaust the likes of which this country has not seen . . . for to millions, Martin King symbolizes the bearing forward of the torch for freedom so savagely wrested from the dying grip of Medgar Evers. American needs and the world cannot afford to lose him to the whims of murderous maniacs."[50]

As the car pulled up to the Collins Funeral Home, Myrlie asked Aaron to arrange a ride home for her and her children, and they were safely at home by the time things went from mournful to calamitous. As the mourners pressed toward the funeral home, a photographer captured Dr. King's look of perturbance as he and other civil rights leaders were physically moved back. Local residents who had not been able to get inside the Masonic Temple were lined up outside the small funeral home to view the body before it left for Washington in six or eight hours.

Ed King said that part of the city's agreement to the funeral procession was that there would be "no singing of freedom songs or hymns or anything."

At the mass meetings, "Medgar had led us every night in singing . . . 'this little light. I'm going to let it shine!' Where? All over Jackson," King said. "And he would point to Jackson's City Hall because that's where we wanted to march. And we would say, 'All over the City Hall, all over Capitol Street, all over the Capitol Building!' And then we would sing, 'All over America, all over Washington!'"

As they approached the funeral home, the crowd began mimicking Medgar's version of "This Little Light" and pointing toward Capitol Street. The three to four hundred police officers lining the streets reacted to the outstretched fingers of the overwhelmingly Black crowd by presuming they were pointing at them. And they reacted.

Before long, they set upon the crowd with nightsticks flying. The crowd reacted by breaking into a run, and shouting: "Let's go to Capitol Street!" which was two blocks away. Police were cutting TV camera wires and clubbing and beating marchers, in a scene of increasing mayhem. Though not a planned demonstration, the postfuneral march was now an illegal one.

As King and the other prominent civil rights leaders were hurried away, the police presence swelled to some two thousand officers. Dozens of people were arrested and hauled off to the fairgrounds outdoor prison, including Salter and Ed King. Police were firing over the heads of the swelling crowds.[51]

President Kennedy and Attorney General Robert Kennedy each placed multiple calls to the Jackson mayor. Medgar's assassination had opened a fresh wound in one of the key racial battlegrounds in the United States, and the protest at his funeral was salting it.[52]

The June 16 *Clarion-Ledger* played up the mayhem with the headline "White-Led Agitation" over an article that said, "A small minority of the marchers led by white Tougaloo staff members turned on police with brickbats Saturday afternoon in a sudden, brisk melee . . . the violent group erupted in a flurry, attacking the police officers at the rear of the process. Dogs, fire trucks and armed men were called but on display only and not used. Dogs on leash patrolled the crowds as they dispersed. Soft drinks bottles had been hurled from the roofs of Farish Street stores."

The "unruly Negroes," as the *Clarion-Ledger* labeled them, were far from a gang of young thugs and white instigators. The songs that rose up from that crowd included "We Shall Overcome" and they were sung not just by college students and impatient young organizers but also by teachers, who had resisted Medgar's pleas to support the cause and who had avoided any association with the NAACP for fear of losing their jobs when Medgar was alive. They were sung by elderly Black men and women who had strained for a lifetime under the yoke of inequality, and who had shied away from Medgar's entreaties to register to vote.

Now that Medgar had sacrificed his own life, people poured out of shops and ran toward Capitol Street in an eruption of song and support. "And before I'd be a slave, I'll be buried in my grave," the crowd sang. As the police chief screamed into a bullhorn, the songs became shouts. "We want freedom!" "We want equality!" "Freedom! Freedom! Freedom!" Around fifty members of the press were forced back by police as their vans converged on the crowd and began hauling people away.

Claude Sitton wrote in the *New York Times* that the police then "went to work in earnest to clear the area. A television cameraman caught in a doorway said a Negro man who did not move fast enough was struck in the face with a shot gun butt by a deputy sheriff. . . . The cameraman said a Negro woman was clubbed by a policeman. She fled to a car but was dragged out and clubbed again. . . . By this time, most of the Negroes had been sealed off in a one-block area. They began throwing bricks, bottles and other missiles at the police. Most fell short of the mark. One group taunted the officers with cries of 'Shoot! Shoot! Shoot!'"[53]

A. L. Ray, the deputy chief of the Jackson Police, screamed into a bullhorn, "You came here to honor a dead man, and you have brought dishonor." The crowd screamed back in a frenzy of shouts, barking police dogs, and the crashing of bottles. John Doar, the Kennedy administration's man in Mississippi, finally stepped out, put his hands up and yelled to the crowd: "You're not going to win anything with bottles and bricks! . . . Is there someone here who can speak for you people?" A young Black man stood beside him, shouting, "This man is right!" Then Doar faced the crowd and yelled, "My name is John Doar—D-O-A-R. I'm from the Justice Department, and anyone around here knows I stand for what is right. Let's disperse now. Go on home. Let's not have a riot here." Black members of the crowd who were known movement leaders began to chime in, and before long, the crowd dispersed. Myrlie later wrote that without Doar, a full-on riot would likely have overtaken Jackson that day.[54]

During the funeral march that turned into an uprising, Medgar's body was quietly taken to the train station in Meridian where it would begin its final journey. Large crowds were waiting for the body, and a large group of Black mourners held a prayer service as the body was loaded onto the train. Thousands would greet the train as it passed through Atlanta as well.[55]

On Sunday, the day after the funeral, CBS ran a previously recorded interview with Medgar, as a kind of obituary. The interview had first aired on June 12, the day he died. But Myrlie hadn't watched. She had shut off the television after the *Today* show and spent the full day wandering in a haze. In the interview, correspondent William Peters asked Medgar about the threats he faced, and Medgar said, "I've had a number of threatening calls—people calling me saying they were going to kill me, saying they were going to blow my home up and saying that I only had a few hours to live."[56]

Peters closed by asking Medgar about the importance of the vote. "I think it's often said that a voteless people are a hopeless people," Medgar replied. "And I think it's true with us or true with anybody or any group of people. So it's necessary that we try to get our hands on the ballot and use it effectively. We're just not interested in voting so that conditions will be improved for Negroes. We want conditions improved for everybody. We feel that in this country that all persons should have an opportunity to register and vote and do the things that the Constitution guarantees them. That's all we're interested in."

"Thank you very much, Mr. Evers," Peters said. This perfectly encapsulated everything Medgar had fought for: the ballot and the betterment of the country, and Peters's use of "Mr. Evers" was the honorific Blacks were denied when they shopped or worked in Mississippi. The interview was evidence that Medgar was on the verge of the kind of national prominence in death that he had not quite achieved in life.

One week after Medgar's murder, Myrlie packed up Darrell and Reena for the trip to Washington, D.C. Medgar had long promised to take them on an airplane one day, and he now kept that promise in death. Charles and Ruby Hurley traveled with them, while Aunt Myrlie and Aunt Francis remained home with Van. Myrlie wrote that the women were afraid to stay in the house, even though she "assured them that no [assailant] would dare return." Still, arrangements were made for twenty-four-hour security guards outside.[57] The NAACP was now providing the security detail they had denied Medgar when he needed it most.

The Evers family was met at the airport by reporters, photographers, and camera crews, along with a delegation from the Washington chapter of the NAACP. Rev. E. Franklin Jackson, the chapter's president and the pastor of John Wesley AME Zion Church, had held a rally the evening before, drawing six hundred people and raising $2,000 for Myrlie and the children.[58] Myrlie was presented with a large bouquet of flowers, and she and the children were ushered into a chauffeured car that Interior Secretary Stewart Udall made available to them during their stay. They were driven to the Mayflower Hotel, where her suite was filled with more flowers "and fruit and nuts, a gift from the manager."[59] They could never have stayed in such a hotel in their segregated home state.

At the Mayflower, silent plainclothes officers lined the hallways to protect Myrlie and her children. Seeing them, Myrlie wrote, "My perverse mind flew back to the nights that Medgar had sped down the dark highways of the delta with a car behind him, 'shaking the car's tail' at pursuers, with only the protection of his wits and his driving skill between him and death. Now he was dead, and we were all protected."[60]

Medgar's body arrived at Union Station on Tuesday and was met by a throng of supporters from CORE, SNCC, and the NAACP. They followed the coffin to a Washington funeral home, and from there to John Wesley AME for a viewing that evening and the next morning.

On Wednesday morning, Myrlie, Charles, Ruby, and the children drove to the church for a procession from there to Arlington National Cemetery. More than twenty-five thousand people gathered on the streets to observe the procession,[61] and Myrlie observed that "block after block, there were people standing, many with heads bowed, many making the sign of the cross as we passed by. Most of them were white."[62] Myrlie felt an immense pride as the car passed the Lincoln Memorial. She knew then that she had made the right decision to have Medgar buried with the full honors his country owed him—not just for serving his country, but for the stated creed of his country, and for trying to force even Mississippi to live up to it.

"My pride in Medgar had never been so great," she wrote. "For somehow this whole experience was the final evidence that the man I had loved and married, the man whose children I had borne, was truly a great American being put to rest in a place with many other American heroes."[63]

That sense of pride couldn't relieve the pain. When they arrived at Fort Myer Chapel for the pre-internment service, Charles was unable to get out of the car for a long time. His strength had finally gone, and he dissolved, immobilized by tears. The Sunday before Medgar died, the brothers had spoken on the phone and talked about a piece of land they'd bought cheap a year before in Brazil, and their dreams of making it their own hunting and fishing paradise. They had been dreamers all their lives. Though Medgar had insisted to the end that he would never call anywhere but Mississippi home.

"A man's state is like his house," he'd said. In that final call the two brothers seemed to talk about everything, from the new Cadillac Charles had bought to the escalating threats against Medgar, and the danger Myrlie and the children were in, as a result. "We both felt the premonition of danger," Charles wrote. "When you have no time to be afraid, what you get are premonitions."[64] The call lasted a long time because neither man wanted to hang up. Now, Medgar had left Mississippi for good.

THE SERVICE AT ARLINGTON WAS BRIEF BUT SOLEMN. AS IT TURNS out, it was the one Medgar had always wanted.

Some two thousand mourners gathered for the burial,[65] yet it felt somehow intimate. The family passed the throng and then walked between a two-line honor guard before sitting down at the gravesite. They were seated among a throng of dignitaries, including Attorney General Robert Kennedy, Secretary Udall, and Senators Jacob Javits and Paul Douglas, along with Major Albert Turner of the Military District of Washington, who was there to represent President Kennedy.

"He is not dead, the soldier fallen here," said Bishop Spottswood. "His spirit walks through the world today." He added: "I hope Medgar Evers will be the last Black American to give his life in the struggle to make the Constitution come alive."[66] It was a prayer that would in just a few years prove rich with irony. Roy Wilkins said Medgar had well shown that he believed in this country, but it remained to be seen if the country believed in him.[67]

After six young white soldiers removed the American flag from the coffin, the sound of three rifle cracks made Myrlie startle instinctively, bringing back the awful memory of the gunshot that took Medgar's life. That was followed by the sound of bugles playing "Taps." Afterward, the cadets handed the flag to Myrlie, who was standing between her elder children. Then Medgar Evers, the love of her life, was lowered into the earth.

Myrlie willed herself to self-control throughout the service, as the cameras continued to examine her every move. But as the casket disappeared belowground, she burst into tears.[68] Beside her, Reena began to sob, and "Darrell sat there, hands together in his lap, the saddest little boy in the world."[69]

Charles could barely stand it. Growing up, Medgar so hated the cold. The thought of his little brother being lowered into the cold ground, with no way for Charles to warm his feet, like he did when they were kids and they shared a bed in Decatur—as close as if they were twins—undid him. His best friend in the world was truly gone.

The last words that day came from Mickey Levine, of the American Veterans Committee, who said "no soldier in this field has fought more courageously, more heroically than Medgar Evers." He pledged that the fight had not ended, that it would go to the Congress and to the people, so that Medgar would not have died in vain. The service ended with "We Shall Overcome," the song that had prompted the Jackson police to batter young protesters during Medgar's funeral procession.

The next morning, June 20, Myrlie, Charles, and the children were taken to the White House to meet President Kennedy. Myrlie noted that Kennedy seemed older and with fairer hair than she'd expected. He was gracious and gave each of the children a small gift—a White House pin for Reena and a PT-boat tie clip for Darrell. They were given a tour of the White House living quarters, and Reena got to sit on the bed Queen Elizabeth had slept on.

President Kennedy had a gift for Myrlie, too: a draft copy of the civil rights bill he had promised the nation on the night before Medgar was murdered. The bill called for an end to segregation in public accommodations and sought to speed up implementation of school desegregation under *Brown*. Medgar and Aaron Henry had been preparing their testimony before the House Judiciary Committee calling for a bill like this on the day of Kennedy's speech, not knowing that one was going to be promised. He had pressed Kennedy personally to take legislative action to protect the rights of Black Mississippians, yet he wouldn't live to see Kennedy try to do it. Kennedy handed Myrlie the draft, which he had signed for her. The bill had been sent to Congress the day before, as Medgar was being laid to rest with full military honors at Arlington.

When they left the White House, Myrlie nearly broke down, as the President's young son ran out onto the lawn to wave goodbye to his father as he departed in a Marine helicopter.[70] The entire situation was surreal. She had come from Vicksburg, a proud but segregated community where on some days, all they had was their faith and their dignified spirits, and Medgar Evers had taken her on a twelve-year journey that had so many ups and downs and so much peril, but an even greater love, and now he had brought her to the ultimate seat of American power. Yet he was no longer there to experience any of it with her. She was walking these grand steps alone *because* he had been murdered trying to save America from itself.

Throughout the trip, the *Life* photojournalist had followed Myrlie for a "picture and text story." Just a few years earlier, the "picture and text" story in *Ebony* had introduced Medgar to a national audience. Myrlie had been a character in Medgar's civil rights story—pretty and smiling as she cuddled her daughter or stood in silhouette at the Civil War memorial in Vicksburg with her husband and their children. This lengthy cover piece had her byline and her words, and the pictures showed a tear streaming down her cheek during the funeral as she comforted a sobbing Darrell. Other pictures showed mourners beside Medgar's open casket, the mass of people marching behind Dr. King, Ralph Abernathy, and Roy Wilkins after the funeral, and Medgar's burial as a hero at Arlington.

Vigils and memorial services were held across the country: in Philadelphia and Atlanta, at the Metropolitan Community Church in Chicago, and in Emmett Till's neighborhood of Bronzeville.

When Myrlie, Charles, and the children arrived home on Friday, the new Jackson airport building was no longer segregated. Built with federal funds, it had to bow to federal law.[71] Medgar had fought for this, and it was another victory he had not lived to enjoy. "I didn't know how I would survive without him," she said. The hospital returned his personal items, and each one flooded her with memories—good ones, like Medgar's favorite photograph of her from their Alcorn days, and ones that were horrific, like the bloodstained five-dollar bill and the blood-encrusted keys Medgar had in his hand when he died.[72]

It was all too much. She had three distraught children to see to, and the endless stream of tragedy tourists pouring onto the block, bothering the children and snapping photos at all hours, thanks to the *Clarion-Ledger* having printed their address on its rancid pages.

TWO NIGHTS AFTER THEY GOT BACK FROM WASHINGTON, ON June 23, the phone rang. It was R. Jess Brown, and the news he had was stunning. The FBI had found Medgar's killer, and he was under arrest. Myrlie dropped the phone on the floor and ran to switch on the television, hunting through the channels for confirmation.[73] She now had a name to affix to her grief and her rage: Byron De La Beckwith.

CHAPTER 9

A Tristate Conspiracy?

"The Negroes are getting too independent," they say. "We must teach them a lesson." What lesson? The lesson of subordination: "Kill the leaders and it will cow the Negro who dares to shoot a white man, even in self-defense."

—Ida B. Wells-Barnett

Nearly everything about how Medgar's murder was handled by the authorities came as a surprise to Myrlie. She was amazed the Jackson police bothered to investigate at all, that the officers who had swarmed her home that night and into the next day lifted a finger to find her husband's killer, that the FBI got involved, that the rifle was found, along with a telescopic scope and a fingerprint, and that anyone bothered to trace it. She had become accustomed to law enforcement doing nothing to bring justice after the murderers of Black men, women, and children. Yet federal law enforcement had done just that.

Byron De La Beckwith was a World War II veteran like Medgar, but five years older and an ardent racist and fascist. He was born in Colusa, California, before his Mississippi-born and reared mother re-turned with him to her home state, after his father died when he was five years old—a detail that allowed the *Clarion-Ledger* to mockingly describe him as a "Californian."[1] The arrest was considered enough of a matter of national importance that J. Edgar Hoover announced the arrest himself.

Jackson police detectives John Chamblee and Fred Sanders, who had arrived at the Evers home soon after the first two responding officers, had taken charge of the investigation. A June 29 report described a visit they made to Greenwood, where Beckwith, who sold fertilizer door-to-door to local farmers—because, according to his fellow workers, it required less contact with "niggers in the field"—was widely known as a vocal segregationist, Citizens' Council member, and Klansman. Chamblee and Sanders's typewritten report stated, "It is the general consensus of the people that [the Evers shooting] was carefully planned and not a quick venture." The report also said, "Most seemed glad to talk to us but could not or would not give us any information concerning De. La. [sic]"[2]

Finding Beckwith was a needle-in-a-haystack operation. After the high-powered rifle was found, Chief Detective M. B. Pierce announced that "all evidence in the case had been sent to the FBI in Washington, including the rifle with a new telescopic sight, a fingerprint from the sight, and the bullet,"[3] which had been damaged as it passed through Medgar's body and ricocheted through the living room and kitchen of the house. It was reported that "there were no substantial leads, but that [Pierce's] men were checking on a few out-of-state people who had been in the area."[4]

The Kennedy administration was inundated by letters and telegrams from Black citizens and interracial and religious organizations expressing outrage and disgust at Evers's assassination. Fearing an outbreak of fresh racial conflict as they faced their first high-profile assassination of a civil rights leader, they made the investigation a priority. Attorney General Robert Kennedy didn't intend to fail, and even Hoover, who viewed the civil rights movement as a hotbed of Communist sympathizers and dangerous would-be "Black Messiahs," put the agency's back into the investigation.

The fingerprint on the rifle scope led agents to Beckwith,[5] and when they visited him at his "deteriorating old house on Greenwood's George Street," to ask if he still had his Enfield rifle, he refused to talk to them. But his military service record included his fingerprints, which matched the one on the scope.

On June 23, a Sunday, President Kennedy was in West Germany being received by huge crowds as he gave a Cold War address. Dr. King was in Detroit leading what was, at the time, the largest civil rights demonstration in U.S. history: the Walk to Freedom, organized by the Detroit Council on Human Rights and joined by clergy, civil rights organizations, and organized labor. After leading 125,000 mostly Black marchers down Woodward Avenue, with many carrying signs declaring "Evers Died for You—Join NAACP for Him," King gave an earlier version of his "I Have a Dream" speech in which he stated that "before the victory is won, some, like Medgar Evers, may have to face physical death. But if physical death is the price that some must pay to free their children and their white brothers from an eternal psychological death, then nothing can be more redemptive . . . I have a dream." King expressed the hope "that there will be a day that we will no longer face the atrocities that Emmett Till had to face or Medgar Evers had to face, that all men can live with dignity."[6]

That same day, Bobby Kennedy appeared on NBC's *Meet the Press* and said there was more evidence against Byron De La Beckwith than has been made public, but that he "was not at liberty to discuss [it] further."

Beckwith's arrest, the *Clarion-Ledger* reported, "capped eleven days of intensive investigation by city, county, state and federal agents."[7]

Hoover said Beckwith had been arrested on a charge of violating the Civil Rights Act of 1957 and that he "and others unknown conspired to injure, oppress, and intimidate Medgar Evers."[8] Beckwith had turned himself in after his neighbors tipped him off that the FBI was watching his house. He was transferred to Jackson and refused to give any statement. At the Jackson police station, he at first refused to pose for a photo, then agreed to do so "when they said they were just doing their job."[9]

Beckwith was clearly a fanatic. One Greenwood resident recalled that after the *Brown* decision, he "stood on the street corner one day selling copies of *Black Monday* by Judge Tom Brady." Beckwith's former employer, Vincent Cascio, told the Associated Press that if anyone mentioned Blacks around Beckwith, "he would fly into a rage."[10] He had a large gun collection and frequently traded firearms to friends and associates.[11]

On June 26, Frank Ellis Smith, a former moderate Democratic congressman from Mississippi, wrote to the assistant attorney general for the Civil Rights Division, Burke Marshall, sharing what he knew about Beckwith. Smith had been appointed by President Kennedy to the board of the Tennessee Valley Authority after losing his seat in the Democratic primary to segregationist Jamie Whitten, three days after Medgar's assassination. He wrote to Marshall that "several years ago, De La (Delay) Beckworth [*sic*] came to my office in Greenwood to ask, in general, why the world was in the hands of the Communists. 'Let me know if I can kill a nigger for you,' were his parting words."[12]

Smith went on to call Beckwith "a product of all right-wing, racist, organizations": a former district treasurer of the Sons of the American Revolution, an associate of the John Birch Society, and someone who "occasionally embarrassed the Citizens Council leaders, but they regularly used him as a promoter and agitator." He also claimed that Whitten had used Beckwith as a campaign operative on the ground.[13]

Detectives also learned that Beckwith had been under psychiatric care, even speaking with a doctor who apparently treated him "for a condition of the mind" for more than a year.[14] Beckwith was all smiles later in July when Sheriff Bob Gilfoy delivered him from the Jackson jail to Whitfield Hospital's maximum-security wing to receive a mental evaluation to determine if he was fit to stand trial. He posed for photographers and joked about his on-again, off-again marriage.[15] He put on quite a show. Few in Jackson's Black and civil rights community believed Beckwith was insane, any more than they were convinced that he had acted alone.

GUYNES STREET RAN STRAIGHT EAST TO WEST, AND THAT EMPTY expanse of trees and honeysuckle bushes that separated the one-block Black development from Missouri Street and commercial Delta Drive now took on an even more sinister posture. "Not a single person lived back there. Nothing but a lot of grass and a lot of trash and what not," Johnnie Pearl Young said. It was next to her home, and she was distressed that the gunman appeared to have used her honeysuckle bushes as cover and pushed the butt of his rifle through her fence, to aim at Medgar through that mounted scope. "I was sitting up there in the kitchen [that night]," she recalled, "looking out the back, and when I heard a shot, I said, 'My goodness, that man came out of . . . that wooded area."

Medgar, Myrlie, and their neighbors knew he was being stalked. Neighbors remembered that in the weeks before the murder a white car, resembling those used by the local white Top Cab company, was parked on the block or was driven up and down it. Young believed the driver "studied the street [for] at least about two weeks before they got a chance to kill him." Medgar repeatedly reported their phone being tapped to the New Orleans FBI office, but they never acted on the complaints. The taps on the phone were a likely product of the Sovereignty Commission, which was hoping to find embarrassing or damning information in order to disparage Medgar's reputation and damage his effectiveness in the movement. The informants feeding information about Medgar's movements included Black informants like Percy Greene.

Medgar was warned by NAACP aides that he had been followed

to the party after Lena Horne and Dick Gregory's appearance at the June 7 mass meeting. He also received threats that were passed along to him through a sympathetic white lawyer. The two Jackson police detectives who primarily worked the case, and who shared their findings with the FBI, took numerous reports about white strangers who appeared at the Masonic Temple that evening, two standing at the back, one smoking a cigarette, while the third man took a seat, "neither clapping his hands, nor laughing at any of the jokes"[16]—prompting Lilian Louie, Medgar's personal secretary, to ask the man if she could sell him a membership. He told her he already had one. She told an associate named Sam Bailey to find out who he was. Bailey "walked over to [the man], and he got up and left in a hurry, and she didn't see him anymore."[17] At least, not that evening.

Hours before Medgar's murder, on June 10, at around 1:00 P.M. or 1:30 P.M., Louie looked out the office window and saw the same man lingering across the street for about an hour. Then he entered the building and came upstairs. Lots of white press men were around, she told the detectives, but this man didn't interact with them, nor did he have a pad or a camera. She asked if she could help him, and he left. Louie's account was corroborated by Doris Allison, a Black housewife who attended the mass meeting that night, along with two other attendees: Marie Bracey and Pearlina Lewis.[18]

All three women identified Brian De La Beckwith from his photograph in the newspaper. So, too, did Leroy Kelly Jr., who saw a man who looked like Beckwith enter the Masonic Temple on the seventh after telling two young Black boys outside that he hadn't been able to get in, to which they told him he could try the back way. Kelly's wife told the detectives that Beckwith unnerved her so much as he sat, staring and unsmiling, that she thought he might throw a bomb at the stage.[19]

Two white cabdrivers, Herbert Speights and Lee Swilley, identified a man they described as "42–44 years of age, 6′2″ tall, dark hair combed back and greying at the temples, wearing dark pants and a sport shirt" who on the Sunday before Medgar's murder came to the Trailways bus station where they were waiting for fares and repeatedly asked, "Where that Evans nigger lived that is the NAACP worker,"[20] apparently mistaking Evers's name. He repeatedly went inside the station to use the phone book and returned three times, giving them possible addresses that they told him couldn't be right because they were in white neighborhoods.

Each person interviewed also identified Beckwith. Witness after witness described the 1962 white Plymouth Valiant, with an unusually long rear antenna and a Masonic emblem hanging from the rearview mirror, which was linked to Beckwith, and which multiple witnesses saw in the Joe's Drive-In parking lot on June 11 and at the Trailways bus station.[21]

No one seemed to doubt that Beckwith had pulled the trigger, but on June 15, the *Mississippi Free Press* reported that "the shooting, which seemed to have involved at least three men, was apparently carefully planned," noting that "J. G. Wells, Houston Wells's brother, said that when he drove down the street near Evers's home, he crashed through a 10-inch-high barricade of tin cans. Wells said he thought that the barricade was part of a trap to facilitate the murder since Evers often went home by that route. Because he returned home from another direction Tuesday night, the barricade was untouched."[22]

The *Free Press* also said, "Mrs. Herbert Bishop, whose home faced the barricade, said that she and her children heard a very loud noise at the time of the killing. Willie Mae Bishop, one of the children, who was watching television, told the [paper] that when they heard the shots, 'we shut off all the lights because we were scared.' She said that when she looked out the window, she saw three men running from the spot where the shot is believed to have been fired."[23] The Bishops were white, which in Mississippi added to their credibility.

Chamblee interviewed a witness who "saw three men sitting in a room with a rifle around the time Medgar was murdered and included in his report that witnesses reported seeing three men walking quickly away from a house on Missouri Street after the shot killing Mr. Evers was fired, and about a suspect who rode a bus into Jackson from Shreveport."[24]

With a man in custody, and despite Hoover's statement about "persons unknown," the FBI appeared to have declared victory on the Evers murder and stopped investigating after Beckwith's indictment. No attempt was made to do a larger inquiry into Klan involvement, even after Chamblee and Sanders reported that a twenty-year-old hotel porter named Estes Knight King had overheard two men discussing killing Myrlie. "The men were standing near the Edward Hotel and . . . they had a suitcase long enough to hold a rifle and were standing beside a red Pontiac." King heard them saying "they were to do away with Evers wife tonight. And that it would be around 2:00 A.M." He then tried to make a phone call from a phone booth, and a man in a mask jerked the phone away and told him not to use that phone again, so he contacted the FBI.

"As a precaution," Jackson police notified all cars to "make a regular check of [the Evers's] address." This also did not prompt any investigation into whether Medgar's murder had been more than the work of a lone fanatic.

Medgar's name was reportedly on the Klan's death lists, as were James Meredith's, John Salter's, and Ed King's. After the Freedom Rides, the lists also included young activist leaders from CORE and SNCC. The *Brown* decision had revived the Klan, which had diminished in membership and power after the Great Depression and World War II. By the 1960s, much of its activity was centered on Mississippi.[25] Many white Mississippians viewed the Freedom Rides as an "invasion" by Northern, Jewish Communists, abetted by a handful of bad, ungrateful, and militant local Negroes like Medgar and outsiders like Dr. King, who they saw as disrupting what they chose to believe was a kindly, Christian, and perfectly fair segregation of the races better known as "the Mississippi way."

Two Klan organizations were active in the South: the original Knights of the Ku Klux Klan, and what Mississippi investigative journalist Jerry Mitchell called "the most notorious Klan organization in the United States: The White Knights of the KKK." The White Knights were led by Sam Bowers, who Mitchell said was "responsible for at least ten murders that we know of here in Mississippi (including the murders of Goodman, Schwerner and Chaney) [and] probably more." Bowers began organizing the White Knights in 1963 in response to CORE's aggressive push for integration in Jackson, where he lived. This was a fight Medgar Evers was intimately involved in.[26]

Mitchell said it was no coincidence that Evers was killed on the night "President Kennedy delivered his first civil rights speech, where he told the nation that grandsons of slaves are still not free."

"The Klan panicked," Mitchell believed, and "they picked that particular night" to show themselves as a national organization. "It was not an accident," he said.

In the same early-morning hours of June 12 that Medgar Evers was bleeding to death in his carport, Bernard Lafayette pulled into his home in Selma, Alabama. A white man approached and asked for help pushing his disabled car. The man went back to his car, but when he returned a second time, he struck Lafayette on his head with the butt of a pistol. Lafayette called to his neighbor, who came outside with a rifle and fired a shot in the air. "Don't kill him," Lafayette shouted, as the man scurried into his car and drove away.

Lafayette was a cofounder of SNCC and the Nashville Student Movement, which saw hundreds of students arrested at sit-ins between February and April 1960. He participated in the Freedom Rides and spent time incarcerated at Parchman. After that ordeal, he helped James Bevel set up the "freedom workshops" for activists emerging from detention as well as new recruits. He was a student of James Lawson, the nonviolence practitioner who had connected with Martin Luther King during the Montgomery Bus Boycott and who also trained fellow SNCC founders John Lewis, James Bevel, and Diane Nash in the Gandhian techniques that prompted him to urge his friend not to shoot and kill his attacker.

Lafayette found out that Medgar was dead while he was still in the hospital. All he could think of was Myrlie and the Evers children, frantic and terrified in what should have been their safe home. Nearly a week later, Lafayette had a visitor: FBI Special Agent Edwin R. Tully,[27] who told him of a "tristate conspiracy" that involved killing CORE activist Benjamin Elton Cox in Louisiana, murdering Medgar Evers in Jackson, and doing "an Emmett Till"[28] on him. Tully said the conspiracy was planned in New Orleans, the original terminus point for the Freedom Rides. Ben Cox had been out of town when the gunmen came for him, so he remained unharmed. Lafayette said such plots were meant to send a strong message to others to warn them away from civil rights activism.[29] If the FBI followed up on this tristate conspiracy, Lafayette never heard about it again.

Even after Beckwith was indicted on July 2[30]—on what would have been Medgar's thirty-eighth birthday—Myrlie and nearly everyone in her community still had little cause to trust the "justice" system in Mississippi. Clyde Kennard certainly hadn't survived it; he died two days later, on July 4 in a Chicago hospital. Cancer had taken what little Parchman Penitentiary had left behind. He was just thirty-six years old, and one of the many millions of Black bodies that had been ground up by "the Mississippi way of life."

MYRLIE WAS IN CHICAGO WHEN THE INDICTMENT CAME DOWN. She had discovered, as had Mamie Till-Mobley, that being a civil rights widow, she was an attractive prospect as a public speaker and a prolific fundraising and publicity tool for the NAACP. When the June 28 issue of *Life* hit the newsstands, with the cover photograph of her consoling Darrell at the funeral, NAACP branches all around the country began requesting that she come and talk about Medgar.[31]

Ruby Hurley and Gloster Current advised her to wait on accepting any offers until after her speech at the organization's national convention, in Chicago, where she was the first week of July. She was accepting the NAACP's Spingarn Medal on Medgar's behalf. Aunt Myrlie traveled with her to look after the children, as did Charles.

Myrlie's speech was scheduled for the evening of July 4, and she had spent the plane ride to Chicago worried about it. The only time she had spoken publicly before had been at the church rally after Medgar died, and now she found it hard to get what she wanted to say down on paper. The emotions were still too raw. How could she, without any display of guile, encapsulate all that Medgar had meant not just to her and to their children, but to the world, and all that had happened in the brief but challenging weeks since his murder? Myrlie was following Roy Wilkins, Fred Shuttlesworth, and then Bishop Spottswood, who would present her with the award.

With Charles, Aunt Myrlie, and her children in their seats, Myrlie stood alone on the outdoor stage. "I remember looking up at the pure blue of the sky with a sense that perhaps Medgar was somehow aware of this day," she wrote later. "I was drawing strength from him and at the same time that I had better do a good job."[32] In her speech, written largely at the last minute and under the pressure of love and legacy, Myrlie said of Medgar: "He made the supreme sacrifice, gave his life for all Americans. I pray his death has shocked the complacent into active participation in achieving the goals for which he died."[33]

She was surprised by the strength of her voice, which was clear and firm. She spoke for ten minutes, and that was followed by a roar of applause. "I turned and saw Aunt Myrlie wiping tears from her eyes," she said. "There were others on the platform similarly overcome. I was dry-eyed and calm."[34]

She thought a lot about the time Medgar asked her: "Myrlie, when you going to learn to stand up and fight for yourself?" She'd taken it as an insult, and shot back, "I do," to which he'd responded flatly, "You don't." "I didn't cry," she later recalled, "which would ordinarily have been what I would've done." Instead, she decided to humor the man who had seemed to take delight in pushing her buttons since they were in college. "Explain to me what you mean," she said.

"He told me that I had strength that I wasn't even aware of," she later wrote. "[He said,] 'Stop backing away from change and challenge.'" During her speech in Chicago, she had plenty of both.

After that, Myrlie was in great demand as a speaker. Public speaking gave her an excuse for being away from home where she was tormented by memories day and night, but it also was a way to earn money and to make good on her promise to Medgar to properly care for their children. It was not lost on her that her husband had sold life insurance in the Delta but died with a lapsed policy of his own. The NAACP, Dr. King, the churches, and sympathetic people of all races and faiths around the country had stepped up to raise money for the family, including funds to ensure the children would be able to attend college. A small policy the NAACP had taken out for Medgar during his employment and their agreement to continue paying his salary to Myrlie would ensure the family would make it,[35] but it wasn't going to be enough.

At first, Myrlie felt that staying at home "served a good purpose," she said, "because it made me determined to make whatever system, whatever people were involved, I was going to make them pay. With my last breath. And I prayed to my God to give me direction and give me strength to see the people who destroyed my husband's body were caught. I was obsessed with that. I tried not to show it every day. That's why I took to the lecture circuit. That was my opportunity to release, with dignity, the hatred that I had inside of me. It is interesting the two opposite forces: love and hate, how those two can drive you to do things ordinarily you wouldn't. I was determined that I was going to live. I was determined that I was going to take care of our three children, without begging. I would work hard. And I was determined that with my last breath I would see that those who were responsible for putting those bullets in my husband's back would pay."

She packed the children off to Vicksburg to stay with Aunt Myrlie for the last weeks of summer and committed herself to the road, where she had quickly become a prolific speaker and the NAACP's most formidable fundraiser. With the children gone, though, when she came home to the empty house, she found herself lost in a spiral of grief. She had not brought herself to pack up all of Medgar's things. His shirts were still hanging neatly in the closet. Sometimes she buried her face in them and hugged them and cried. It was a special torment, as she remembered those last few days when he thanked her for ironing them.

Her friends worried about her. Dr. Britton prescribed sleeping pills but gave her only a few at a time, fearing what she would do with a full bottle.[36] There were days of darkness, when she found it hard to get out of bed. And she worried about her children. Reena was able to cry, and sometimes find a night's peace. She mothered her brothers obsessively, though she was the middle child, but that seemed to comfort her. Van was so young his resiliency came from a lack of memory. The hardest part with him was his constant demand to be told, again, whether his daddy was coming back. That was torture for her, but a healthy expression for her little boy.

Darrell was another story. He seemed to be retreating further into himself, sometimes refusing to eat, or speak. Medgar had been his hero, and he seemed completely lost without him. Photos of Darrell in newspaper and magazine articles show a distant, brooding boy. He seemed unable to confront the depth and power of his emotions over the loss of his father, and nothing seemed to penetrate his silence.[37] At times he sat in the carport for hours and stared at the place where his father had fallen. Myrlie asked him what was wrong, and he answered, "Nothing." Every single night, he slept with his toy rifle, and he rarely slept through the night without nightmares.

When Myrlie was packing to go away on another speaking trip, Darrell—the ten-year-old man of the house—chastised her and accused her of going away all the time, just like Daddy did. Sometimes he threw in, "The same thing that happened to Daddy is going to happen to you." She tried telling him she was traveling to places where people felt and behaved differently than they did in Mississippi, and she was going away to help them, and to remind people about their daddy. Nothing seemed to comfort her sad little boy.[38]

Myrlie felt broken, angry, and lost without Medgar. She thought often of taking her own life, sometimes driving fast and erratically down dark highway roads or pouring whatever pills were around the house into her hand and cradling them in her palm, only to be jerked out of her trance by the thought of her children losing their one remaining parent.[39]

The stress was such that in mid-July, Myrlie miscarried.[40] Medgar had worried aloud about bringing a fourth child into the cruel world that Mississippi offered his family, and despite the pain, and the fresh state of grieving forced upon her, she felt a kind of relief. One less person to need her.

Between the travel and the loneliness, Myrlie had come to a frightening place where she wasn't sure she could keep her promise to Medgar to care for their children. She placed a tearful call to Charles's wife, Nan, begging her to take the children, for their sakes. Nan understood her. They were close in age, and Nan was a realist, but also sensitive to her pain. She told Myrlie she would take care of her children, "but only if she had to." In the meantime, Nan told her sister-in-law that she needed to take real care of herself and heal. "Your children need you, not someone else, to rear them," she said.[41]

Caring for herself seemed especially difficult with Medgar's ghost everywhere. She felt him holding her when she buried her face in the sheets of their bed. She took out the letters and postcards he'd written her over the years and read and reread them.[42] She couldn't stop hearing that rifle shot, or seeing him dying, drowning in blood reaching for the door, for her. She lived in a nightmare and couldn't wake up from it. She had hoped the speaking assignments would ease the pain, but they forced her to relive it onstage.[43]

Still, she kept up a furious pace, including an engagement in Boston that caused her to miss the March on Washington, which left her with pangs of guilt and regret. The event was for the Negro Elks of Boston, and it included a $4,000 scholarship for each of her children. As a mother, she simply could not responsibly renege.

Organizers of the March had been fueled by the national anger over Evers's slaying. "Originally it was conceived of as a march for jobs, but as '63 progressed, with the Birmingham demonstrations, the assassination of Medgar Evers and the introduction of the Civil Rights Act by President Kennedy, it became clear that it had to be a march for jobs and freedom,"[44] said Rachelle Horowitz, an aide to March organizer Bayard Rustin.

President Kennedy had been a fitful friend of the movement. Despite big promises during his campaign, the early years of his administration had been marked by diffidence. He spoke sympathetically with civil rights leaders and used his executive authority to push through desegregation when confronted by violent Southern resistance. But he also had reelection in mind, and he believed an historic income tax rate cut was key to boosting the economy ahead of the 1964 campaign. Meanwhile, the turbulence in the streets of Mississippi and Alabama was not just an international embarrassment, it was a bad mark on his administration. Yet he had to be as careful in his pleas to Southern senators as he was with Southern Democratic governors, as the former held his legislative future in their hands.

The March on Washington, particularly after Medgar's assassination, was meant not just to call for civic and economic justice for Black Americans, but also to push the Kennedy administration and Congress on the Civil Rights Act, which had become mired in the House as President Kennedy quietly pushed for his tax cut bill to be passed first.[45] Medgar's final telegram to President Kennedy had been sent eleven days before his assassination, calling on the administration to intervene in Mississippi, where young Black marchers were being abused and incarcerated as they marched for justice and equality. He believed in local action—in the rising up of Black Mississippians to claim equality and dignity for themselves. But he also believed in the federal government's power and responsibility to enforce the rule of law, and the edicts of the federal courts.

"Medgar Evers' death was a subtext of the march," then Tougaloo student activist Joyce Ladner said. "Everyone was aware that one of the truly great heroes in the Deep South had just been murdered. And therefore, Mr. President, your request that we go slow doesn't make sense."[46]

Myrlie returned to the hotel from her speaking engagement as the March was well underway. Darrell and Reena were watching it unfold on television. Darrell pointed and exclaimed "Momma, you're supposed to be in Washington. They're calling your name right now!" Her heart sank.[47] NAACP activist Daisy Bates, an architect of the Arkansas school integration movement and advisor to the Little Rock Nine, delivered a short speech in Myrlie's place, and Josephine Baker, in full French military uniform, took the stage to greet the massive crowd. They were the only women the 250,000 assembled on the National Mall heard from that day. Coretta Scott King would later recall her irritation that none of the battle-worn female veterans of the movement, from Fannie Lou Hamer to Ella Baker to Diane Nash, Gloria Richardson, and Dorothy Height (the lone female member of the "Big Six" organizers and the godmother of the civil rights movement) was allowed to give a major speech at the March. "That's how chauvinistic leadership was at the time," she wrote.[48] In fact, Myrlie's name had only been suggested after Anna Arnold Hedgeman of the National Council of Churches objected to the all-male lineup, in response to which Roy Wilkins put in Myrlie's name.

The demands of the March matched the NAACP's consistent demands of the Kennedy White House: that the Kennedy civil rights bill include federal enforcement of desegregation of all public facilities; a federal ban on employment discrimination by race; and voting rights protection for Black Americans, particularly in the South. The administration had feared the March; worrying that it could descend into violence and give the world another Jackson or Birmingham. Instead, it was peaceful, soaring, and it elevated Dr. King to international and iconic status as a moral leader. After the March, President Kennedy invited movement leaders to the White House to discuss advancing the civil rights bill. Among them: Dr. King; Roy Wilkins; John Lewis of SNCC; Whitney Young of the National Urban League; Mathew Ahmann of the National Catholic Conference for Interracial Justice; A. Philip Randolph; and labor leader Walter Reuther; along with Floyd McKissick of CORE; and W. Willard Wirtz, Kennedy's secretary of labor.

Ten days later, the Kennedy bill cleared its first hurdle in the House. Images of the Woolworth's sit-in mayhem were distributed to members during the summer hearings, and the outrage over Medgar's murder hung over the proceedings, as the national civil rights groups pushed hard on the White House and the Congress for the bill. Then at just after 10:00 on Sunday morning, September 15, the KKK responded in kind: laying dynamite on the site of the 16th Street Baptist Church in downtown Birmingham, which had been a launch point for civil rights marches, including those led by Dr. King. The explosion killed four young Black girls who were inside the choir dressing room on the church's lower level, and nearly blinding a fifth. The bombing added a fresh shock for a nation that had seen what felt like a year of racial siege. With a horrified nation looking on, and a feeling of near civil war wafting across the American South, House Judiciary Committee chairman Emanuel Cellar, a liberal New York Democrat, author of the 1957 Civil Rights Act and the bill's champion in the House, opted to send an even stronger bill to the Rules Committee, whose chair was a segregationist Virginia Dixiecrat named "Judge" Howard W. Smith. The date of the bill's arrival to the Rules Committee was set as November 19. After that, its next destination would be the House floor.

ON NOVEMBER 22, A FRIDAY, REENA WAS HOME SICK WITH A COLD, and Myrlie was leaving the next day to speak in Chicago and New York. Myrlie telephoned her hairdresser Alleyne "Skeet" French to see if she could fit her in. She left Van next door with the Wellses and went to her appointment. She was lost in an issue of *Look* magazine—the one with John F. Kennedy and his son on the cover—and she and Skeet were commenting on what a beautiful child John Jr. was when the phone rang.

Myrlie guessed, "I'll bet that's Reena," who hated being in the house alone. Skeet picked up the phone, and then she screamed. Myrlie panicked, as Skeet snapped on the radio. President Kennedy had been shot as his motorcade moved through Dallas, Texas—Vice President Lyndon Johnson's home state. Myrlie dissolved into a mass of hysterical tears, reliving every moment of Medgar's murder and being overwhelmed by fear.

Skeet held Myrlie and rocked her back and forth, begging her not to cry herself sick. Finally, Myrlie composed herself enough to call Reena and told her to turn off the television and wait for Mama to come home. She called the Wells house and asked Carolyn to go next door and check on Reena. Then she climbed into her car and began what felt like an endless drive home. She thought of Jackie, and Caroline, and John-John. She prayed they would not soon be living her nightmare. Darrell was still at school, and she hoped the nuns were comforting him.

When she arrived home, Reena was in bed, convulsing in tears, and all Myrlie could do was take her daughter in her arms, lead her gently into the living room, and turn on the television, in time to hear Walter Cronkite deliver the news that President Kennedy was gone, shot dead with a high-powered rifle with a telescopic sight, just like Medgar had been.[49]

Darrell came home, went into his room, and closed the door. The next day, Myrlie was in Chicago, feeling utterly dejected. When a group of women said Mrs. Kennedy would be fine because she was rich, Myrlie lost her composure and yelled at them that Mrs. Kennedy had just lost her husband and the father of her children. Money was hardly the point. She stormed out of the room and went back to her hotel. It felt like the second longest night of her life.

Myrlie was convinced that the same forces that had taken Medgar had gotten Kennedy. The president had announced on the night of June 11 that he would send a sweeping civil rights bill to Congress, making law what National Guardsmen had made fact on campuses from Arkansas to Mississippi to Alabama since *Brown v. Board* and right up to the day of his speech. On June 12, a Klansman killed Medgar in front of his own home. On September 15, Klansmen blew up a church in Birmingham, killing four little girls, just two weeks after the August 28 March on Washington. Now Kennedy was dead, too. Nowhere in the American South was safe for Black people or for anyone who sympathized at all with them.

During Medgar's last national trip, he had written his family a sweet letter, hoping for a wonderful Christmas with Myrlie and their children. Instead, the year would end as it had begun: with violence, agony, turbulence, and death.

THE TRIAL OF BYRON DE LA BECKWITH BEGAN ON JANUARY 28, 1964, and it went about as Myrlie expected. The Greenwood White Citizens' Council set up a legal fund, with the town's three bank presidents as "acting financial advisors," so Beckwith could afford an expensive three-man defense team consisting of Greenwood's city attorney, Hardy Lott; Stanley Sanders, a former DA; and Hugh Cunningham, a partner in Governor Barnett's law firm and one of the state's top defense lawyers. Of the pool of nearly two hundred male potential jurors (women couldn't serve on Mississippi juries until 1968) only a handful were Black, and they were systematically excluded by the defense. After four days of selection, the jury consisted, as was the Mississippi way, of twelve white men.

William Waller, the thirty-seven-year-old district attorney, was asking for the death penalty, but Myrlie saw him as just another face of white Southern injustice. He was a segregationist and had no trouble telling her so. That didn't mean he wasn't also ambitious, and he made it clear he intended to win the case, which was being closely watched in Washington, D.C.

Myrlie was being called as a witness, and when she asked how she would be addressed in court, Waller dismissively told her not to expect to be called "Mrs." or "Ms." She was in Mississippi, after all. "When in Rome, do as the Romans do," he told her. "You were born and raised here. You know what the customs are."[50] Whites referred to Black adults as Aunt or Preacher, boy, girl, or Nigger—always by their first names. Myrlie let Waller know she would brook no such disrespect, that her husband had lived and died for this. He asked if she'd rather be called "Mrs. Evers or win a conviction." She wanted both and let him know she assumed he would do just enough during the trial to satisfy the press and no more.[51]

The trial included more than a dozen prosecution witnesses, from people at the Evers home that night to police officers, detectives, forensic pathologists, medical and fingerprint experts. Waller presented testimony from the man who traded the gun to Beckwith, his fingerprint on the scope, and evidence of his obsession with maintaining segregation. Several Guynes Street neighbors testified about that night, as did the police officers who responded and the detectives who investigated the case and found the rifle. The cabdrivers identified Beckwith as the man who came looking for the Everses' address.

Myrlie was the second prosecution witness, and neither side addressed her by name at all. She described that agonizing night and the telephone threats they had received for months. The defense team quizzed her about her and Medgar's attempts to integrate Jackson public schools, Medgar's application to Ole Miss, and about why Darrell's middle name was Kenyatta. The FBI's New Orleans office, via an agent observing the trial in Jackson, sent teletypes summarizing each day's testimony to the New York office. This included defense attorney Hardy Lott's attempts to impeach Jackson police officer Ralph Hargrove, who photographed Medgar's body at the University Hospital, for being a graduate of a correspondence school and having no more than a high school education, and attacking the police identification of the latent fingerprint on the scope as Beckwith's.[52]

Beckwith's defense consisted almost solely of testimony from two Greenwood police officers who claimed they saw him in his hometown, eighty miles from Jackson, around the time Medgar was killed, just after midnight. Beckwith was the last to testify, and he denied killing Evers, though he admitted to owning lots of guns, including an Enfield .30-36 rifle, which he claimed was stolen before June 12. He even admitted to trading for a telescopic sight like the one that killed Evers, though Cunningham dismissed this, saying the fingerprint proved "the defendant may have had the telescope—not the gun—in his hand."[53] Beckwith also claimed he got the bruise over his eye, which matched what the shotgun sight recoil would cause, at a shooting range.

Beckwith seemed delighted when some of his racist tracts about "opposing the evils of segregation" were read back to him—including a January 1963 letter to the National Rifle Association which said, "we in Mississippi are going to have to do a lot of shooting to protect ourselves against 'bad Negroes.'" In a January 1964 letter to *Field and Stream,* Beckwith proposed an article on "varmint hunting at night in summertime in the South," and another letter said he was writing a book titled *My Ass, Your Goat and the Republic, dealing with states' rights and integration.*[54]

Beckwith's demeanor as each piece of evidence was presented was jaunty and relaxed; he seemed full of confidence that he would soon be free. *Time* wrote that Beckwith "performed more like a circus clown than a defendant in a first-degree murder case. Constantly shooting his French cuffs, he propped his feet up on a nearby chair, swigged soda pop, glowered at Negro newsmen, hallooed to white spectators, was once restrained by a bailiff from sauntering over to the jury box to chat with his peers, and with the exaggerated Southern courtliness upon which he so much prides himself, even offered cigars to prosecutor William L. Waller."[55]

In summation, Hardy Lott told the jury that "not a single witness" had put [Beckwith] at the scene. Waller portrayed Beckwith as a fanatic who "did not come to Jackson just to kill Medgar Evers," but to "kill evil" as he saw it "and to get the number one man." He told jurors he had never seen more evidence in a felony case, and likened the defendant to the killers of Emmett Till, who sold their story to *Look* for $4,000, without using Till's name, saying Beckwith had "gotten a real big kick out of being a martyr," adding, "What worries me is that two or three months from now, I will pick up a *Saturday Evening Post* and read 'My True Story.' He's already written it."[56]

On February 6, the day the jury was to begin its deliberations, Governor Barnett appeared at the courthouse pledging full cooperation with the federal government. But he also came to the courtroom and warmly greeted Beckwith and shook his hand. Myrlie later wrote, "If there had ever been a question of where the governor of Mississippi stood, it did not survive that scene."[57] She believed that Barnett belonged in the docks with Beckwith, and that Mayor Thompson and William Simmons, the head of the White Citizens' Council, did, too. She was convinced they had conspired to murder her husband.[58]

The next morning, Beckwith got another high-profile visitor when Gen. Edwin A. Walker strode into the courtroom to take his turn shaking Beckwith's hand. Walker was a West Point graduate and Korean War veteran who in 1957 had been forced, as the commander of the Arkansas Military District in Little Rock, to help break Gov. Orval Faubus's eighteen-day-long refusal to accede to the desegregation of Little Rock Central High School by nine Black children. Soon afterward, President Dwight Eisenhower relieved Walker of his command when it was discovered that, as a John Birch Society member, he was indoctrinating his troops using the group's racist literature. In 1962, Attorney General Kennedy issued a warrant for his arrest on seditious conspiracy charges after he helped organize the violent protests against James Meredith's admission to Ole Miss, leading him to declare himself a political prisoner of the Kennedy administration, whose members he accused, along with other northern Democrats, of being Communist sympathizers for supporting integration.[59]

The trial's biggest surprise however, came from the jury. Rather than the quick acquittal that was expected, this jury, after twenty-two hours of deliberations over three days, announced that they were hopelessly deadlocked, prompting Circuit Judge Leon Hendricks to declare a mistrial, which, in Mississippi, was the equivalent of an earthquake.

Prosecutors tried again in April, and Beckwith seemed to take it more seriously, as did his racist supporters. The Ku Klux Klan burned crosses in Jackson on the first day of the trial, perhaps to send a message to Beckwith's second jury. Hugh Cunningham took the lead this time.[60] The final jury panel was again all white and all male, and it included seven college graduates and two Northern transplants.

The second trial began on April 6, 1964, and a new development included testimony from Fred Beard, the manager of Jackson's WLBT, who described the threats that poured in after the TV station aired Medgar's speech on May 20, 1963. Beard recounted people vowing to "do bodily harm to Evers."

The then assistant district attorney, John Fox III, solicited testimony from Herbert Speight—one of the two cabdrivers—that Beckwith (or, according to Speight, "if it was not Beckwith . . . his twin brother") had asked him and a fellow cabdriver at the Trailways terminal for Evers's address—and that he had been "beaten up as a result of the testimony he previously gave." Even so, Speight gave the same testimony in the second trial. A coworker of Beckwith also testified that Beckwith "brushed it off" when he asked about the scar left by the scope over his eye.

Testimony this time also alluded to a conspiracy to kill Medgar Evers, or to cover it up. Mrs. A. W. Branch and her son, Charles Branch, of Sidon, Mississippi, said that on the night of Sunday, June 9, three days before Evers was killed, they saw an individual getting in or out of Beckwith's white Valant while it was parked on a lot adjacent to the

Greyhound bus station in Greenwood; and that Charles Branch told Beckwith, who was inside the station, that he'd seen this, and that Beckwith went outside and talked to this unknown individual. A note in an FBI file during the trail said this was not developed to any significant degree.[61]

In the prosecution's closing arguments, Assistant DA Fox called the Evers killing "the worst crime, the most cold-blooded killing I've ever seen," adding, "It is not a crime of passion or revenge. It is one man's short-lived hold on destiny in which he can become a big, big martyr."[62] He then asked the jury, "Does [Beckwith] come to you in any manner of innocence? Rather, he sat upon that throne of glory and reveled in it, and his attitude was almost beyond comprehension to me."[63]

On April 17, 1964, Beckwith's second trial also ended with a hung jury. This time a grinning Beckwith was released on $10,000 bond, and he returned home to Greenwood and to his job selling fertilizer. He would bask in the glow of his new status as a conquering hero of the white, segregationist South. "Beckwith's trip from Jackson to Greenwood was covered later on television," Myrlie wrote. "Smuggled out of town hiding on the floor of an unmarked car, the drive turned into a triumphant 'welcome home' as he neared" his hometown. "Crowds stood along the highway, some with large welcome signs, cheering and calling to him as the car went past. Beckwith told reporters it brought tears to his eyes."[64]

He remained under indictment, and under Mississippi law he could remain so until his case reached some form of conclusion. Waller was dubious about trying him a third time. "I think the defense case was much better this time," Waller told reporters. "I don't see any reason to assume we can put on a better case; I don't know what my attitude will be in the future."[65] Justice would not only *not* be done for Medgar, it would be delayed into nonexistence.

In Meridian, Sgt. Wallace Miller, a Mississippi National Guard veteran who served the police department by day and was a senior official of the White Knights of the Ku Klux Klan at night, celebrated the jury's failure to convict Beckwith and his release by planning a cross burning in front of a Black church in Lauderdale County. Miller had been the Klan's first recruit in the county and was considered its best promoter. He tipped off Meridian newspapers to the cross burning and posted photos of himself with the charred cross after the flames died away. The Klan wanted their victory over desegregation to be widely known.[66]

One month later, though, the lawsuit filed by Medgar, Myrlie, and the other Black parents desegregating Jackson schools came to fruition. The city's schools were ordered to desegregate starting at kindergarten, to allow Black children to catch up academically. By the time desegregation reached Reena and Darrell, they would have been ready for college. For Myrlie, the victory was bittersweet because desegregating Mississippi schools was something Medgar had wanted so badly.

"Segregation was finally broken in Mississippi public schools," she wrote. And the wins kept coming. "Medgar was dead, and suddenly there were victories on every side. . . . The Jackson police department hired Negro policemen," she wrote. "Some schools were desegregated. The airport was integrated."[67] Freedom Summer launched in June 1964, led by Bob Moses, Julian Bond, and fellow SNCC organizers, and it led to federal registrars being sent to register Black voters in several Mississippi counties. The national media swarmed back into Mississippi, as it became the center of civil rights attention again.

The assassinations of Medgar Evers and President John F. Kennedy also galvanized Lyndon Johnson.

Johnson was in the Oval Office with Presidents Eisenhower and Kennedy as the three men conferred on solving the seemingly unsolvable riddle of how to accommodate the legitimate demands of Black citizens without setting the South, and the country, on fire. Kennedy had hoped for a calm in the storm of Southern protest and "massive resistance" in order to introduce the civil rights bill that the NAACP, King, and the other major civil rights organizations were demanding;

instead he'd gotten Bull Connor unleashing dogs, batons, and water hoses on Black marchers in Birmingham in May 1963 and Gov. George Wallace blocking the doors of the University of Alabama on June 11. The subsequent, relatively peaceful desegregation of the university with the help of the federalized Alabama National Guard—unlike the deadly chaos at Ole Miss—seemed to provide that window. But the Klan had moved to slam it closed forever. Medgar's assassination was meant to send a message to Kennedy and other national leaders that the South would not come to heel, that it was willing to shed blood to prevent desegregation from proceeding at Washington's demand.

Johnson, a man of the South, understood that Washington needed to respond. A country ruled by violence and repression couldn't remain a country for long, that was a lesson the nation ought to have learned during the Civil War. Kennedy had mounted a lobbying campaign among major business and among governors and mayors across the South, urging them to commit to voluntary desegregation and come out publicly in support of the bill, and gotten assassinated for it. He had simultaneously hesitated to push the bill in Congress, lest it jeopardize the tax cut bill that his fellow Democrats in the House and Senate—the ones from the South—had the power to kill. Johnson also planned to force Kennedy's bill through the House and Senate. He would leave the lobbying to the civil rights groups.

In a meeting at the White House on November 29, 1963—the day after Thanksgiving—Johnson told Roy Wilkins what he intended to do. "He said he could not enact it himself," Wilkins later recalled. "He was the President of the United States. He would give it his blessing. He would aid it in any way in which he could lawfully under the Constitution, but that he could not lobby for the bill. And nobody expected him to lobby for the bill, and he didn't think we expected him to lobby for the bill. . . . He was asking us if we wanted it, if we would do the things required to be done to get it enacted."[68] Roy Wilkins and Clarence Mitchell got to work on liberal Northern and Republican members of Congress. Besides Mitchell's uniquely effective persuasive skills, the men had the moral authority of the NAACP, which was further enhanced by the shock and outrage over the assassination of Medgar Evers, a World War II veteran who had been buried with the nation's highest honors.

On July 2, which would have been Medgar's thirty-ninth birthday, President Lyndon Johnson signed the Civil Rights Act into law.

THE CIVIL RIGHTS ACT OF 1964 WAS A MONUMENTAL AND historic achievement. After it passed, the back of segregation began to break, even in Mississippi. "Negroes were admitted to theaters, restaurants, motels, hotels and parks," Myrlie wrote. "Medgar had fought for all these things, had given eight and a half years of his life to lead the fight. There are those who said that his death and the outrage that attended it throughout the country had been the final straw that broke the back of the opposition."

THAT SUMMER—WHICH HAD BEEN DESIGNATED AS "FREEDOM Summer" by COFO—brought more than one thousand volunteers from around the country to Mississippi to join with local organizers to register voters. The legislative victory in Washington had been bittersweet, in that the Civil Rights Act lacked a strong voting rights enforcement section; a compromise from the original bill that had been needed to get it through. But the summer of 1964 would also bring fresh tragedy. On June 21, CORE workers Andrew Goodman and Michael Schwerner, two young Jewish activists from New York City, and James Chaney, a twenty-one-year-old local Black civil rights worker, disappeared into the Delta night.

Schwerner, twenty-four, had, like Medgar before him, joined the top of the Mississippi Klan's death list. As a white leader of CORE, he was especially derided by the Klan simply as "Goatee." Chaney had been a youth activist in his hometown of Meridien. At fifteen, he'd been suspended from his segregated Catholic school with a handful of friends for affixing handwritten NAACP badges on their shirts. He later joined CORE, and became a liaison between local activists and Schwerner. Goodman, twenty, hailed from an affluent, liberal family in Manhattan and had grown passionate about the civil rights struggle as a high school student. He'd attended a three-day training program in Ohio for the Freedom Summer project. He was murdered on his first day in Mississippi.

Myrlie was in Washington, addressing the NAACP convention when she learned of the disappearances. "We should have known this would happen again,"[69] she said in her speech. The Johnson administration sent former CIA director Allen W. Dulles to assist in the search,[70] but Myrlie knew in her heart what the outcome would be. The NAACP, led by Aaron Henry and Charles Evers, called on President Johnson to extend federal protection to Black voters in Mississippi, and they led a protest outside the Justice Department over the missing activists,[71] whose youthful faces were by then splashed across the pages of national and international newspapers.

The general public was more alarmed by the men's disappearance because two of them were white. The administration's urgency soon included the attention of Robert Kennedy and his Justice Department aides Burke Marshall and Nicholas Katzenbach,[72] but none of this could change the facts of life in Mississippi. The bodies of Goodman, Schwerner, and Chaney were found forty-four days later, on August 4. They had been lynched and discarded in an earthen dam.[73]

Myrlie was exhausted. Her world oscillated constantly between violent reminders of hate in Mississippi and of the progress Medgar would never enjoy. Their home was a torment of memory. The carport still bore a faint stain of Medgar's blood as he dragged himself from the driver's side of his car to the entry door. She was not comforted by the plum and fig trees Medgar planted, nor by the hackberry tree or the oak tree she and the children planted in the front yard to remember him. She was being too protective and too dependent, especially on young Reena, who was just nine years old but had become her emotional support. Cars still drove slowly past the house, sparking fresh fears of another shooting or firebombing. The ugly calls still filtered through her attempts to ignore the phone. Sometimes, one of the children picked up the line.[74] It was all just too much.

Myrlie began to consider a plan of escape.

She briefly weighed returning to Vicksburg, to a house Aunt Myrlie had renovated for her and the children, but she dreaded becoming "poor, unfortunate Myrlie" who had to return home to Auntie and Mama. The notion felt infantilizing. New York, where the NAACP headquarters were, felt too big and overwhelming. Eventually she settled on California, which Medgar had visited and loved. California felt somehow magical. The state had become a magnet for Black people seeking a respite from the inchoate violence of the American South. It had racial discrimination, like everywhere in America, and deep social and economic inequalities, but it felt like a land of possibility.

Myrlie had been there a couple of times, including to Los Angeles, where Althea Simmons of that city's NAACP office gave her the grand tour. In 1963, three Black members had been elected to the city council, including future mayor Tom Bradley. But the city, with its teeming and struggling Watts neighborhood and growing gang crisis, didn't seem appealing. If she were going to go west, it needed to be to a place where her children would feel safe, secure, and free. Ultimately, she settled on Claremont, in eastern California, "in the lower slopes of the San Gabriel Mountains . . . with tree-lined streets, plentiful parks, and well-maintained homes, all conveying a sense of safety and propriety."[75] The schools were excellent, which was important to her.

Claremont was also about as far from Mississippi as she could get.[76] Myrlie took the money she had saved from her speeches, and the little bit left over from Medgar's salary, and put a down payment on a modest house. She didn't even notice, until it was almost closing time, that the neighborhood she had chosen was almost entirely white. As word got around, some NAACP colleagues criticized her. Why not live in predominantly Black Pomona? Did she think she was too good? Did she want to be *white*? She was so stung by this she came close to forfeiting her deposit.

In the end, she stood beneath her and Medgar's plum tree in the backyard of their Jackson home, and she asked for his approval. His was the only one that mattered to her. She had promised to raise their children and to keep them safe. She knew that in Claremont, she could accomplish that.[77]

Reena and Darrell most decidedly did not want to leave their home and their block on Guynes Street, their school, and their friends. "There were lots of boo-hoos," Reena recalled. Who would she ride bicycles with? Play jacks with? Have watermelon-seed fights with? "This is our house," she protested,[78] but her mother insisted it wasn't safe to stay.

The Evers children were not the only ones devastated by the news that they were leaving. "This block was a family," Dennis Sweet III said.

Jean Wells and Johnnie Pearl Young were losing their dear friend. Carolyn Wells recalled that after the shooting, Myrlie was a constant fixture at their home, when she wasn't traveling. Houston and Jean Wells would sit with her on the front steps trying to console her. "Then she decided to move to California."[79]

"I remember [thinking] . . . why are they leaving us?" Sweet Owens said. "It just looked like they just up and left, and they were gone."

Charles had been trying to fill in, not just at the NAACP, where he declared himself Medgar's successor as field secretary, but also on Guynes Street. "He was trying to [help us] heal," Dennis Sweet III said. "He knew we were hurt. We were terrorized. He would pick us up, the boys, especially, [and take us out]. He'd bring us gifts like Mr. Evers used to do—bring balls to play with and stuff."

Even "Uncle Charlie," as the kids called him, couldn't make up for the loss of their friends, the Evers kids. "It was traumatic for us because Reena and I were close. We were the same age and [in] the same class. We were best buds."

Also, Charles wasn't Medgar. In Chicago, he'd returned to the hustle, working various odd jobs, marrying and divorcing, and eventually drifting into the numbers racket, returning to bootlegging, running nightclubs, and even delving into "running girls" on the side. According to a later interview in *Playboy*, he also found time to teach history and physical education in a majority Black town called Robbins, outside Chicago. Returning to Mississippi was not something he'd planned. Nor had he relished the notion of taking up Medgar's role at the NAACP. He did it anyway, but with more anger than relish.[80]

On moving day, Myrlie panicked, suddenly racked with doubt. Althea Simmons of the Los Angeles NAACP office had come to help with the move. A moving van was parked outside, and Reena was tearfully grabbing the remainder of her things. Darrell, now eleven years old, was away at a summer camp sponsored by NAACP supporters. Myrlie recalled sitting "like a zombie on a windowsill, watching my life of twelve and a half years disappear."[81]

"I can't leave, Medgar," she moaned. He had vowed never to leave Mississippi and always said he wanted to raise his children here—yet now she was ripping them away from their home. *His* home.

"No," Myrlie protested. "I'm not leaving." But Althea urged her on, and before long, they had loaded Reena and Van into Medgar's powder-blue Oldsmobile, and they were wheeling down Guynes Street and on to California.[82]

CHAPTER 10

Justice

I have learned over the years that when one's mind is made up, this diminishes fear; knowing what must be done does away with fear.

—Rosa Parks

Reena and Darrell were the first Black children to attend Claremont Public Schools, and they did so without Myrlie having to file an injunction or even having the overt intent. Most of their white neighbors had been welcoming, as had all but a handful of people at the local, very white, Baptist church. On their first Sunday there, one woman recoiled when Myrlie tried to shake her hand. She spat out that she didn't want to touch Myrlie, as if her brown skin would wear off onto her hands. "I stepped toward her, giving it a second try," Myrlie later wrote. "Oh, the devil in me! She nearly fell into the shrubbery, backing up to avoid me. I laughed at the sight of her."[1]

She and the children traveled frequently to Los Angeles, to visit friends and to participate in Black and Brown California culture. She tried to have fun with the children: dancing in the living room to Motown records and leaving them little love notes when she was out of town. She said good night to them, one by one, with a kiss on the forehead. She wanted them always to know they were loved and cherished.[2] She also accepted their little rebellions as part of the lingering trauma over losing their father so violently.

There were incidents. When a group of white boys drove past Darrell, shouting "Nigger!" he, every bit an Evers, dared them to say it to his face as they drove on. He played football, as his father's son, and sometimes the Black Pomona players ridiculed him as a "Tom" for playing for a white team. After the Watts riots in August 1965, Myrlie and Reena were riding their bikes and heard a group of young boys, screaming, "Nigger, nigger, nigger, go back to Africa!" Myrlie was furious, and with Reena begging her to just go home, she stormed over and demanded that a sheepish neighbor, who had heard what was said, let her know who lived in the house where the boys were. The man insisted that the family was good and decent and wouldn't approve of what their boys had done. Myrlie reported the incident to the NAACP anyway, and she wanted to call the police. The next Sunday, the boys' father stood up in church and publicly apologized to her and Reena. It was a small gesture, but a big step for Claremont.[3]

Myrlie suffered bouts of depression, and to chase away the memories, she sometimes still needed sleeping pills to drift off at night. Still, she was determined to make California work. She put Van in daycare and started taking classes at Pomona College, fulfilling her promise to Medgar, the women who raised her, and herself, to complete her degree. She briefly considered a music major but ultimately settled on sociology. Several students and professors stared at her because they recognized her from her picture in the papers. As a student just over thirty years old and a mother of three, she felt out of place and overwhelmed some days on a campus full of twentysomethings. She settled into a routine of dropping the kids at school and daycare, going to class, back home, study, prepare dinner, spend time with the children, and then study again.

The deep and sometimes violent American resistance to change was never-ending. On February 21, 1965, Malcolm X was murdered in Harlem. A pair of Black Muslims connected to the Hon. Elijah Muhammad, from whom Malcolm had become estranged, were arrested, tried, and convicted (they were later exonerated). "I felt these claws of pain that just rip you apart,"[4] Myrlie later recalled about hearing the news of Malcolm's murder. She was heartbroken for Betty Shabazz and watched as she composed herself for the cameras and answered reporters' questions just as she had done. Myrlie felt almost as if she were reliving her own horror in knowing that another young wife and mother had heard the rat-tat of gunfire and seen her husband bleed and die in front of her and their children. When the gunmen charged toward the stage, Betty pushed her children to the floor and shielded them with her body. Black America now had a second nationally known freedom widow.

Myrlie was haunted by Medgar's killer. She and the children returned to Mississippi at least three times a year, to Vicksburg during the holidays, and to Jackson, for the children to reconnect with the "Guynes Street gang." Her other motive was to keep tabs on Beckwith.

She subscribed to Mississippi newspapers and plumbed her information network. In phone calls to Mississippi, she asked, "have you heard anything about Beckwith? Has he talked?"[5] Beckwith was an ardent fame seeker and grew even more fanatical each year. Myrlie knew his inability to keep his mouth shut would eventually undo him. He ran unsuccessfully in the Democratic primary for lieutenant governor in 1967, a year after being called before the House Un-American Activities Committee alongside Klan leader Sam Bowers to testify about Klan activity. He refused to answer any substantive questions.

On April 4, 1968, the earth seemed to shift irrevocably. Martin Luther King Jr. was in Memphis to organize a strike among Black sanitation workers who were being abused financially and racially at work; so much so that many of them were living in poverty and subjected to daily degradation. He was shot with a high-powered rifle as he stood on the balcony of his room at the Lorraine Motel. Coretta Scott King was left with two boys and two girls, aged five to twelve. America was continuing to indulge its habit of murdering the men who strove to save the country from, as King warned, going to Hell.

King's assassination touched off a nationwide wave of anger, grief, and rebellion in Black communities in two hundred cities from New York to California. According to the Smithsonian Institute, "around 3,500 people were injured, 43 were killed and 27,000 arrested. Local and state governments, and President Lyndon Johnson, would deploy a collective total of 58,000 National Guardsmen and Army troops to assist law enforcement officers in quelling the violence."[6]

Dr. King's Poor People's Campaign and the March on Washington had been rooted in the battle for economic as well as racial justice. Malcolm had preached economic, as well as social, liberation for the "so-called Negro." Medgar had fought to lift the Black masses out of poverty and rejection. Ed King recalled Medgar saying that "we can't just focus on voting. We can't just focus on school desegregation or employment. They're all important . . . [and] we've got to focus on what the media is doing locally and nationally." Now the whole world felt like it was in flames.

On June 5, Robert Kennedy, after winning the California primary for president, was shot dead by a Palestinian militant. The King and Kennedy assassinations left fifteen fatherless children, and Ethel Kennedy was pregnant with the couple's eleventh child when her husband was murdered.

Charles Evers said he became close to Bobby, whom he called "his best friend in the world" after Medgar.[7] Earlier that day, Charles had ridden with Kennedy through Black neighborhoods, and that evening he watched the returns with Kennedy and his staff, Ethel Kennedy, and NFL player Rosey Grier, before Bobby was cut down in the kitchen after his victory speech at the Ambassador Hotel.[8]

Charles later wrote that Bobby's death shook him harder in a way, because he hadn't had to see his brother fall with his own eyes.[9] Kennedy had had a steep learning curve on matters of race, but at the time he was murdered, Charles saw him as "the most trusted white man in Black America"[10] and someone who related to the community's anguish over Dr. King's assassination.

Malcolm spoke to young Black America's raging heart in ways that were matched only by his old friend, Muhammad Ali, the young militants of SNCC and CORE, and the Black Panther Party. Medgar had flirted with similar ideas of Black revolution and separatism in his early, most militant days. Yet King laid down the connective thread that wove the national civil rights movement together, sometimes as volubly as a small ship on an ocean, but he had done it. Malcolm and Martin had caused J. Edgar Hoover to fear the emergence of a Black messiah. Medgar had admired them both as his brothers in the at-home war for the soul of America. Now they were all gone.

In a July 1968 interview with *Esquire*, James Baldwin summarized America's situation bluntly. "For me, it's been Medgar. Then Malcolm. Then Martin," he said. "And it's the same story. When Medgar was shot they arrested some lunatic in Mississippi, but I was in Mississippi, with Medgar, and you don't need a lunatic in Mississippi to shoot a cat like Medgar Evers, you know, and the cat whoever he was, Byron de la Beckwith, slipped out of the back door of a nursing home and no one's ever heard from him since. I won't even discuss what happened to Malcolm, or all the ramifications of that. And now Martin's dead. And every time, you know, including the time the President was murdered, everyone insisted it was the work of one lone madman; no one can face the fact that this madness has been created deliberately."[11]

Myrlie knew of Betty and Coretta as fellow civil rights wives, but she did not meet them before their husbands were murdered. She admired both women from a distance, particularly their dedication to their children, but there was no network of leaders' wives. After the assassinations, the three women were thrown together in the minds of the media, the public, and the civil rights establishment—branded as a tripart sisterhood as they moved from speech to fundraiser to movement event. "It is a private club," Myrlie wrote in a foreword to a biography of Betty Shabazz, "but open to new members—if one is willing to pay the price. It is a club, as my daughter Reena puts it, 'that no one wishes to join.'"[12]

The three widows chose divergent paths in writing their martyred husbands' names into American legacy. From the moment Coretta Scott King got the call she had feared for more than a decade, she was poised, methodical, and relentless. "The news media and Civil Rights establishment projected Mrs. King as the maximum Civil Rights widow after Martin's assassination," wrote Russell J. Rickford, author of the Betty Shabazz biography. "She rose to the station instantly and elegantly, in the nostalgic style of Jackie Kennedy."[13] Coretta became the voice of her husband's grandest ideals—integration and equality—and not of the protests, marches, and boycotts. She threw herself into building the King Center in Atlanta and to securing a federal holiday for Martin to "Institutionaliz[e] the Dream."[14]

This, according to Rickford, led to a quiet, early rivalry with Betty. "The two widows," he wrote, "operated in the late 1960s and 1970s like emissaries of distant lands. Blacks and white liberals who accepted nonviolent, integrationist struggle hailed Mrs. King, while Afro-Americans who believed in militant resistance to white supremacy elevated Betty."[15] Myrlie was somewhere in between. "We were friends," she said of the women's relationship in those early years, "but I wouldn't say we were close friends. But through these tragedies that we all suffered we became *very* close friends."

Myrlie watched as events seemed to wash Medgar's memory out of the national consciousness. Freedom Summer in 1964 was followed by the Mississippi Freedom Democratic Party disruption of the 1964 Democratic Convention. The party had been formed by activists who emerged from the COFO coalition Medgar had helped seed in Mississippi, including Fannie Lou Hamer, Rev. Ed King, and Aaron Henry (the two men were eventually seated as at-large delegates by reluctant party leaders), to challenge the whites-only Democratic Party's right to send a segregated slate to a national party in the post–Civil Rights Act era. Then came Malcolm's murder, the passage of the landmark Voting Rights Act of 1965 and the violence in Selma that preceded it, plus the cataclysms over the assassinations of President Kennedy, Dr. King, and Bobby Kennedy. Each new assassination brought back the shock and grief of June 12, 1963, while making justice seem more distant and unattainable. Myrlie became even more determined to see justice done, particularly after James Earl Ray was sentenced to a ninety-nine-year term in prison in March 1969 for the murder of Dr. King.

EARLY IN THEIR MARRIAGE, MEDGAR HAD ASKED, "ISN'T THERE anything you believe in strongly enough to fight for it?" For Myrlie, that was their children, who "meant everything to the two of us," but she also wanted to fight to see that the person who killed Medgar was punished. Friends begged her to let it go, but she had a mission, and its name was Byron De La Beckwith.

Myrlie graduated from Pomona in 1968 with her bachelor's degree and was offered an administrative position as a planning director at the Claremont Colleges. She had also cowritten *For Us, the Living,* about her and Medgar, and it was selling. *Ladies' Home Journal* offered her a position as contributing editor, allowing her to write articles and make suggestions. She even convinced them to use Black models for the first time. Myrlie was spreading her wings and feeling truly independent. She applied for her first credit card, despite Mama's invocations against debt, yet as Mrs. Medgar Evers, she couldn't obtain one. A married woman was required to have her husband's signature at that time. As Myrlie Evers, though, she could open a checking and a savings account, and savings accounts for each of the children.[16]

"Someone asked me, a friend of mine, 'Do you think it was God or the Devil that kept you going?' I said, 'Quite frankly, I don't know, but one of them. Or maybe both of them.' So, with everything that God allowed me to do from that point on: rear my children, give them the best life that I could, go back to college, get my degree, run around the country lecturing . . . for the NAACP, it was important to me and I needed to do it—I always asked my God to show me the way. And I stepped out on faith. It took a long time."

In 1970, Myrlie decided to stop observing and take action: announcing she was running for Congress in California's Twenty-Fourth Congressional District. The seat had been vacated by the death of a Republican, Glenard P. Lipscomb, but the partisan lean of the district didn't deter her. It was something she couldn't have imagined herself doing even a year before. She was feeling her independence—and some fundamentals in the country had changed. The Voting Rights Act had created space for Black political power, from California to Mississippi.

Myrlie felt buoyed by the tide of events that used to overwhelm her. She posed for a UPI photo with her new dog, Honey Bun, and confidently addressed the media. "I wish we'd stop wasting time dividing ourselves into white and black camps," she told reporters that March. "There's so much we can do together."[17] Her campaign printed up red and white buttons with her picture in profile, reading: "MYRLIE EVERS FOR CONGRESS: In a Time of Crisis, A Voice for Peace." Her run made the *New York Times* and the cover of *Jet*.

The campaign was a test for the family as well. The children were at formative points in their lives: Darrell was seventeen, Reena sixteen, and Van just ten. And a campaign meant pulling them into back the public spotlight, where they might not want to be. But they supported their mother's ambitions and were helpful and proud. At least as much as a pair of teenagers and a boy more focused on football than campaigns could be.

Myrlie didn't win the race, but she became one of the first African American women to run for Congress, two years after Shirley Chisholm made history as the first Black woman to be elected to the body, joining the only other woman of color, Patsy Takemoto Mink of Hawaii. Two years later, three more Black women were elected to Congress: Barbara Jordan of Texas, Cardiss Collins of Illinois, and Yvonne Braithwaite Burke of California, and Chisholm ran for president. Alongside her, Myrlie joined the National Women's Political Caucus, the feminist organization formed by Gloria Steinem, Bella Abzug, and Betty Friedan.[18] History was moving, nationally and personally, for Myrlie.

William Waller, the prosegregation prosecutor who had surprised Myrlie with his aggressive prosecutions of Byron De La Beckwith, was the Democratic nominee for governor of Mississippi in 1971, and he was elected. Facing him on the ballot, as an independent, was Charles Evers, who had been elected mayor of Fayette, Mississippi, in 1969 and named that year as the NAACP's Man of the Year. Much was changing in Mississippi and across America. That March, the Congressional Black Caucus was formed, and its thirteen members secured a meeting with President Richard Nixon.

As the 1970s rolled on, Myrlie let her hair go natural. Medgar had teased, "You should wear your hair nappy," when they were at Alcorn, knowing how horrified she was by that. Now she embraced it. She was still the NAACP's most prodigious fundraiser. She resented that among the organization's most valuable "commodities" were pictures of her and her children at Medgar's funeral, but she understood that it kept Medgar's name and legacy alive and helped to keep her children fed and clothed. She even said yes to a date or two, wading through her elder children's disapproval. Reena would make it clear where she stood by strutting into the living room holding a framed photograph of her daddy when a gentleman would come calling.

Myrlie also solidified her sisterhood with Betty Shabazz in the 1970s. They had in common the experience of being present with their children at their husbands' murders. Of Coretta King, Myrlie later said, "At least she was spared seeing it. We literally got our husband's blood on us."[19]

The two women truly connected over both having returned to

school after losing their husbands. Betty eventually earned her doctorate in education. When she was looking for a job that befit her newly earned degree, she came upon Medgar Evers College in Brooklyn, New York. It was created after student protests in 1968 on behalf of the Black and Puerto Rican struggle against poverty and for equal access to education brought classes at Harlem's City College to a standstill, forcing the City University system to capitulate to student demands. They agreed in February 1968 to create a new campus in Brooklyn's Bedford-Stuyvesant neighborhood, one of the country's largest Black and Brown communities. Betty was drawn there because the students there were overwhelmingly Black, working-class, and largely drawn from Caribbean backgrounds, like Malcolm had been. The faculty was comprised mostly of Black women, and she had been looking for a job that befit her newly earned degree. Her admiration for Medgar sealed the deal.

When Betty invited Myrlie to come to the college and speak, they discovered how much they liked each other. Betty liked Myrlie's independence and her irreverence. Myrlie said of herself: "I was not always the quiet, long-suffering little woman behind the great man. I was not the always hopeful, always strong single mother. I was not always nice and forgiving, compliant and ladylike." Betty liked that about Myrlie.[20]

They laughed about the media rushing to Coretta when the three widows were thrown together as "the trio," sometimes with Mamie Till-Mobley or Rosa Parks added to the group. Coretta acknowledged the disparity, too, later reflecting that "when Martin died, it was almost like I was embraced by the whole world, and 240,000 people came to Atlanta for the funeral. Betty didn't have that." Betty was denied the media support and sympathy draped on Coretta. "The world wanted me to be perceived as being alone," Betty later said.[21]

She and Myrlie, though, could chat about single motherhood, about lean times and making neckbones stretch by doing them as a stew with beans and rice. They talked about finding male figures to include in their children's lives, and they cried into their phones about the nightmares they still endured about feeling the warmth of their husband's blood in their hands. Betty encouraged Myrlie to date, rejecting the idea that movement widows were condemned to live like royal spinsters or lonely saints. "Step on out there, kid," Betty told her. "You're just getting older and uglier every day," and they burst into laughter on the phone. Myrlie said, "Absolutely no envy existed between us. She could have seen me as competition. But that was not Betty."[22]

The true sisterhood with Coretta came later, as Myrlie and Betty saw through her perfect hair and makeup and the steely determination to her pain. In many ways, Coretta bore more national responsibility as a national civil rights widow and wore the cruel crown that Jackie Kennedy had worn. As they became not just the trio of "movement widows," but a true sisterhood, Myrlie discovered she could turn to Betty and Coretta for a unique comfort.

"They were my support system, and I like to think I was a part of their support system as well," Myrlie said. "We could call each other and cry. They probably wouldn't like it if I said this, but I'm going to say it. We called each other and cursed. . . . We would talk about various ways of punishment [for our husband's killers]. Who in which community was helping the other. It was like an underground network. . . . It was a sisterhood of widows."

Over time, and with her children getting older and more focused on their own young lives, Myrlie began to accept that she needed a support system that went beyond her good girlfriends. Despite Betty's encouragement, she remained reticent about introducing a new man into her life and the lives of her children. Besides, no man alive was Medgar.

She relented when she met Walter Williams in 1975, whom she described as "a very fine man who, interestingly enough, was a follower of Medgar's." Standing at six feet, four inches, Walter was an NAACP man and a union organizer who had battled discrimination against Black and women dockworkers in California since the 1940s. He introduced himself to Myrlie after watching one of her speeches in Los Angeles, and at first she was characteristically polite but dismissive. Walt, as she called him, was a cofounder of the Victory Committee, "an early effort to promote voter registration among African American citizens. When businesses balked at hiring black employees, he organized pickets and boycotts,"[23] she said.

He was also persistent. The two soon became the best of friends and constant companions. Some in her circle scoffed at the idea of Myrlie being in a relationship with a longshoreman. In their view, his was not a high enough calling to befit Myrlie's stature. But Walt was smart and moral, and he cared about civil rights. She respected him, as she had Medgar. And he was kind to her and her children. That mattered most to her. And her true friends understood and were supportive. Better yet, her children approved of Walter and recognized that he would protect their mother and keep her from having to fight so many battles alone.

Medgar's memory lingered, which at times seemed terribly unfair to Walt. But he knew Medgar was the love of Myrlie's life, and was at peace with that. "I asked him at one point, 'Why are you here?' [And] you know what this man told me? 'Because I admired, respected, and loved your husband. And I wanted to be sure I could do something to help his children.' I said, 'Oh? What about me?' 'Myrlie,' he said, smiling, 'for goodness' sake, let me alone. You were just part of the package.'" Myrlie thought his answer would have amused Medgar, who spent so much time teasing her. She could only laugh, too, because she knew Walt really wanted to make sure that the children had all they needed, and to be there for her. The two married at a ceremony at Pomona College in 1976.

"I knew that if I were gone, [Medgar] probably would not remain single," she said. "But he would be so careful in the woman that he would choose to be with my children. And it was the same way with me." Her marriage to Walter was very blessed, she said, "but Medgar Evers was my life. Even with our three children, I would've given my life for his because I knew he would be the best father ever. I loved the man, I still do. I can't help it."[24]

Life continued its relentless march for the Evers family. There would be annual commemorations of Medgar's life in Jackson and long drives to Vicksburg to look in on Aunt Myrlie and Mama, the loving, aging roommates in their impeccable home. As they increasingly struggled to care for themselves, Myrlie hired a series of home nursing aides, each of whom rarely lasted more than a week.[25] She faced painful decisions, including moving Mama to Shady Grove Nursing Home. After Myrlie woke up in what used to be Aunt Myrlie's room to see her elderly aunt standing in the doorway, brandishing a gun, and demanding to know who she was and what she was doing in her home, she moved Aunt Myrlie there, too.[26]

These women had taken such great care of her, and now Myrlie, even from thousands of miles away, was determined to take care of them.

But there was more than family love that kept calling her back to Mississippi.

Still loving Medgar Evers meant continuously pursuing his killer, and Myrlie had never stopped asking about him. She still ordered the Jackson newspapers and kept in contact with friends, peppering them with question: Had they heard anything new about Beckwith? Had any new information emerged about who he talked to or associated with before killing Medgar?

Beckwith's car had been pulled over on September 27, 1973, and a six-stick dynamite bomb was found inside. He was thought to be headed to the home of Adolph (A. I.) Botnick, the regional director of the Anti-defamation League of B'nai B'rith.[27] The FBI charged him with possession of explosives. He was acquitted in federal court, but in August 1975, he was convicted on state charges and sentenced to five years in prison. Myrlie savored her newfound happiness even more, knowing Beckwith would lose his freedom at least for now, even if not for Medgar's murder. Even better: the state jury that convicted him included five Black women.[28]

In 1977, with his appeals exhausted, Beckwith finally went to prison. But he would come back to haunt her again and again.

Even behind bars, Beckwith couldn't hold his tongue. In a letter to the editor published in the white supremacist magazine *Attack!*, Beckwith referred to Medgar Evers as "Mississippi's mightiest nigger," saying, "We have had no trouble with that nigger since they buried him—none!" He was released after three years and returned to Greenwood, remarried, and moved to Signal Mountain, Tennessee. Myrlie tracked his every move.[29]

In March 1979, Myrlie's reality changed again, as an era that defined her entire life came to an end. Annie McCain Beasley, born in 1881 in rural Mississippi, had lived ninety-eight years, into a new century with its new realities and shifting possibilities for daughters of the enslaved, like her, and for their granddaughters, like the little girl she took in and called Sister. Mama had been known for her moral austerity and a kind of majesty that belied her financial circumstances: the neatness of her garden, the care she took with her home, and her insistence on educational excellence and discipline under her roof. But for Myrlie, it was the love that she remembered most from this fearsome church mother whose fiercest passions were for her son, and her two Myrlies.

Aunt Myrlie followed in 1985. Myrlie had brought her to Los Angeles to live with her after Mama's passing. Aunt Myrlie's husband was long dead by then, and they had no children, besides Myrlie, of course. She had lived to be eighty-one years old. Myrlie savored the knowledge of these women's long lives, which seemed an even greater miracle for Black people in America. "I can recall now," said Myrlie, "the number of wonderful messages sent to the family when she passed away, of people who were successful who had been her students in school and praised her for the success they had had in their lives."

If she had gotten her grit and discipline from Mama, it was "Auntie" who gave Myrlie the gift of music. She recalled her as the organist for her childhood church: Mount Heroden Baptist. "Could she ever play that organ!" Myrlie said. It was Aunt Myrlie, the schoolteacher, choir director, and great lady of the Black Vicksburg community who funded the piano lessons after she left off teaching Myrlie herself. And it was Aunt Myrlie who took her and Mama in and cared for them until it was time for Myrlie to care for both her "mothers."

But Myrlie had also been shaped by M'dear, who had been more of an elder sister than a mother to her and who, like Medgar, had died so young. For all the limited time they had together, she had come to appreciate her deeply, and treasure her childhood memories of their shared time across the street at Big Mama's. "She was a good-looking woman and very stylish," Myrlie recalled. "And I recall her buying cloth at Woolworth's and bringing [it] home, particularly on a Saturday, and she would put the cloth down on the floor and cut out a pattern without a paper guide . . . hand-stitch that dress and wear it that night. I was always amazed at how she could do that because I never learned to sew!" But it was her loving understanding of why Myrlie had to defy Mama and Aunt Myrlie and pursue her love for Medgar that had truly bonded them, just as it was M'dear's loving sacrifice that made Myrlie's improbable life possible.

"As I grew older, her strength to be able to turn me over to my grandmother to rear me, was something marvelous [to me] because she knew that my grandmother could do a much better job in rearing me than she could. I will always be thankful to her for that," Myrlie said. "I loved her dearly, but it wasn't until I was an adult that I understood the loss that she felt when she turned me over to my grandmother." She recalled M'dear once explaining her choice at sixteen years of age this way: "Baby, I did what was best for you, and I dealt with my pain of not having you in my care every day."[30]

And now these three women who had so shaped her were all gone. Returning with Walt and the children to California after each of Mama's and Aunt Myrlie's funerals created a fresh wave of grief. But it also made her determined to do something that would make all those who had loved her, and who were now her heavenly choir, proud.

In 1987, Myrlie decided to try her hand at politics again. She joined the primary for a council seat in Los Angeles. She would be one of thirteen candidates for the seat in the city's majority Black Tenth District, which also included Hispanic and Jewish enclaves and an Asian American neighborhood known as Koreatown. Tom Bradley had been the councilman for the Tenth District before becoming Los Angeles's first Black mayor. But he was supporting another candidate: a longtime political ally. Myrlie had the support of a handful of women legislators including California state senator Diane Watson and an assemblywoman named Maxine Waters (both future U.S. congresswomen), plus the sitting assembly Speaker, Willie Brown.[31] But she was considered an underdog in the nonpartisan race.

Still, she threw herself into the campaign, taking time off from her job as the national community affairs director for Atlantic Richfield Company to walk the district and listen to the concerns of longtime renters, homeowners, and business owners. Walt was a great support and de facto campaign manager: always eager to hand out her blue campaign buttons reading: "We All Agree—Myrlie Evers for the 10th Council District" and to give great advice. Luckily for Myrlie, he was a civil rights man and therefore an organizer.

The issues in the race were mostly about decline. The Tenth had been home to Black American greats like Joe Louis and Nat King Cole, and once boasted thriving Black-owned shops in the downtown section nicknamed Sugar Hill. But the Eisenhower administration's national highway program had done to the area what it had in so many majority Black and Latino enclaves: vivisected it with freeway on-ramps, and leaving blight and dying businesses behind. Plus the onset of the crack epidemic had mired the district in misery, poverty, and crime. And tensions between the Black and Asian communities were simmering, almost to a boil.[32]

But Myrlie faced resistance from some locals who viewed her as an outsider, trading on the surname of her martyred husband to push a political bid in a town she wasn't from and had only recently moved to—despite the fact that she moved from Pomona to Los Angeles in 1975. Some even criticized her use of "Myrlie Evers" rather than Myrlie Williams, even though it was Walt who suggested she hyphenate her surname in tribute to Medgar.[33] The criticisms stung, particularly those about her name. Myrlie had been clear in her own mind, and with Walt, that she would never let go of Medgar. Yet who in their right mind would trade on the agony of June 12, 1963? The attacks, particularly from Black people, brought disappointment and even anger, but it was a single incident that left her feeling something coldly familiar: fear.

After a forum with the twelve other candidates, a young white man walked up to her, unsmiling. She put out her hand, but he refused it and then repeated, over and over: "You have to stop this." When she referred him to her campaign headquarters, he screamed: "You *have* to stop this! You keep doing it to my family! The Beckwiths are my family!"[34]

Hearing "Beckwith" nearly drained the blood out of her. The young man had his hand near his waist, and she thought this was it. It would end for her the way it had for Medgar. Her children would lose both their parents. Then someone who overheard the commotion called out, and the man disappeared. Police later discovered he had rented a dingy single room nearby, whose walls were papered with pictures of Medgar, newspaper articles about him and about Myrlie, and sketches of the Beckwith family tree. He had been stalking Myrlie. It was sobering, and then enraging. The investigating detectives all but accused Myrlie of provoking the attack herself. Matters grew worse when other candidates, most of whom were Black, accused her of staging the incident as a publicity stunt.[35]

The threats had slowed but never stopped. Walter worried about her and the children, particularly Van, who was then just nineteen, and Myrlie felt continually surveilled. Even this far from Mississippi, cars sometimes still rolled slowly by her house, and there were still clicking sounds on the phone. She lost the race, finishing third. In a way it was a relief. Her focus shifted back to seeing that Medgar's killer was punished. She kept asking questions, the way Medgar had done in so many investigations in the Delta.

But she also kept busy. While she didn't win the council seat, Mayor Bradley appointed Myrlie to the Los Angeles Board of Public Works, overseeing a $1 billion budget. She had gone from Medgar's secretary at Magnolia Mutual and the NAACP, to executive, to leader, wielding power that she couldn't have imagined as a young, skinny Black girl in Vicksburg, Mississippi.

"My grandmother was [known for] quoting scripture," Myrlie said. "And she probably would have said, 'The Lord works with those who work with Him.'" She lived in a constant balance between gratitude and seething, with each new step forward mitigated by the one thing she still lacked: justice for Medgar. With Beckwith free again, having been paroled from Louisiana's notorious Angola prison in 1980, she could never truly rest on her victories.

"It is interesting how I found I could hate so deeply and believe so strongly," she said. "But I kept working. I kept praying. People told me to let it go. . . . I smiled and said 'Thank you. I talk to Medgar every night, it isn't crazy, just a little conversation.'"

Myrlie spent two years on the commission and the work was familiar. But on a trip with Walt to visit friends in Oregon, she seized on a new idea.

Medgar had loved Mississippi: not because it was kind to him—far from it. He loved it for its space; space to roam, space to hunt, space to fish, and space to be. In the quiet moments in the wilderness, when no one was around: no sneering sheriffs, marauding Klansmen, or rude shopkeepers, and so no racism or cruelty to contend with, Mississippi was a beautiful place. It was why he had always vowed to stay. Walt was the opposite; born and raised in Los Angeles, and steeped in city life and city conflict, space to roam was something of a luxury. When they visited Oregon, they felt a spark of inspiration. And when they found *their house:* high on a hill with a mountain view, it was "love at first sight."[36]

The town of Bend, Oregon, had a tiny population of about twenty thousand, mainly white residents. When Walt and Myrlie bought that house and moved in, early in 1989, they were mostly welcomed, as Myrlie and her children had been in Claremont. There were the occasional fractures, but for the most part, they stayed in love with Bend. Walt found that he had a passion for fishing, just as Medgar had. Myrlie indulged her passion for peace—and the idea of a peaceful place to come home to. Her children were grown and gone and living their own lives. This was an opportunity to live her best one.

Then on October 2, the phone rang. It was a Mississippi reporter named Jerry Mitchell, and he asked if he could fax her his story that had run the day before. His emergence into her life presented Myrlie with two challenges. First, he was a white Southern man (though he was originally from Missouri, not Mississippi). For Myrlie, that was reason enough to be wary. Second, he worked for the *Clarion-Ledger*, which for years had tormented Medgar and her. The newspaper had changed dramatically since the racist Hederman family sold it to the Gannett company for $100 million. Rea Hederman, a third-generation member of the family who left Mississippi, returned and took charge in 1982, determined to transform the paper into a home for journalism rather than hate. Mitchell joined in 1986 and quickly developed a specialty in investigating racist murders. He tracked down Klan connections to the Goodman, Schwerner, and Cheney lynching as well as to Beckwith. He got and exposed the Sovereignty Commission files and confirmed Medgar's reports to the FBI that he was being spied on and his phones were being tapped. The Sovereignty Commission might not have outwardly been the Klan, but as Grace Britton Sweet said, they were the Klan in suits, with ties to the violent white supremacist organization that were as fine as reeds.

"It's not just that these guys got away with murder," Mitchell said of the Mississippi Klan. "It was the fact that everybody knew these guys got away with murder. This was thumbing your nose at justice in the worst way imaginable, and that's what happened in [the Medgar Evers] case." When the Mississippi Legislature dissolved the Sovereignty Commission in 1977, it sealed its spy records for fifty years. Mitchell developed sources that "began to leak me the files, and what they show is [that at] the same time the State of Mississippi was prosecuting Byron De La Beckwith for the murder of Medgar Evers, this other arm of the state, the Sovereignty Commission, was secretly assisting the defense," vetting potential jurors, "trying to get Beckwith acquitted."

"When Jerry asked if I thought his findings warranted reopening the case, I let out a resounding 'Yes!'" Myrlie wrote.[37] Two days later, the paper ran a response column from her that called on Ed Peters, the Hinds County district attorney, to reopen the Beckwith murder case. "At the time that the story ran, odds were a million to one against the case ever being reopened and re-prosecuted," Mitchell said. "I mean, there was no murder weapon, no evidence in the vault, no court transcript, nothing of any value in the court files. I think like ten pages maybe."

By December, Myrlie was flying to Jackson to lobby the district attorney.[38] She brought with her Morris Dees, the civil rights attorney from the Southern Poverty Law Center, to meet with Peters and Assistant District Attorney Bobby DeLaughter. At first, she let Dees do most of the talking. Peters seemed skeptical about reopening the case, and the meeting got heated, as Dees threatened a lawsuit to force the DA's office to act. Myrlie eventually stepped in and calmly informed Peters and DeLaughter, who was from Vicksburg, that she had heard what they'd said. "Now, tell me what you are going to do to carry forward the pursuit of justice. If you don't, with my full support, Mr. Dees will,"[39] she said.

Myrlie had material that could help. Aaron Henry had given her the transcripts of the previous trials, which the state of Mississippi had discarded, but which she now gave to DeLaughter. "Myrlie Evers believed, and she prayed, and some amazing things happened," Mitchell said. She also believed that the murder weapon could not have just disappeared. She was right.

In the mid- to late 1960s, according to Mitchell, trials in the murders of Black citizens carried little importance in states like Mississippi. And so after Beckwith's second trial, "they were just getting rid of the evidence, and guns having a certain value, someone obviously asked, 'Hey, who wants the gun that killed Medgar Evers?'" The person who took it was Judge Russell Moore, who was responsible for sending some of the Freedom Riders to Parchman Penitentiary. Judge Moore also happened to be Bobby DeLaughter's father-in-law. "And really, thank God," Mitchell said, "because it wasn't lost, and it happened the family still had it . . . I mean, you can't make it up."

DeLaughter called his brother-in-law, Matthew Moore, who said he knew nothing about the gun. DeLaughter next visited his mother-in-law's house—the serial number of the murder weapon in hand—and found the lost Enfield rifle in her storeroom. He took it home that night, but instead of logging it in at the Jackson Police Department the next day, he kept it, fearing that if Beckwith learned the district attorney's office had the rifle, he would "clam up."

Whatever the true story, Mitchell believed there was "something kind of poetic about the fact that Medgar Evers tried to find witnesses in the Emmett Till case"[40]—another case in which everybody knew who the killers were—and that the weapon in his own murder was found in the home of a judge.

Beckwith was arrested in Tennessee, and his third trial for the murder of Medgar Evers was scheduled to begin on January 31, 1994. This trial would take place in an entirely different atmosphere in Mississippi. With the Sovereignty Commission gone and no longer able to bring Ku Klux Klan pressure to bear, the jury, which had been chosen from Panola County, 140 miles north of Jackson, was made up of eight Black and four white members. ("The foreman of the jury actually had cut Dr. King's hair just days before he was assassinated," Mitchell said.)

Beckwith could no longer count on the Citizens' Councils for legal support, and rather than the high-powered attorneys who aided him in 1963 and 1964, he was represented by a pair of public defenders. The courtroom—the same one where Beckwith had previously put on a white supremacist show in 1964—was now filled with Black onlookers.

The Evers family had to endure the trauma of having Medgar's body exhumed[41] at the insistence of DeLaughter, who wanted to ensure they had usable forensic evidence; the originally autopsy conducted in 1963 had gone missing along with the trial transcripts and other key evidence.[42] Van, who was then thirty-four years old, insisted on accompanying the body, later telling his mother that Medgar was almost perfectly preserved, but for some moisture on his fingertips. The forensic pathologist, Michael Baden, agreed, "It was as though Medgar had remained intact long enough for his youngest child to see and visit with him."[43]

When the trial began, the prosecution called the now-retired police detective Ralph Hargrove, who had saved the crime scene photos and other evidence in a box he left behind at the Jackson police station when he retired. They also called Thorn McIntyre, who testified for the third time that he traded the 1917 Eddystone Enfield rifle, designed for soldiers fighting World War I, to Beckwith in exchange for fertilizer for his farm, and that "the next time [he] heard about the gun was in June 1963 in the *Jackson Daily News*."[44]

The prosecution had more than the old forensic evidence this time. They now had Byron De La Beckwith's inability to keep quiet about murdering Medgar Evers. In the end, his own braggadocio undid him.

Beckwith's nephew, Reed Massengill, testified that Beckwith "had tried, on a number of occasions . . . to have a book written about his life."[45] As part of the effort, Beckwith provided Massengill "on a quite regular basis with racist propaganda, Christian Identity tapes, with copies of letters he had written and had published in newspapers; the manuscript of a book that had been written about him by an author he had worked with; and letters he had written to local townspeople in Signal Mountain about the fluoridation of their water."[46] Massengill provided a letter Beckwith wrote to a local newspaper in June 1957, in which he said: ". . . the NAACP, under the direction of its leaders, is doing a first-class job of getting itself in a position to be exterminated."[47] Beckwith vowed that "soon the cancerous growth, the NAACP, shall be cut out of the heart of our nation, and we will all live happily ever after."[48]

In a letter Beckwith wrote to his son on November 22, 1963, he heralded the murder of President Kennedy, saying whoever shot him, "did some fancy shootin'—to be sure," and he added, "Well, I guess when a few more of our enemies are gone then this will be a real fine world we get to live in—Wonder who will be next? I bet ole Medgar Evers told Kennedy when he got down there, I thought you'd be along pretty soon—Haw, Haw, Haw."[49]

Mark Reiley of Chicago, a thirty-six-year-old air traffic control equipment manager, testified that when he was an impressionable twenty-one-year-old guard at the Angola State Penitentiary ward at Earl K. Long hospital in Louisiana, he was assigned to guard Beckwith, who was imprisoned at Angola after being convicted of carrying explosives, allegedly to blow up Anti-Defamation League leader A. I. Botnick's home. He said that when Beckwith was hospitalized at Earl K. Long, he and the elder man developed a close, father-son relationship, and he testified that Beckwith told him, "Black people were . . . beasts of the field," and that white people were "chosen to rule over the earth and to be in charge of the beasts of the field."[50]

Reiley related an incident in which he rang for a nurse, and a Black nurse's aide responded. Beckwith "was very polite" but said "he would rather a nigger not wait on him or take care of him." A screaming match ensued, Reiley told the court, at the end of which Beckwith told the nurse's aide: "If I could get rid of an uppity nigger like Nigger Evers, I would have no problem with a no-account nigger like you."[51] On another occasion, according to Reiley, Beckwith said that if he hadn't had the "power and connections," "he would be serving time in jail in Mississippi for getting rid of that nigger, Medgar Evers."[52]

Reiley was followed by numerous other witnesses who described Beckwith proclaiming that not only had he shot and killed Medgar Evers, but that he'd been able to get away with it in the state of Mississippi. Also featured was the testimony of Delmar Dennis, who joined the Klan in March 1963 but soured on the idea when he realized it was a violent organization and not just devoted to the interests of white people. He became an FBI informant and infiltrated the Klan. Dennis testified that he met Beckwith in 1965 when Beckwith spoke at a meeting. He recalled Beckwith "admonishing Klan members to become more involved, to become violent, to kill the enemy . . . to kill from the top down." Dennis repeated the line that "killing that nigger Evers didn't cause me any more physical harm than your wives have to have a baby for you."[53] Dennis got Beckwith's autograph at the meeting, and that was introduced as evidence of the men's acquaintance.[54]

DeLaughter in his closing asked jurors "what Evers had done to deserve assassination," answering: "What he did was have the gall, the *uppitiness*, to want for his people—what? To be called by his name instead of 'Boy'? . . . To go into a restaurant? To go into a department store, to vote, and for your children to get a decent education in a decent school?" When it was Ed Peters's turn, he said Evers's calls for equality for Black Mississippians "so offended this defendant that he couldn't take it."[55]

The mood was tense when the jury went into deliberations. Mitchell believed the state had "put on a good case," but he knew the jury would still have to consider that the police officers "lied and claimed Beckwith was up in Greenwood" at the time of the murder. Mitchell recalled that "there was even a press pool on when the jury was going to come back, and everybody was saying, 'Oh, two hours, three hours . . .' So, a little over three hours . . . maybe a little more than that, the jury comes back in. We still haven't had a decision yet, but what you could see is some of the jurors were just red-faced like they had been arguing. Like they were angry. I was like, 'Oh, no. Beckwith is going to walk,' And . . . from a selfish perspective I thought everybody's going to blame me. . . . He's going to walk away and everybody's going to [say], 'Jerry, what'd you do this for?' I shouldn't have thought in those terms, but I did."

Myrlie wasn't worried. When she and Mitchell spoke that evening, "[she just repeated,] 'We've won,'" Mitchell said. "She believed they'd won just by having the trial. I didn't see it that way at all. I made some reference about her getting beyond hate and all that stuff, and she said, 'I don't know that I've gotten beyond it.'" She shared with Mitchell her truth about wishing she had a machine gun on the night Medgar was murdered to mow down all the policemen milling around on her lawn.

"And in that moment," Mitchell said, "I realized I had no idea what she and her family had gone through. None. Zero. How dare I think that I know? I think if there were a lesson to this, it would be that all of us in America could understand the pain these families went through and begin to understand our history for what it is, and not for what we may try to want it to be."

On Saturday, February 5, 1994, Byron De La Beckwith was convicted of murdering Medgar Evers, and immediately sentenced to life in prison. The seventy-three-year-old, who wore a Confederate flag pin throughout the trial, smiled slightly when the verdict was read.

"The verdict sent up a cheer among the mostly Black crowd attending the trial," the Associated Press reported. It "brought to a close one of the longest and most painful sagas of the civil rights movement."[56] After decades of carefully honed public self-control, after Medgar's homegoing and his burial, after speeches and fundraisers and board meetings and on the campaign trail, Myrlie finally let go. "Mrs. Evers, usually a rock of composure, broke into tears after the verdict was read," the report said. "She clasped the hand of her daughter, Reena Evers-Everette, while her son, Darrell Kenyatta Evers, clapped in jubilation."[57]

Myrlie went outside the courthouse, which had been the focus of so much pain, disappointment, and injustice for so many Black families, and celebrated. "It's been a long journey," the Associated Press reported that Myrlie said, arms locked with her children's and tears streaming down her face. "'Medgar,' she added, eyes heavenward, 'I've gone the last mile.'"[58] Reena's thoughts were also for the heavens. "'Hi Daddy,' she said in a voice choked with emotion. 'We did it.' She said the pain of her father's death 'cannot be erased . . . but now it can be soothed. And I got a whole lot of medicine soothed on me today.'"[59]

Darrell had attended the trial with a goal as singular and furtive as his childhood determination to kill his father's murderer with the toy gun Myrlie bought him. He wanted to force the coward De La Beckwith to look at his face and to see Medgar Evers staring back at him. "He never saw my father's face" when he shot him, Darrell told reporters after the verdict. "All he saw was his back. I wanted him to see the face . . . to see the ghost of my father come back to haunt him." Darrell Kenyatta Evers was forty-one years old; three years older than his father had been when he died. He had chosen to become an artist, not an activist. But in his manner and demeaner, and, yes, in the face that so resembled Medgar's, the sad little boy from the cover of *Life* magazine had grown up to be every bit his father's son.

With the thanks of the court, the jurors were released and taken home by bus to Panola County. The verdict would be their only comment. "They were exhausted. They were just drained," Panola County sheriff David Bryan said of the jurors.[60]

From Jackson to Greenwood, no Klan crosses were burned in outrage or in honor after Beckwith's belated conviction. He had emerged from this very courthouse in 1964 as a white nationalist folk hero. Now, he was just an old man—an opportunity he had stolen from

Medgar. He was going to spend the rest of his unhappy life behind bars.

For the prosecutors, the triumph, thirty years after this notorious crime, brought notoriety, books, movies, and, for DeLaughter, an elevation to a judgeship (which years later would end in scandal). In noting the criticism some leveled for his decision to bring the case after so long, DA Peters said, "I feel like it should have been done a long time ago. But by waiting we were able to get some new witnesses, so maybe it's a blessing it took so long."[61]

MYRLIE FELT THAT AT LAST SHE HAD FINALLY AWAKENED FROM the shock of Medgar's murder, and the rage and sorrow that consumed her afterward. She could finally revel in the triumphs and accolades his sacrifice had earned, without that extra pang of bitterness that remembering him entailed.

In 1992, Delta Drive, near the Evers home in Jackson, had been renamed Medgar Evers Boulevard, and a statue to Medgar was erected downtown. (Guynes Street would be renamed for Margaret Walker Alexander.) Betty Shabazz helped secure a street named for Medgar in Brooklyn, New York, one year later. There were several movie portrayals of their family, including a Hollywood production: *Ghosts of Mississippi* in 1996, which brought director Rob Reiner, Whoopi Goldberg (as Myrlie), Alec Baldwin (as Bobby DeLaughter), and James Woods (as Beckwith) to Guynes Street and saw Darrell playing himself on-screen. And there was a 1997 Mississippi Supreme Court denial of Beckwith's appeal.

Medgar and Myrlie's children were thriving in adulthood. While Darrell focused on his artistic pursuits, Reena worked in the travel industry and eventually became head of the foundation Myrlie created to honor Medgar. Van excelled as a photographer—one of Medgar's favorite hobbies besides fishing and hunting. Myrlie served on corporate boards and had stints as an advertising executive and a corporate consumer affairs officer, and she wrote a second book. Life was busy, but it finally had become fulfilling.

Myrlie had one more mission, and it would bring her full circle.

EVERY YEAR ON JUNE 12, MYRLIE EVERS-WILLIAMS, OFTEN WITH her family, or friends, and sometimes in solitude, alone, would visit Arlington National Cemetery in Washington, D.C. It was her chance to remember Medgar, to sit with him, and to honor him. It was the day she set aside to reconvene with the grief that she had received blessed respite from since she succeeded in seeing his killer dispatched to prison.

On her 1994 visit, she was accompanied by Walt and by a friend: Joe Madison, a former General Motors PR man who in 1973 had been named executive director of the NAACP branch in Detroit at age twenty-four. Now a popular radio host whose latest show aired on Washington, D.C.'s WWRC-AM, he remained involved in the civil rights organization as a member of the NAACP's national board of directors, which Myrlie had also been sitting on since the early 1990s.

The visit came during a turbulent time for the NAACP, which had become mired in financial and sexual scandal. The organization was $4.7 million in debt. Its executive director, Benjamin Chavis Jr., had recently been fired over accusations he covered up sexual harassment allegations and paid off the woman who made them using organization funds without the knowledge of or permission from the board. This was followed by a sexual harassment lawsuit brought against the organization alleging not just a culture of harassment, but also of denying advancement opportunities to women. The term of the current chairman of the national board, Dr. William F. Gibson, was set to end in 1995 unless he was reelected, which seemed unlikely as he, too, faced financial scrutiny over the alleged abuse of his NAACP expense account.[62] Myrlie had been publicly critical of the organization being unable to "get its house in order." She punctuated her public statements by charging that the NAACP did not generally treat women, who made up two-thirds of its membership, fairly.[63]

Chavis had succeeded Roy Wilkins, who retired in 1977 following a string of victories including the Civil Rights, Voting Rights, and Fair Housing Acts, but also seasons of tragedy in the assassinations of Medgar, Malcolm, Dr. King, the Kennedy brothers, and so many more; and Benjamin Hooks, who presided over some of the organization's most turbulent years, marked by internal and financial struggles, and who endured a series of targeted bombings aimed at civil rights leaders. By the 1990s, the organization seemed rudderless. It no longer commanded the attention of much of Black America, as many questioned the organization's relevance[64] and turned instead toward younger, brasher civil rights leaders like Rev. Jesse Jackson (whom Chavis defeated for the executive director's role) and Rev. Al Sharpton of Harlem, both heirs to the work of Dr. King. Even the word "Colored" in the name spoke of the past.

Madison picked Myrlie and Walt up from their hotel to drive with them to Arlington. Before getting into the car, though, he took Walt aside. He had a question he wanted desperately to ask Myrlie, but he didn't dare until he knew whether he would have an ally in Walt. Madison wanted Myrlie to run for executive director, to succeed Chavis. Madison thought Myrlie was the only person who could right what was wrong at the NAACP: both its financial standing and its standing with its female members. He was convinced that Myrlie was the only choice for an organization that needed to prove its relevance again. She had been its most prodigious fundraiser. She had worked side by side with its bravest field secretary, Medgar. Her story, and her moral voice, Madison believed, could rescue the NAACP. But he needed Walt to agree to help him lobby Myrlie. "Do you think she'll do it?" Madison asked. To his surprise and relief, Walt was all in.

During the twenty-minute ride to Arlington, the question was poised on his lips, but Madison was afraid to ask it. Myrlie was sixteen years his senior, and he had deep respect for not just her legacy, but also her well-earned peace. He was also aware of how turbulent Medgar's relationship had been with Roy Wilkins, Gloster Current, and the other NAACP leaders, who had all but ordered him to cut his ties to the direct-action efforts of groups like SNCC. Indeed, Myrlie had mixed feelings about the organization that she believed chose not to protect Medgar when it counted but also put a financial floor under his wife and children once he was gone. Despite Medgar's struggles with the leadership, she and he had developed long and enduring friendships inside the organization. It was a complicated picture.

Madison put out a feeler. He brought up the Chavis resignation, Gibson's troubles, and the general state of the NAACP, to which Myrlie chimed in that *he* should run for chairman of the board. Madison and Walt exchanged knowing looks. He told her *she* should run. Walt agreed.

When they arrived at Arlington, they were escorted on a personal tour by Arlington officials, who walked them through the gravesites to the Tomb of the Unknown Soldier, a memorial with a sarcophagus perched on a hill, with catacombs underneath. They then arrived at Medgar's grave, where they stood alone for a long time, surrounded by reverent silence and markers of the sacrifice of thousands of men like Medgar, who had fought America's wars abroad while some like Medgar had been forced to fight anew at home. Myrlie always wept at Medgar's gravesite. Just being there, amid all that silent grandeur, reminded her of what a great man she'd married and how much she missed him.

She began to talk about their life together, and to recall the pain of having to send his body on its journey from Jackson to here, and the agony of having to exhume him as a necessary step for achieving justice. Her reverie emboldened Madison, who reiterated that she simply had to run for NAACP chair. "Medgar would want you to do this," he told her. "We need you. *We need you.*"[65] Medgar had died for the NAACP, Madison told her. Only she could prevent the nation's oldest civil rights organization from dying.[66]

Myrlie promised to give it serious consideration.

When she and Walt returned to Bend, they had a heart to heart. Walt had recently been diagnosed with cancer, and just the idea of throwing herself into another campaign when she had him to take care of seemed absurd. But he summoned her to think about what her mission ought to be. She had toiled as a typist in the Jackson NAACP office not just because Medgar needed her, but because Jackson did, and Mississippi did. And all she had accomplished since that time spoke to her unique abilities, to speak, to cajole, to fundraise, to manage enormous financial resources, and to inspire. In short, Walt finished what Madison had started and talked Myrlie into it. As always, he would be there to help manage her campaign.

The campaign to lead the NAACP waded into the internecine rivalries at the highest echelons of the NAACP. During the meeting in New York to decide Gibson's fate, and Myrlie's, Julian Bond and Hazel Dukes, two activists who had previously been ousted over disputes with Gibson, were returned to their seats on the board. Following a spirited meeting that included a vote of "no confidence" in Gibson by the rank-and-file membership, Myrlie was elected chair by a single vote—30 to 29 among those who cast a ballot—as her supporters among the seven hundred assembled members chanted "Clean House Now!"[67] Twenty members of the sixty-four-member board were women.[68]

This was her third campaign, and this time she was victorious. "It is time to heal our wounds," an emotional Evers-Williams told the NAACP membership after the vote. "We will move forward because we are family."[69]

She then addressed the assembled media, echoing Joe Madison's words a year earlier at Arlington: "Medgar died for the NAACP. I will live for the NAACP."[70] In the end, she stepped into the role out of a sense of duty, becoming just the third woman board chair of the civil rights organization since its founding in 1909.

Walt had insisted that she press forward, telling her, "This is the last thing I'll ever ask you to do. Run and win!"[71] But they both understood that his situation was dire. He died of prostate cancer just two days after her election, at seventy-six years old.

MYRLIE WAS ON HER OWN AGAIN AND FACING MANY OF THE CHALlenges Medgar had confronted with an organization whose mission—equality for African Americans—they both supported, even though its execution of that mission sometimes left folks wanting. For Myrlie, it was as if everything Medgar Evers lived and died for was coming to fruition in her hands. She received congratulatory calls from seemingly every NAACP branch in America, and from President Bill Clinton. But she had no doubt about the difficulty of the task ahead of her.

The first step was to get the organization's fiscal house in order. She began to make the rounds to the organization's traditional donors and found many doors closed. "All of the foundations and organizations that I personally went to, to raise funds, I was told that the NAACP was dead. And I received no contributions," Myrlie later said. "Only Ford Foundation stepped up and said: 'We will provide you with the funds.' It was not healthy."[72] Gibson's alleged profligacy was part of the challenge with donors. Chavis's relationship with Minister Louis Farrakhan of the Nation of Islam was another. Both scared major donors away. It was left to Myrlie to convince potential funders that she could bring the NAACP back on mission.

With a Republican-led Congress poised to attack many of the programs the NAACP had fought for—and Medgar, King, and others had died for—Myrlie felt passionately that the NAACP was still needed. "We may be a dinosaur, as some people say, but we're not going to be extinct," Myrlie told the Associated Press. "As long as there is racism and unfair treatment, not just for African Americans, but for all people, there is going to be this organization."[73]

Myrlie was sworn into her new role on May 14, 1995, Mother's Day, at Washington's Metropolitan AME Church. This was the church where Frederick Douglass prayed. And it seemed fitting to be near Baltimore, where the NAACP had moved its headquarters from New York in 1986, and where Clarence Mitchell Jr., the architect of the NAACP's legislative strategy and the man who had so gently counseled Medgar and Myrlie during some of the toughest times in their marriage, lived. More than a thousand people packed into the church to cheer her on, and seven federal judges, six current and one retired, swore Myrlie in. Coretta Scott King came to support Myrlie. "Over the years, I have witnessed the remarkable dignity, integrity and courage of Myrlie Evers-Williams," she said. "No one is better prepared to lead this great ship of hope into the next century."[74] And Myrlie vowed to restore the moral course of the organization for which her husband had given his life, and in a nod to Medgar's life mission, she also vowed to reach out to young activists and include their voices in the mission.

Money flowed in along with joy and enthusiasm for Myrlie, as Black sororities—including her own, Delta Sigma Theta—fraternities, and professional organizations joined banks, businesses, and individuals in pledging hundreds of thousands of dollars to the revived NAACP. It felt like a revival for the organization and its nearly seven hundred thousand members.[75]

Within a year, the NAACP had a new president and CEO: Maryland congressman Kweisi Mfume (who many years later would himself resign in scandal), and with Myrlie's steadying hand in place, its finances were revived. By the organization's October 1996 board meeting, the NAACP had retired its $4 million–plus debt.[76]

Medgar would have been so proud. He would challenge Myrlie sometimes about her fiscal prudence, and she would stand strong in her confidence that she knew how to manage their small income and still support his work, the dinners with James Baldwin and Lena Horne at the house, and feed and care for their children. Their life together had taught her how to manage the business of their lives. He would push her to be stronger and more self-confident, and she had become both almost instinctively. Now, at sixty-three years old, Myrlie had taken the activist mission that they shared to its pinnacle.

In May 1997, Myrlie, Betty, and Coretta embarked on a trip to Florida; one of the "girls' weekends" they would occasionally treat themselves to, "on the pretext of losing weight and eating healthy," Scott King wrote in her memoir, noting that they rarely achieved their fitness goals, but "oh what fun we had."[77] One of the Kings' daughters, Dr. Bernice King, recalled that "whenever my mother had time with people like them" and other Black women friends who lived their lives in public view, like Maya Angelou or Oprah Winfrey, she was like "a giddy little girl, because it afforded her an opportunity to . . . let [her hair] down and really relax."[78] According to King, the idea for this trip came from Ingrid Saunders Jones, a Black woman executive at the Coca-Cola Company's headquarters in Atlanta, who even secured a grant to pay for it. The plan was to meet at the Doral Country Club and Spa near Miami Beach for a "ritual of connection, girl talk and rare self-indulgence,"[79] as Myrlie described it. There, they could be something other than civil rights widows. Hidden from the cameras, reporters, and onlookers, "We were not Mrs. King, Mrs. Shabazz, or Mrs. Evers," Scott King wrote, "just Coretta, Betty, and Myrlie."[80]

"Myrlie arrived first," wrote Russell J. Rickford, author of *Betty Shabazz: Surviving Malcolm X—A Journey of Strength from Wife to Widow to Heroine*. And as she could swim, she headed straight to the pool. "By the time the other two showed up, she had already had a powerful massage. They discovered her on the spa's exercise and sauna wing, droopy-eyed and weaving."[81] Betty knew Myrlie didn't drink, so she knew for sure that her friend wasn't inebriated. "Honey, what happened to you?" she asked. "The same thing that's about to happen to the two of you," Myrlie answered.

At their first day lunch, Betty jokingly needled the waiter over the too-small "gourmet" portions, and the women abandoned the five-mile walk with the other guests for a quiet saunter for three. They signed up for an aerobics class, and Myrlie and Betty giggled in their baseball caps, as Coretta arrived in full makeup. Betty soon turned the class into an impromptu "Achy Brakey" dance, to her friends' absolute delight.

That first night, they curled up in Coretta's suite, watching a Chicago Bulls NBA game on TV. "We screamed, we hollered; it didn't matter who won," Coretta wrote. "That wasn't what we'd come for. We came to enjoy not being in charge of anything. We came because we loved one another unconditionally, despite negative news reports about how we'd tried to upstage or jealously compete with one another over the limelight. Imagine that anyone would actually want to rise to prominence on the basis of losing the man she'd loved! . . . When you can relax, let your hair down, and share your secrets—that's real friendship."[82]

As the weekend went on, they broke their pact not to talk about the men they had lost. They talked about the pain of sharing their brilliant, visionary husbands with the world, and the ache of knowing from the start that they would never really have them to themselves. They talked about the fleeting, agonizing nature of spectacular love and loss. They shared stories about their late husbands as men and not as heroes.[83] And they talked about their children—thirteen between them—who had been "united by accidents of birth and the misfortunes of death," and thus had "grown up plagued by visibility and violence."[84] They laughed together, and they cried together. And for those few glorious days, they were as free as can be.

They had so much fun that when the weekend was over, they immediately began planning another trip.[85] It was not to be. A week after returning to their homes, Myrlie and Coretta learned that Betty Shabazz had been hospitalized for severe injuries she suffered in a fire at her home. The fire had been set by her twelve-year-old only grandson, whom his mother, Qubilah, had named Malcolm.[86]

Myrlie called Coretta. "What does God have in mind?" she asked her friend. "What lesson are we supposed to take from this?" The women had no answers. Instead, they were soon gathering for a funeral. Each had visited Betty in the hospital, and Myrlie got there a week before Betty died on June 23, 1997. At her bedside, Myrlie had teased her heavily bandaged and deeply sedated friend, saying "Okay, girl, let's get it on," which had been their cue to keep going when they were weary.[87]

"I remember having the urge to put my arms around her and say, as I did, 'I love you, Betty,'" she wrote in the foreword to Mrs. Shabazz's biography.[88] These women's lives had been punctuated by great love and great loss, and for the moment, loss was victorious again.

A YEAR LATER, IN 1998, MYRLIE STEPPED DOWN AS NAACP BOARD chair, with one year left in her tenure. She felt that her job was done, and she was ready to spread her wings yet again.

"When first elected chairman, I promised to work with the board and our members to restore credibility, financial integrity and focus to the NAACP," she said. "Together, we have accomplished this mission. I've worked 18-hour days, year in and year out. I've traveled around this country countless times in this volunteer, non-salaried position. I've been able to bring us through the darkest moments of this organization's history. Now it's time to move on."[89]

At sixty-four years old, she had accomplished so much, but still had a hunger in her. She planned to write a second memoir, and to work with Reena at the family foundation in Jackson, to preserve Medgar's legacy and her own. She was awarded the Spingarn Medal—the NAACP's highest award, which Medgar had received posthumously in 1963. Myrlie thus joined not just Medgar, but also Roy Wilkins, Rosa Parks, and Walter F. White. It was heady company. But there were still more honors to come.

CHAPTER 11

Carnegie Hall

You can kill a man, but you can't kill an idea.

—MEDGAR EVERS

The first time Medgar Evers kissed Myrlie Louise Beasley she was playing the piano. He pretended to be enjoying her classical music, and that was their first flirtation, and his excuse to be near her. Music was the catalyst for their love and for their lives—whether it was the Motown songs they danced to in their living room on Guynes Street, the organ music Myrlie played at the start of a mass meeting at the Masonic Temple, or the gentle music she played on their piano just for Medgar as he dozed off, exhausted, on the couch.

Music was, in fact, Myrlie's first love, even before Medgar.

"My grandmother saved her pennies and her quarters and paid for my music lessons every week. My aunt . . . was the one who made me squirm, sitting on the piano stool practicing. And they never lost faith in me. 'Come on baby, you can do it. You can do it,'" they would say." The women who raised Myrlie "had this picture in their minds that one day that little skinny girl with long pigtails would be performing at Carnegie Hall," she said.

Back then Myrlie obediently replied, "Yes, Mama. Yes, Auntie," but she never actually believed it. Her only complaint at the time was that she was only permitted to play classical music, but not jazz.

In December 2012, Myrlie Evers-Williams found herself in New York, preparing to fulfill the dream Mama and Aunt Myrlie had for her. Back in Jackson, Jerry Mitchell, who had become close friends with Reena, took a phone call from her. "She calls me, [and] she goes, 'Okay, you can't tell anybody, but Mom is going to play Carnegie Hall in New York.' I was like, 'That's so great. I want to be there!'"[1]

Mitchell remembered Reena throwing in what she assumed was a curve ball. "And she's playing with a group you've never heard of, Pink Martini,"[2] he recalled her saying. She didn't know Mitchell was a big fan of the Oregon-based orchestra that blended classical, jazz, Latin music, and pop. Myrlie had gotten to know members of Pink Martini because of the home she and Walt had purchased in Bend, Oregon—the state where the group was based. Mitchell booked his tickets right away to come to New York to attend the concert.

If Myrlie's nerves were jangling, she certainly didn't intend to show it. She had become an expert at public performance. In the hours after Medgar was lost, she had stepped into Pearl Street Baptist Church and poured out her anger and pain as a means of rousing the people of Jackson to continue her husband's work. She had deployed her gift of public speech for decades for the NAACP. And long before that, back in Vicksburg, she had sung with the Chansonettes, and for that she had been possessed of poise, grace, and, of course, talent.

"We were kind of an exclusive group that performed wherever we had a chance to perform," Myrlie recalled of her childhood girl group. "We performed in churches, we performed for . . . civic groups who wanted music . . . and to pinpoint the talent of teenagers in our community. We even performed at a couple of weddings, as I recall. We performed everywhere except funerals."[3]

The Chansonettes were well known in Vicksburg. "Our teacher and pianist was Ruth Roanne Sanders," Myrlie said, "and she was the daughter of one of the presidents of Fisk University, so we were well acquainted with the classics, as well as folk songs and everything else. Fortunately, we all had good voices.

"All of us were students of music, two of voice, and myself and one other in piano. . . . One of our singers, Josephine Springs, was our soprano. She had a beautiful voice," Myrlie recalled. "It was an exciting adventure for us because we got a chance to have a new gown, a long dress made for us, for each occasion. There was always a photographer there to take our photograph. And those photographs were placed in the 'colored newspapers.' We were kind of popular, and we loved it!

"Foolishly, foolishly at that time, all of us had hoped to become concert pianists. Not one of us made it, and it wasn't because at least one person, [especially] our soprano, wasn't good enough, [or] studied music long enough to have been an excellent concert singer. But with a segregated society . . . there was no opportunity for that. At that time, the ultimate goal was to finish college and to become a teacher."

Mama and Aunt Myrlie instilled in Myrlie the possibility that she could become a concert pianist. "I don't know where they got that idea, but that was one that they pursued." It "encouraged them to make me practice the piano, at least two hours every day. . . . [And] I was darn good . . . I'll tell you that." Unfortunately, the opportunities just weren't there back then for even the most talented Black girls in Mississippi. So Myrlie and her group contented themselves with playing at local venues.

"My intent, my hope, my prayer," she remembered, "was that I could go to Fisk University and study music there, and hopefully from that point, someone would recognize my talent, and I would become a concert pianist, even if I were limited only to playing to audiences of my color, and that usually meant [playing] at churches around the counties where I lived."[4]

Much had changed by the time Myrlie made it to Carnegie Hall in December 2012.

The airport in Jackson, which opened in 1963 and had been named for Jackson's segregationist mayor Allen C. Thompson, was renamed Jackson–Medgar Wiley Evers International Airport in December 2004. It was yet another triumph of Medgar Evers over his racist tormentors—and yet another he never lived to see.

Four years later, a new Navy ship was designated to be named in Medgar's honor. The U.S. Navy secretary who made the decision and the announcement was Ray Mabus, a former governor of Mississippi who was a fourteen-year-old living in a northern county of the state the year Medgar was assassinated.[5] And in a reality few could have conceived of back then, the commander in chief Mabus served under was Black.

America had entered a new century and seen the election of its first Black president: Barack Hussein Obama—the son of a Kenyan father and a white American mother, and whose name was as unfamiliar to white American ears as "Kenyatta" had been when Medgar had insisted on that being Darrell's middle name. When Robert Kennedy had his disastrous meeting in May 1963 in New York with James Baldwin, Lorraine Hansberry, Harry Belafonte, and the other Black cultural and social leaders, he had suggested the country could have a "Negro president in forty years," hoping this would endear him to the room. It didn't work that night,[6] but his prediction had come true.

On the night after Obama's election on November 4, 2008, Myrlie sat for an interview with National Public Radio. Sitting beside Rev. Jesse Jackson, Dr. King's former aide, a civil rights leader in his own right, and a two-time presidential candidate, she took out a poll tax receipt she frequently carried with her that had Medgar's blood on it. "It's not to be sad and to stay in the past all of the time," she said, "but it's a constant reminder that we have to move forth." She said she had shed tears of "absolute joy" at Obama's election, but not tears of surprise. "I knew that that would happen, that the day would come, but I wasn't sure that I would live long enough to see it."[7] She had lived to see and do so much. She couldn't help but think of those who weren't there to enjoy it all with her.

Now, as she took her place on the Carnegie Hall stage with Pink Martini and the New York Pops behind her, under that towering, ornate ceiling that stretched over balconies stacked to the heavens, absent were Mama, Aunt Myrlie, M'dear, Big Mama, and the men who had loved her: her strong but sometimes disappointing father, Jim, the patient and ever-supportive Walt, and, of course, Medgar. She stood on that stage on her own. Reena and Van were in the audience. Dear, sweet Darrell was not.

Medgar had often rubbed her belly when she was pregnant with their firstborn child, saying, "There's my little football player in there." Darrell had grown to be athletic and independent, deeply spiritual and quiet; handsome like his father and a strong man who brooked no disrespect, to him or his family. Early on, he had found a career in a computer-related field, founding a DVD company in California with his wife, Lauren. But art was his passion and true vocation. It was the way he spoke to the world. And his work, searing and avant-garde, had made its way into the collections of Henry Luce II and Vidal Sassoon. But of Medgar and Myrlie's three children, Darrell had seemed to bear his father's assassination the hardest, often in stoic silence, followed by floods of pent-up tears. He had been plagued by nightmares and bouts of vengeful anger, but also a determination to seek justice that would have made Medgar proud. In many ways, he had indeed become his father's apparition, the man of the house while still a child, Myrlie's occasional scold, and a seemingly eternal mystery behind the closed door of his room.

Now he was gone too. In January 2001, Darrell succumbed to colon cancer. He was just forty-seven years old, with a son of his own, named Keanon. He had lived to see his father's assassin convicted and outlived—by just one month—the man who had terrorized his family.

Like Medgar, he would never become an old man, or get to watch Myrlie fulfill her dream.[8]

On the Carnegie stage, Myrlie wore a floor-length sequined gown custom made for her by designer Ikram Goldman. She had told him she had "always wanted to stand in the curve of a big grand piano in a slinky red dress and sing torch songs."[9] She gathered all the strength and poise Mama and Aunt Myrlie had fed into her and, with a wink, told the packed audience, "If I stumble and fall, you applaud. If I sing off key, you applaud. If I forget my words, you applaud even harder and sing along with me. Thank you for your friendship, thank you for your prayers, and—oh, my—thank you for your patience."[10]

"The only accident that night proved to be a happy one," the *Wall Street Journal* reported. "When a cell phone ringtone cut through the room, Ms. Evers-Williams ad-libbed *'Mama?'*—as if addressing her late grandmother, to whom she had dedicated the Debussy performance just moments before. The house exploded in laughter."[11]

"It was wonderful," Mitchell said. "She was fantastic."

Myrlie had brought her and her family's dreams, and the dreams she and Medgar dreamed together, painfully, lovingly, and with their whole hearts, full circle. And she was a hit.

A month later, on January 21, 2013, Myrlie Evers-Williams returned to Washington and to the United States Capitol, where she delivered the invocation at President Obama's second inaugural. Her address was watched by 1.8 million people in person, but the total who watched was 20.6 million, per Nielsen, and she became the first woman, and the first layperson, to give the invocation at a presidential inauguration.[12]

Then on June 4, Myrlie, Reena, Van, and their families returned to Arlington National Cemetery to honor the contributions Medgar made to create an America where Black voters could cast ballots for a Black president, even in Mississippi. The attorney general who greeted them at the ceremony was Eric Holder, a Black man who had been drawn to the legal profession inspired by men like John Doar, Burke Marshall,

Robert Kennedy, and Nicholas Katzenbach, and by a Justice Department that presided over the desegregation of Southern universities. Holder's sister-in-law, Vivian Malone, was one of the two brave young Black students, along with James Hood, who endured the gauntlet of screaming segregationists and Gov. George Wallace's defiant "stand in the schoolhouse door" at the University of Alabama. Malone and so many other Black Americans had gotten to taste some of the "first-class citizenship" Medgar talked about when he gave his own historic televised address calling for desegregation and full equality for Black Mississippians.

The *New York Times* reported that other speakers at the commemoration included Navy Secretary Mabus and Benjamin Todd Jealous, the then executive director of the NAACP,[13] who a month earlier had apologized to Myrlie and her family during an NAACP national board meeting in Jackson for the organization's failure to protect him.

"He put his speech aside," Myrlie told radio host and civil rights activist Mark Thompson regarding Jealous. "And he stood there, and he said, 'I have an apology to make.' And he apologized to me and my daughter and other family members for what the Association leadership, top leadership, said to Medgar and the way they treated him. . . . I don't think there was a dry eye in the place at that time. Because people didn't know."[14]

Medgar would have reveled in everything that was happening, because he had contributed to making these once-inconceivable events possible.

After the Arlington burial in 1963, Myrlie, Darrell, Reena, and Charles had been invited to the White House by President Kennedy. This time, in 2013, the family was welcomed by President Obama. Myrlie told the *Michigan Chronicle,* "Being able to be here and visit with President Obama with my family . . . speaks to the change in America, but it also speaks to the changes that need to come."[15]

President Kennedy had given gifts to the children, but this time, Myrlie brought gifts for the president. Van, who had turned his father's fascination with photography into his profession, presented President Obama with two inscribed black-and-white portraits he'd taken: one of Rosa Parks, and the other of his mother with Coretta Scott King and Betty Shabazz. The president's senior advisor, Valerie Jarrett, who hailed from one of the most prominent Black families in Chicago, told Myrlie the president planned to hang the portraits in his private office.[16]

Myrlie Louise Evers Williams had climbed from a humble Black enclave in Vicksburg to the grandest heights of American power, to secure the legacy of Medgar Evers, who had fought for his country and ultimately died trying to save it from its own demons. She had convened with three presidents, and challenged and changed the NAACP. She had been "Woman of the Year" (*Ms.* magazine, 1998) and one of the "100 Most Fascinating Black Women of the 20th Century" (*Ebony*, 1998). She'd written two biographies and helped to edit her husband's, collecting his papers and preserving the memory of the dangerous, valiant work he did for Mississippi and America. But the greatest gift she had received, in all her years of struggle and striving, the anger and the quest for vengeance, and the pain and loss she had endured, was the gift of love.

"I'm blessed," Myrlie said, sipping a hot cup of tea in Van's tidy California backyard, nearly sixty years after Medgar was gone. "Many a battle, but I don't think I ever fought one that I could not win. . . . I'm still fighting as best as I can at this age. . . . [And] I will fight until I take my last breath. . . .

"Medgar Evers was and is the love of my life," Myrlie said, smiling deeply as the afternoon wore on and the air cooled to a chill. "There has never been a day in my life that I have not been loved. . . .

"I will tell you this," she said. "The best thing . . . is remembering little details, small little details, about the love of my life, and the life that we had, and how blessed I am to have known that man—to have loved him, and to have had his children and walked through life with him."[17]

Many thanks.

There are almost too many people to thank for their support and assistance in bringing this project to life. But I will begin with Mrs. Myrlie Evers-Williams, who gave so generously of her time, on the phone and in person, to talk with me about her remarkable life and marriages. My dear Soror, you are the best of Black women, of all women, of civil rights leaders, and of icons. Thank you for your voice—for its rich melody and resonant strength. You inspire me and make me want to make more of my own life and contributions to the world. Bless you in all things.

Many thanks also to Ms. Myrlie and Medgar's children: sweet Darrell in spirit, who spoke so powerfully in his life, as an artist, as a man, and as a survivor; and in the living realm: James Van Dyke "Van" Evers and Reena Evers Everette, who helped to facilitate my interviews with Ms. Myrlie and, in Reena's case, guided me and my team toward so many remarkable people in Jackson, Mississippi, who knew and loved the Evers family. Reena, thank you for sharing your story, your childhood home, the incredible museum you and your family birthed, and your precious family archives with us, and for allowing me to commune with so many change makers, your amazing mom included. Van, thank you for sharing your home, your beautiful family, and your mom's illustrious presence. I also thank the great Chris Fleming, who is as great a coordinator and connection maker as there is in the world, and whose love for Ms. Myrlie and the Evers family radiates through everything he does.

I cannot leave out the fabulous Evers cousins: Carolyn Evers Cockrell, Charlene Evers Kreel, Sheila Evers Blackmon, and Wanda Evers, plus the entire team and staff at WMPR, the late Charles Evers's forever radio home. Thanks also to the Evers Institute and the Mississippi Department of Archives and History and its patient and kind deputy director of programs and communications, Stephanie Morrisey, for all her help and guidance.

Thanks also to Keena Nichell Graham of the National Parks Service, whose loving care of the Evers home and brilliant insights into its and the Evers family's history is steeped in unteachable grace. *Whadatah,* my sister!

And now to the Guynes Street gang! I salute the late and fabulous Johnnie Pearl Young, who welcomed us into her home and gave so generously of her time to share her story with us—in glorious red lipstick, I might add! And the wonderful Carolyn Wells Gee, who shared her home and her memories of her precious parents, to tell the story of the singular trauma of her youth. Thank you so much to the Sweets: Grace Britton Sweet; her son, Dennis Sweet III; her daughter, Judge Denise Sweet Owens; and to all the residents of this miraculous Black community.

Many thanks also to the great Jerry Mitchell, who shared so much journalistic and personal wisdom, and who was an invaluable resource in writing this book. Thanks also to the many warriors of the movement: Hezekiah Watkins, James Meredith and Hazel Meredith Hall, Bernard Lafayette, Fred Douglas Moore, Wendell Paris, Rev. Amos Brown, Sen. Michael Mitchell, Rev. Shirley Harrington, Fred Clark, Flonzie Brown-Wright, Dr. Robert Smith, Rev. Daphne Chamberline, the wonderful Frank Figgers, who was our constant guide and conscience in Jackson, and Rev. Ed King, who had so many stories to tell, I couldn't fit them all in this book. Many thanks also to Glendora mayor Johnnie B. Thomas; Mound Bayou mayor Darryl Johnson and his brother and museum director Herman Johnson; the fabulous Dr. Cassie Sade Turnipseed, assistant professor of history at Jackson

State University's Department of History and Philosophy, who shared her knowledge of Mississippi's "cotton kingdom" and the incredible work of sculptor Ed Dwight with us; Dr. J. Janice Coleman of Alcorn State University; Pamela Junior, director of the Mississippi Civil Rights Museum; and Tougaloo professor Daphne Chamberlain; as well as Mrs. Annette Collins-Rollins of Rollins Funeral Home.

I cannot confer enough thanks to my incredible and diligent research team and road warriors: Dr. Angela Pashayan (the ultimate planner and organizer), king of the deep-dive historical spreadsheet; Kamryn Nelson, my phenomenal fact checker and friend; Sharon Gaffney; and my partner in crime, genealogy research guru, and personal superhero, Shauntay Hampton Prewitt; along with *her* assistants, Kaiah Amira Warr and Justice D. Prewitt, as well as Joseph Ryals and Jason, my thirty-plus-year friend who wielded the camera on our incredible journey to Jackson.

Many thanks also to the wonderful people of the Mississippi Delta: Betty Campbell, Otha Campbell, and all the folks at Betty's Place in Indianola, who showed us such a great time and taught us what it's like to experience true Mississippi Delta hospitality; chef Enrika Williams, who kept our bellies full and our cheeks sore with smiles in Jackson (as well as her amazing mama); Tracy Beal, who guided us through these communities with an easy, informative flair; and Gary, whose home, in the shadow of a former residence of a Mississippi Sovereignty Commission founder, was our refuge.

A salute through the universal plane goes to the late Manning Marable, who collaborated with Ms. Myrlie to compile a phenomenal catalog of Medgar's letters, NAACP field reports, and documentation of his brief but powerful life journey, as well as to the late John Salter, James Baldwin, Lena Horne, Dick Gregory, Charles Evers, and Tom Dent, whose insights I scoured the archival universe for and who were such an important part of Medgar and Myrlie's story. And in this earthly plane: Dr. Bernice King, Minyon Moore, Bishop William Barber, Latosha Brown, former Maryland state senator Michael Bowen

Mitchell, Rev. Mark Thompson, Joe Madison (the Black Eagle), Derrick Johnson, and Ben Jealous of the NAACP.

And now to my book team: the amazing Henrys—Henry Ferris, my indispensable and indefatigable editor, three books and counting, who makes my lengthy thoughts concise, and sidelines as my cheerleader, collaborator, and coach; and Henry Reisch, who does triple duty as my agent, big brother, and friend. And in the pantheon of great and good people, my literary agent, Suzanne Gluck, stands as tall as she is diminutive in real life. Thank you always for making a path for me. And Mariner Books' Peter Hubbard, I cannot thank you enough for believing in what I can do and for giving me the space and grace to do it.

I close with endless thanks to my best friend, documentary film collaborator, coparent, and amazing husband, Jason Mark Anthony Reid—who has been on this journey with me for three decades running—and who played a vital role in this ongoing mission to bring new life to the Evers story, including documenting on video the key interviews for this book. And to the sources of my joy: Winsome, Jmar, and Miles Reid, thank you for keeping me smiling, laughing, and posting silly things to the family group thread through every trial and turn. I love my family and they are my light.

I dedicated this book to Prudence Gibbs Gilbert, otherwise known as my sweet Auntie Dolly, because she is the person who loved romantically with the greatest fearlessness and ferocity of any of the women I know. And like Miss Myrlie, she endured the loss of great love twice. And in my siblings' darkest hour, when we lost our beloved mom, her big sister, she opened her home to three young people in desperate need of the shelter of love. I love you madly, Auntie Dolly.

And last, I send up thanks and praises into the eternal universe to Medgar Wiley Evers. Thank you for fighting for our freedom, for loving your family, your country, your state, and your people unapologetically, and for showing us how to do the same. Thank you for *being*.

Notes

PROLOGUE: LOVE

1. Medgar Evers, as told to Francis H. Mitchell, "Why I Live in Mississippi," *Ebony*, November 1958, 65–70.
2. W. J. Weatherby, *James Baldwin: Artist on Fire: A Portrait* (New York: Donald I. Fine, 1989), 3.
3. Associated Press, "Violence Feared; Murder Rifle Is Found," *Record* (Hackensack, NJ), June 13, 1963, https://www.newspapers.com/image/491097683.
4. Ibid.
5. Associated Press, "Jack Appalled by Barbarity, *Springfield Leader Press*, June 13, 1963, https://newspapers.com/image/299347227.
6. Associated Press, "Ike, JFK Discuss Race Rift, Kennedy 'Appalled' at Evers Killing," *Miami Herald*, June 13, 1963, https://newspapers.com/image/619610635.
7. AP, "Jack Appalled by Barbarity."
8. McKenzie Jean-Philippe and Jane Burnett, "30 Civil Rights Leaders of the Past and Present: We'll Feel Their Impact for Generations to Come," *Oprah Daily*, February 8, 2023, https://www.oprahdaily.com/entertainment/g35181270/civil-rights-leaders.

CHAPTER 1: MISSISSIPPI *GODDAMN* . . .

1. Tom Dent, "Portrait of Three Heroes," *Freedomways*, Second Quarter, 1965, https://www.crmvet.org/info/65_dent_3heroes.pdf.
2. Author interviews with Myrlie Evers, 2021. They were based on what she heard from Medgar's brother, mother, and friends over the years.
3. Medgar Evers, as told to Francis H. Mitchell, "Why I Live in Mississippi," *Ebony*, November 1958, 65–69.
4. Ibid.
5. Oral history interviews, "Behind the Veil: Documenting African-American Life in the Jim Crow South," Duke University, John Hope Franklin Research Center, records 1940–1997 and undated, bulk 1993–1997; Jack Young interview, 19–20.
6. "World War II: D-Day, The Invasion of Normandy," National Archives, Dwight D. Eisenhower Presidential Library, Museum & Boyhood Home, https://www

.eisenhowerlibrary.gov/research/online-documents/world-war-ii-d-day-invasion-normandy.

7. Jordan Ginder, "Biographies: Medgar W. Evers," National Museum United States Army, February 5, 2023, https://www.thenmusa.org/biographies/medgar-w-evers.
8. Charles Evers and Andrew Szanton, *Have No Fear: The Charles Evers Story* (New York: John Wiley and Sons, 1997), 47.
9. Ibid., 48.
10. James Campbell, "Black American in Paris," *Nation,* September 9, 2004, https://www.thenation.com/article/archive/black-american-paris.
11. C. Evers and Szanton, *Have No Fear,* 6.
12. M. Evers and Mitchell, "Why I Live in Mississippi," 65–70.
13. Myrlie Evers-Williams and Manning Marable, *The Autobiography of Medgar Evers: A Hero's Life and Legacy Revealed Through His Writings, Letters, and Speeches* (New York: Basic Civitas Books, 2005), 367.
14. M. Evers and Mitchell, "Why I Live In Mississippi," 65–70.
15. C. Evers and Szanton, *Have No Fear,* 3.
16. Jack Mendelsohn, *The Martyrs: Sixteen Who Gave Their Lives for Racial Justice* (New York: Harper and Row, 1966), 64.
17. Ibid., 64–65.
18. Ibid., 64.
19. C. Evers and Szanton, *Have No Fear,* 6.
20. Ibid.
21. Ibid., 24.
22. Ibid.
23. Ibid.
24. Ibid., 8.
25. Mendelsohn, *Martyrs,* 64–65.
26. C. Evers and Szanton, *Have No Fear,* 40.
27. Ibid., 11–12.
28. Eric Norden, "The Playboy Interview with Charles Evers," *Playboy* (website), October 1, 1971, https://www.playboy.com/read/the-playboy-interview-with-charles-evers.
29. Ibid.
30. 1965 U.S. Civil Rights Commission report on voting in Mississippi, https://www2.law.umaryland.edu/marshall/usccr/documents/cr12v94.pdf.
31. U.S. Census Bureau, Historical Census Statistics on Population Totals by Race Table 39 Mississippi—Race and Hispanic Origin: 1800–1990, 67, https://www.census.gov/content/dam/Census/library/working-papers/2002/demo/POP-twps0056.pdf.
32. Ibid.
33. BlackPast historical online archive, https://www.blackpast.org/african-american-history/digital-archives.
34. Matthew S. Shapanka, "White Primary," Mississippi Encyclopedia, Center for Study of Southern Culture, http://mississippiencyclopedia.org/entries/white-primary (published July 11, 2017, last updated April 15, 2018, accessed February 5, 2023).
35. C. Evers and Szanton, *Have No Fear,* 29.
36. Ibid., 30–31.

37. Ibid.
38. Ibid.
39. Ibid.
40. Ibid.
41. Ibid.
42. "Mississippians Vote Despite Bilbo Threats," *Jackson Advocate,* July 6, 1946, https://www.newspapers.com/image/748320428.
43. "The South: Present Laughter," *Time,* December 16, 1946, https://content.time.com/time/subscriber/article/0,33009,934699,00.html.
44. "Fair Weather for Tuesday Voting Is Late Forecast," *Clarion-Ledger* (Jackson, MS), July 2, 1946, https://www.newspapers.com/image/202693740.
45. Ibid.
46. C. Evers and Szanton, *Have No Fear,* 60.
47. Ibid., 61.
48. M. Evers and Mitchell, "Why I Live in Mississippi," 65.
49. C. Evers and Szanton, *Have No Fear,* 61.
50. Ibid.
51. Ibid.
52. Ibid., 62.
53. Ibid., 58–64.
54. Juan Williams, "Men Changed by War Fight to Be Equals," *Washington Post,* July 26, 1995, https://www.washingtonpost.com/archive/politics/1995/07/26/men-changed-by-war-fight-to-be-equals/ff719d33-91ab-4420-a88c-a038a33bcfc6.
55. C. Evers and Szanton, *Have No Fear,* 64.
56. "New Bilbo Probe Looms as Negro Protests Location," *Clarion-Ledger* (Jackson, MS), November 18, 1946, https://www.newspapers.com/image/202713645.
57. "The South: Present Laughter."
58. National Parks Service, "Medgar Wiley Evers," https://www.nps.gov/memy/learn/historyculture/medgar-evers.htm.
59. C. Evers and Szanton, *Have No Fear,* 57.

CHAPTER 2: MEDGAR AND MYRLIE

1. Myrlie Evers-Williams and Melinda Blau, *Watch Me Fly: What I Learned on the Way to Becoming the Woman I Was Meant to Be* (Boston: Little, Brown, 1999), 52.
2. Author interviews with Myrlie Evers-Williams, 2021.
3. Evers-Williams and Blau, *Watch Me Fly,* 52.
4. Ibid., 23–24.
5. Ibid., 53.
6. Ibid., 54.
7. Ibid., 33.
8. Charles Evers and Andrew Szanton, *Have No Fear: The Charles Evers Story* (New York: John Wiley and Sons, 1997), 69.
9. Evers-Williams and Blau, *Watch Me Fly,* 57.
10. Author interviews with Myrlie Evers-Williams, 2021.
11. Bilal G. Morris, "The Legend of Ben Montgomery: From Enslaved Man to One of the Richest Merchants in the South," *NewsOne,* June 13, 2022, https://newsone.com/4354023/ben-montgomery-davis-bend.

12. Milburn Crowe, John Martin, and Luther Brown, "The Mound Bayou Story," The Delta Center for Culture and Learning, Delta State University (Cleveland, MS), revised 2019 by Linda and David Beito, https://www.earlyblues.com/Mound_Bayou_Story_1-compressed.pdf; Melissa Block and Elissa Nadworny, "Here's What's Become of a Historic All-Black Town in the Mississippi Delta," March 8, 2017, WUBR, NPR News, https://www.wbur.org/npr/515814287/heres-whats-become-of-a-historic-all-black-town-in-the-mississippi-delta.
13. Brian Gann, "T. R. M. Howard (1908–1976)," June 19, 2011, BlackPast.org, https://www.blackpast.org/african-amercican-history/howard-t-r-m-1908-1976.
14. Dr. T. R. M. Howard Papers, 1929–1976, Chicago Public Library, https://www.chipublib.org/fa-t-r-m-howard-papers.
15. David T. Beito and Linda Royster Beito, "An Unlikely, Unsung Civil Rights Champion," *Los Angeles Times,* August 28, 2009, https://www.latimes.com/archives/la-xpm-2009-aug-28-oe-beito28-story.html.
16. Interviews with Mound Bayou historians Mickey Johns and Darrell Johns.
17. Dr. T. R. M. Howard Papers, 1929–1976, Chicago Public Library.
18. Author interviews with Myrlie Evers-Williams, 2021.
19. Evers-Williams and Blau, *Watch Me Fly,* 61.
20. Myrlie Evers-Williams and Manning Marable, *The Autobiography of Medgar Evers: A Hero's Life and Legacy Revealed Through His Writings, Letters and Speeches* (New York: Basic Civitas Books, 2005), 20.
21. Author interviews with Myrlie Evers Williams, 2021.
22. Evers-Williams and Blau, *Watch Me Fly,* 58.
23. Ibid., 59.
24. Ibid.
25. Author interviews with Myrlie Evers-Williams, 2021.
26. Ibid.
27. Evers-Williams and Blau, *Watch Me Fly,* 59-60.

CHAPTER 3: EMMETT TILL

1. Jack Mendelsohn, *The Martyrs: Sixteen Who Gave Their Lives for Racial Justice* (New York: Harper and Row, 1966), 67.
2. "State NAACP Officer Conference Listed," *Jackson Advocate,* February 9, 1954, https://www.newspapers.com/image/835011623.
3. Charles Evers and Andrew Szanton, *Have No Fear: The Charles Evers Story* (New York: John Wiley and Sons, 1997), 77–78.
4. Ibid.
5. Author interviews with Myrlie Evers-Williams, 2021.
6. C. Evers and Szanton, *Have No Fear,* 77.
7. Valerie Wells, "News Wars: The Rise and Fall of the *Clarion-Ledger," Jackson Free Press,* September 7, 2011, https://www.jacksonfreepress.com/news/2011/sep/07/news-wars-the-rise-and-fall-of-the-clarion-ledger.
8. David G. Sansing, "Hugh Lawson White," Mississippi Encyclopedia, Center for Study of Southern Culture (published July 11, 2017, last updated April 15, 2018, accessed February 5, 2023), http://mississippiencyclopedia.org/entries/hugh-white-lawson.

9. "Bi-Racial Board Urged by Negroes," *Clarion-Ledger* (Jackson, MS), July 26, 1954, https://www.newspapers.com/image/185234029.
10. Charles Bolton, "*Brown v. Board of Education*," Mississippi Encyclopedia, Center for Study of Southern Culture (published July 10, 2017, last updated February 24, 2020), https://mississippiencyclopedia.org/entries/brown-v-board-of-education.
11. Myrlie Evers with William Peters, *For Us, the Living* (Garden City, NY: Doubleday, 1967), 118.
12. Myrlie Evers-Williams and Manning Marable, *The Autobiography of Medgar Evers: A Hero's Life and Legacy Revealed Through His Writings, Letters and Speeches* (New York: Basic Civitas Books, 2005), 14.
13. Ibid., 17–20.
14. Ibid.
15. Ibid.
16. Federal Bureau of Investigation, *Prosecutive Report of Investigation Concerning [the Lynching of Emmett Till]*, February 9, 2006, https://vault.fbi.gov/Emmett%20 Till%20.
17. M. Evers with Peters, *For Us, the Living*, 120.
18. Ibid., 122.
19. Ibid., 131–32.
20. Ibid, 132.
21. David T. Beito and Linda Royster Beito, "The Grim and Overlooked Anniversary of the Murder of the Rev. George W. Lee, Civil Rights Activist," George Washington University, Columbian College of Arts and Sciences, History News Network, https://historynewsnetwork.org/article/11744.
22. Ibid.
23. Ibid.
24. Author interview with Rev. Amos Brown, April 2023.
25. Ibid.
26. *American Experience: The Great Migration; From Mississippi to Chicago*, season 15, episode 6, "The Murder of Emmett Till," directed by Stanley Nelson, written by Marcia Smith and David C. Taylor, featuring Andre Braugher, Pat Antici, and Oudie Brown, aired January 20, 2003, on PBS, https://www.pbs.org/wgbh/american experience/films/till/#part01.
27. Ellen Barry, "Rumor of a Key Witness," *Los Angeles Times*, July 30, 2005, https://www.latimes.com/archives/la-xpm-2005-jul-30-na-johnny30-story.html.
28. Linda Royster Beito and David T. Beito, "Emmett Till, a New Investigation, and Vindication of T. R. M. Howard," Independent Institute, August 13, 2018, https://www.independent.org/news/article.asp?id=1047.
29. Sam Roberts, "Simeon Wright, Witness to Abduction of Emmett Till, Dies at 74," *New York Times*, September 6, 2017, https://www.nytimes.com/2017/09/06 /obituaries/simeon-wright-witness-to-abduction-of-emmett-till-dies-at-74.htm.
30. Federal Bureau of Investigation, *Prosecutive Report of Investigation*.
31. Author interview with Mayor Johnny B. Thomas, 2022.
32. Roberts, "Simeon Wright."
33. *American Experience*, "The Murder of Emmett Till."
34. Dave Tell, "Robert's Temple Church of God in Christ," Emmett Till Memory Project, https://tillapp.emmett-till.org/items/show/20.

35. Evers-Williams and Marable, *Autobiography of Medgar Evers*, 34–35.
36. C. Evers and Szanton, *Have No Fear*, 86–87.
37. L. R. Beito and D. T. Beito, “Emmett Till, a New Investigation.”
38. Transcripts of testimony in the trial of Roy Milam and J. W. Milam, September 19–23, 1955, https://diginole.lib.fsu.edu/islandora/object/fsu%3A390158.
39. From interview with Mayor Johnny B. Thomas, 2022.
40. “Charleston Sheriff Says Body in River Wasn’t Young Till,” *Memphis Commercial Appeal*, September 4, 1955, https://www.newspapers.com/image/769909130.
41. *American Experience*, “Murder of Emmett Till.”
42. L. R. Beito and D. T. Beito, “Emmett Till, a New Investigation.”
43. John Edgar Wideman, “A Black and White Case,” *Esquire* (website), October 19, 2016, https://www.esquire.com/news-politics/a48989/black-and-white-case.
44. Martin Luther King Jr., “Recommendations to the Dexter Avenue Baptist Church for the Fiscal Year 1954–1955,” Dexter Avenue Baptist Church, Montgomery, Alabama, September 5, 1954, Stanford University, The Martin Luther King Jr. Research and Education Institute, King Papers, Bin 2, 290.
45. Evers-Williams and Marable, *Autobiography of Medgar Evers*, 67–69.
46. Federal Bureau of Investigation, *Prosecutive Report of Investigation*.
47. Evers-Williams and Marable, *Autobiography of Medgar Evers*, 21–27.
48. C. Evers and Szanton, *Have No Fear*, 95–96.
49. Michael Newton, *The Ku Klux Klan in Mississippi: A History* (Jefferson, NC: McFarland, 2010), 113.
50. Author interview with Myrlie Evers-Williams, 2021.

CHAPTER 4: THE HOUSE ON GUYNES STREET

1. Myrlie Evers-Williams and Melinda Blau, *Watch Me Fly: What I Learned on the Way to Becoming the Woman I Was Meant to Be* (Boston: Little, Brown, 1999), 64.
2. Fifty-six dollars in 1956 would be the equivalent of about $610 today.
3. Myrlie Evers with William Peters, *For Us, the Living* (Garden City, NY: Doubleday, 1967), 136–37.
4. Ibid., 131.
5. Ibid., 64.
6. Evers-Williams and Blau, *Watch Me Fly*, 66.
7. Ibid., 67.
8. Author interviews with Myrlie Evers-Williams, 2021.
9. Ibid.
10. Ibid.
11. Author interviews with Ms. Grace Britton-Sweet, March 2021.
12. Myrlie Evers-Williams and Manning Marable, *The Autobiography of Medgar Evers: A Hero’s Life and Legacy Revealed Through His Writings, Letters and Speeches* (New York: Basic Civitas Books, 2005), 54–55.
13. Ibid.
14. Medgar Evers, telegram to President Dwight D. Eisenhower, dated October 25, 1956. Quoted in Evers-Williams and Marable, *Autobiography of Medgar Evers*, 58–59.
15. Evers-Williams and Marable, *Autobiography of Medgar Evers*, 58–59.
16. Medgar Evers, “1955 Annual Report: Mississippi State Office, National Association for the Advancement of Colored People.”

17. Ibid.
18. Evers-Williams and Marable, *Autobiography of Medgar Evers*, 64.
19. Ibid., 73–74.
20. Medgar Evers, as told to Francis H. Mitchell, "Why I Live in Mississippi," *Ebony*, November 1958.
21. Ibid.
22. Ibid.
23. Ibid.
24. Darrell Evers interviewed by Orlando Bagwell, April 3, 1986, in *Eyes on the Prize: America's Civil Rights Years, 1954–1965*, Film and Media Archive, Washington University in St. Louis, American Archive of Public Broadcasting (GBH and the Library of Congress), Boston and Washington, D.C., http://americanarchive.org/catalog/cpb-aacip-151-cv4bn9xv7m.
25. Rep. Bennie Thompson, interview, in *Spies of Mississippi*, directed by Dawn Porter, PBS, February 10, 2014, https://www.pbs.org/independentlens/documentaries/spies-of-mississippi.
26. John Herbers, "Moderate Stand Give Negro Leaders Humes, Green Hot Time," *Delta Democrat-Times*, July 28, 1957, https://www.newspapers.com/image/22364680.
27. Associated Press, "Sovereignty Commission Records Show Owner of Black Newspaper Worked for Group," July 30, 1989, https://web.archive.org/web/20230623051312/https://apnews.com/article/2a4fd050a3da9757dd79536c94fe228f.
28. "Lisa K. Speer, Mississippi Encyclopedia, Center for Study of Southern Culture (published July 11, 2017, last updated April 14, 2018, accessed February 5, 2023), http://mississippiencyclopedia.org/entries/percy-greene.
29. Editorial, *Mississippi Free Press* archives, Vol. 1, No. 1, December 16, 1961, https://www.crmvet.org/docs/mfp/611216_mfp.pdf.
30. Ibid.
31. Carol Nunnelley, "Hazel Brannon Smith," Encyclopedia of Alabama (published November 4, 2008, last updated March 27, 2023), http://encyclopediaofalabama.org/article/h-1826.
32. Author interview with Rev. Ed King, 2021.
33. Carol Dalton Lyon, "Rev. Edwin King," Mississippi Encyclopedia, Center for Study of Southern Culture, https://mississippiencyclopedia.org/entries/ed-king.
34. Evers-Williams and Marable, *Autobiography of Medgar Evers*, 163.
35. Ibid., 199.
36. Mathew J. Mancini, "Pig Law," Mississippi Encyclopedia, Center for Study of Southern Culture (published July 11, 2017, last updated April 14, 2014), https://mississippiencyclopedia.org/entries/pig-law.
37. Evers-Williams and Marable, *Autobiography of Medgar Evers*, 201.
38. Ibid., 107–8.
39. Ibid., 202–3.
40. Ibid., 204.
41. Ibid., 202–11.
42. Author interview with Frank Figgers, Jackson, Mississippi, 2021.
43. Author interview with Derrick Johnson of the national NAACP, April 2023.
44. In 1946, the U.S. Supreme Court ruled in *Morgan v. Virginia* that segregation in interstate transportation was unconstitutional. This was followed in 1960 by the

Court's ruling in *Boynton v. Virginia* that segregation in the facilities provided for interstate travelers, including bus terminals, restrooms, and restaurants, was also unconstitutional. Morgan v. Virginia, 328 U.S. 373 (1946); Boynton v. Virginia, 364 U.S. 454 (1960).

CHAPTER 5: MISSISSIPPI FREEDOM

1. Author interviews with James Meredith, 2021.
2. Myrlie Evers-Williams and Manning Marable, *The Autobiography of Medgar Evers: A Hero's Life and Legacy Revealed Through His Writings, Letters and Speeches* (New York: Basic Civitas Books, 2005), 127.
3. Author interview with James Meredith Jackson, Mississippi, 2021.
4. "Early Year Rumors Prove to Be Correct," *Star-Herald* (Kosciusko, MS), June 8, 1961, https://www.newspapers.com/image/274134389.
5. BlackPast, historical online archive, https://www.blackpast.org; Evers-Williams and Marable, *Autobiography of Medgar Evers,* 228.
6. Ibid.
7. Ibid.
8. Sophia Gardner, Brie Thompson-Bristol, and Kathy Roberts Forde, "How the Tougaloo Nine Transformed History," *Washington Post,* May 23, 2021, https://www.washingtonpost.com/outlook/2021/05/23/how-tougaloo-nine-transformed-history.
9. Rev. Edwin King, interview, in "Behind the Veil: Documenting African-American Life in the Jim Crow South," Duke University, John Hope Franklin Research Center, records 1940–1997 and undated, bulk 1993–1997.
10. Evers-Williams and Marable, *Autobiography of Medgar Evers,* 228.
11. Ibid.
12. Edmund Noel, "Nine Jailed in 'Study In,'" *Clarion-Ledger* (Jackson, MS), March 28, 1961, https://www.newspapers.com/image/180073038.
13. Gardner, Thompson-Bristol, and Forde, "How the Tougaloo Nine Transformed History," https://www.washingtonpost.com/outlook/2021/05/23/how-tougaloo-nine-transformed-history.
14. Author interviews with Myrlie Evers-Williams, 2021.
15. Myrlie Evers-Williams and Melinda Blau, *Watch Me Fly: What I Learned on the Way to Becoming the Woman I Was Meant to Be* (New York: Little, Brown, 1999), 69.
16. Ibid.
17. Ibid.
18. Ibid., 68–71.
19. Ibid., 70–71.
20. Author interviews with Myrlie Evers-Williams, 2021.
21. "John Michael Doar," University of Mississippi, UM History of Integration, https://50years.olemiss.edu/2012/07/18/john-michael-doar.
22. FBI Files, Medgar Evers. Part 4 of 5, https://vault.fbi.gov/Medgar%20Evers.
23. FBI Files, Medgar Evers. Part 3 of 5, https://vault.fbi.gov/Medgar%20Evers.
24. "Mississippi Shocks Entire Nation," *Arizona Sun,* April 6, 1961, https://www.newspapers.com/image/847353021.
25. "NAACP Operation Mississippi Gets Off to Fast Start Here," *Jackson Advocate,* April 29, 1961, https://www.newspapers.com/image/835023028.

26. "Police Dogs Incidents Puts City in Spotlight," *Jackson Advocate,* April 8, 1961, https://www.newspapers.com/image/835022881.
27. Ibid.
28. Evers-Williams and Marable, *Autobiography of Medgar Evers,* 229.
29. Ibid.
30. Ibid., 225–26.
31. Ibid.
32. Ibid., 226.
33. Raymond Arsenault, *Freedom Riders: 1961 and the Struggle for Racial Justice* (Oxford, UK: Oxford University Press, 2006), 535.
34. *American Experience,* season 23, episode 13, "Meet the Players: Freedom Riders," directed and written by Stanley Nelson, aired May 16, 2011, on PBS, https://www.pbs.org/wgbh/americanexperience/features/meet-players-freedom-riders.
35. Ibid.
36. Ibid.
37. Evers-Williams and Marable, *Autobiography of Medgar Evers,* 160–61.
38. Author interviews with Bernard Lafayette Jr., 2021.
39. Associated Press, "Stay in Non-Violence Workshop to Cleanse Self for Goal Ahead," *Greenwood Commonwealth,* May 23, 1961, https://www.newspapers.com/image/256012497.
40. "Ross R. Barnett, "Oral History Interview—5/6/1969," interview by Dennis O'Brien, May 6, 1969, John F. Kennedy Presidential Library and Museum, John F. Kennedy Library Oral History Program, https://www.jfklibrary.org/asset-viewer/archives/JFKOH/Barnett%2C%20Ross%20R/JFKOH-RRB-01/JFKOH-RRB-.
41. Marian Smith Holmes, "The Freedom Riders, Then and Now," *Smithsonian Magazine,* February 2009, https://www.smithsonianmag.com/history/the-freedom-riders-then-and-now-45351758.
42. Bernard LaFayette Jr. and Kathryn Lee Johnson, *In Peace and Freedom: My Journey to Selma* (Lexington: University Press of Kentucky, 2013), 38.
43. Author interview with Fred Douglas Moore Clark Sr., 2021.
44. Author interview with Hezekiah Watkins, 2021.
45. Arsenault, *Freedom Riders,* 535–86.
46. Evers-Williams and Marable, *Autobiography of Medgar Evers,* 233.
47. Ibid.
48. Roy Wilkins, letter to Harris Wofford, April 5, 1961, Papers of John F. Kennedy, Presidential Papers, White House Staff Files of Harris Wofford, Alphabetical Files, 1956–1962, Roy Wilkins, December 1, 1960–March 15, 1962, https://www.jfklibrary.org/learn/education/leaders-in-the-struggle-for-civil-rights/roy-wilkins.
49. Evers-Williams and Marable, *Autobiography of Medgar Evers,* 233.
50. Telephone Recordings: Dictation Belt 22B, John F. Kennedy Presidential Library and Museum, Papers of John F. Kennedy, Presidential Papers, President's Office Files, https://www. jfklibrary.org/asset-viewer/archives/JFKPOF/TPH/JFKPOF-TPH-22A-4/JFKPOF-TPH-22A-4, and Part 2, https://www.jfklibrary.org/asset-viewer/archives/JFKPOF/TPH/JFKPOF-TPH-22B-1/JFKPOF-TPH-22B-1.
51. Ibid.
52. Evers-Williams and Marable, *Autobiography of Medgar Evers,* 233.
53. Ibid.
54. Ibid., 238.

55. Ibid., 236.
56. Ibid.
57. Marian Wright Edelman, "The Courage and Vision of Medgar Evers," *Huffington Post,* February 8, 2013, https://www.huffpost.com/entry/the-courage-and-vision-of_b_2649092.
58. Evers-Williams and Marable, *Autobiography of Medgar Evers,* 237–39.
59. Ibid.
60. "NAACP Files Suit to Desegregate Recreational Facilities in Jackson," *Mississippi Free Press,* Vol. 1, No. 6, January 20, 1962, https://www.crmvet.org/docs/mfp/620120_mfp.pdf.
61. Evers-Williams and Marable, *Autobiography of Medgar Evers,* 243.
62. Myrlie Evers with William Peters, *For Us, the Living* (Garden City, NY: Doubleday, 1967), 255.
63. Ibid., 254.
64. Author interview with Frank Figgers.
65. Jerry Mitchell, interview, in *Spies of Mississippi,* directed by Dawn Porter, PBS, February 10, 2014.
66. Rick Bowers, interview, in *Spies of Mississippi.*

CHAPTER 6: FREEDOM FROM FEAR

1. "Ole Miss Will Integrate in July: NAACP Attorneys Gain 2–1 Decision. Meredith to Begin with Summer Session," *Mississippi Free Press,* June 30, 1962, https://www.crmvet.org/docs/mfp/620630_mfp.pdf.
2. Charles Evers and Andrew Szanton, *Have No Fear: The Charles Evers Story* (New York: John Wiley and Sons, 1997), 117.
3. John R. Salter, Jr. (Hunter Gray), "Remembering Medgar Evers," *Against the Current,* no. 165, July–August 2013, https://againstthecurrent.org/atc165/p3935.
4. Ibid.
5. Myrlie Evers with William Peters, *For Us, the Living* (Garden City, NY: Doubleday, 1967), 242.
6. Ibid., 242–44.
7. Ibid.
8. Ibid.
9. Meredith Coleman McGhee, *James Meredith: Warrior and the America That Created Him* (Jackson, MS: Meredith Etc., 2013), 100–102.
10. Telephone Recordings: Dictation Belt 4C.1 (portion of telephone conversation between President Kennedy, Attorney General Kennedy, and Governor Barnett, September 28 or 29, 1962), John F. Kennedy Presidential Library and Museum, Papers of John F. Kennedy, Presidential Papers, President's Office Files, https://www.jfklibrary.org/asset-viewer/archives/JFKPOF/TPH/JFKPOF-TPH-04A-1/JFKPOF-TPH-04A-1.
11. M. Evers with Peters, *For Us, the Living,* 244–45.
12. Ibid.
13. "Two Killed in Outbreak of Bias Riots at Ole Miss," *Courier-Post,* October 1, 1962, https://www.newspapers.com/image/180764234.
14. Tom Dent, "Portrait of Three Heroes," *Freedomways* (September 1965), https://www.crmvet.org/info/65_dent_3heroes.pdf.

15. "About James Meredith," University of Mississippi, UM History of Integration, https://50years.olemiss.edu/james-meredith.
16. Ibid.
17. McGhee, *James Meredith: Warrior*, 77.
18. "Meredith Case Gets Publicity," *Star-Herald* (Kosciusko, MS), December 20, 1962, https://www.newspapers.com/image/274717943.
19. McGhee, *James Meredith: Warrior*, 77.
20. C. Evers and Szanton, *Have No Fear*, 116.
21. Nia Decaille, "Dorothy Gilliam Confronted Racism and Sexism as the First Black Female Reporter at the *Washington Post*," *Washington Post*, March 7, 2019, https://www.washingtonpost.com/nation/2019/03/08/double-handicap-dorothy-gilliam-being-first-black-female-reporter-washington-post.
22. Author interviews with Myrlie Evers-Williams, 2021.
23. M. Evers with Peters, *For Us, the Living*, 228.
24. Darrell Evers, interviewed by Orlando Bagwell, April 3, 1986, in *Eyes on the Prize: America's Civil Rights Years, 1954–1965*, Film and Media Archive, Washington University in St. Louis, American Archive of Public Broadcasting (GBH and the Library of Congress), Boston and Washington, D.C., http://americanarchive.org/catalog/cpb-aacip-151-cv4bn9xv7m.
25. "Petition to Integrate Schools—Parents Want Equal Education for Children. 15 Students Also Sign; Enthusiasm High," *Mississippi Free Press*, Vol. 1, No. 36, August 18, 1962, https://www.crmvet.org/docs/mfp/620818_mfp.pdf.
26. Ibid.
27. M. Evers with Peters, *For Us, the Living*, 249–50.
28. Ibid., 250.
29. United Press International, "Mississippi Negroes Urged to Boycott State Fair," *New York Times*, October 11, 1962, 30, https://timesmachine.nytimes.com/timesmachine/1962/10/11/94303185.html?pageNumber=30.
30. "Black Students, Community, Allies Begin Desegregating Jackson, Mississippi, 1962–1963," Swarthmore College, Global Nonviolent Action Database, https://nvdatabase.swarthmore.edu/content/black-students-community-allies-begin-desegregating-jackson-mississippi-1962-1963.
31. Myrlie Evers-Williams and Manning Marable, *The Autobiography of Medgar Evers: A Hero's Life and Legacy Revealed Through His Writings, Letters and Speeches* (New York: Basic Civitas Books, 2005), 264.
32. Ibid., 265.
33. James Baldwin, forward to *Blues for Mister Charlie* (New York: Dell, 1964), 7.
34. Dent, "Portrait of Three Heroes."
35. Evers-Williams and Marable, *Autobiography of Medgar Evers*, 273.
36. Ibid.
37. M. Evers with Peters, *For Us, the Living*, 224–25.
38. "James Meredith Goes to College—Another Negro Went to Prison," *The New Republic*, reprinted in the *Vancouver Sun*, November 15, 1962, https://www.newspapers.com/image/491684358.
39. Ibid.
40. Evers-Williams and Marable, *Autobiography of Medgar Evers*, 273.
41. "Kennard Is Free," *Mississippi Free Press*, Vol. 2, No. 8, February 2, 1963, https://www.crmvet.org/docs/mfp/630202_mfp.pdf.

42. Ibid.
43. "Barnett Orders Negro's Release," *Pensacola News,* January 29, 1963, 6, https://www.newspapers.com/image/263473373.
44. Larry Still, "Cancer-Stricken Miss. Prisoner Fights for Home State Education," *Jet,* January 24, 1963, 20–23.
45. Dent, "Portrait of Three Heroes."
46. Evers-Williams and Marable, *Autobiography of Medgar Evers,* 270.
47. Ibid.
48. Dent, "Portrait of Three Heroes."
49. "Kennard Is Free," *Mississippi Free Press,* Vol. 2, No. 8, February 2, 1963, https://www.crmvet.org/docs/mfp/630202_mfp.pdf.
50. "Greene's Ole Miss Bid Goes to Court," *Mississippi Free Press,* Vol. 2, No. 9, February 9, 1963, https://www.crmvet.org/docs/ mfp/630209_mfp.pdf.
51. "Courts to Be Asked to Open P. S. Here," *Mississippi Free Press,* March 2, 1963.
52. M. Evers with Peters, *For Us, the Living,* 245.
53. Adele Norris, "Anne Moody's Coming of Age in Mississippi: Seeing Anne's Struggles as Our Own," July 10, 2020, African American Intellectual History Society, Black Perspectives, https://www.aaihs.org/anne-moodys-coming-of-age-in-mississippi-seeing-annes-struggles-as-our-own.
54. "Local Jaycees Pledge Support to Thompson," *Clarion-Ledger* (Jackson, MS), May 21, 1963, https://www.newspapers.com/image/185692469.
55. M. Evers with Peters, *For Us, the Living,* 256–57.
56. Ibid.
57. Black students, community, allies begin desegregating Jackson, Mississippi, 1962–1963, Global Nonviolent Action Database. Swarthmore College, https://nvdatabase.swarthmore.edu/content/black-students-community-allies-begin-desegregating-jackson-mississippi-1962-1963.
58. M. Evers with Peters, *For Us, the Living,* 259.
59. Author interview with Rev. Ed King, 2021.
60. Ibid.
61. M. Evers with Peters, *For Us, the Living,* 259.
62. Hunter Gray, "Cracking a Closed Society," *Against the Current,* no. 98, May–June 2002, https://againstthecurrent.org/atc098/p1264.
63. M. Evers with Peters, *For Us, the Living,* 258–61.
64. "Rights Group Demands End to Bias; Mayor Say All Is Fine," *Mississippi Free Press,* May 18, 1963, https://www.crmvet.org/docs/mfp/630518_mfp.pdf.
65. M. Evers with Peters, *For Us, the Living,* 266–67.
66. Evers-Williams and Marable, *Autobiography of Medgar Evers,* 280–83.
67. Ibid.
68. Ibid.
69. Ibid.
70. M. Evers with Peters, *For Us, the Living,* 268–69.

CHAPTER 7: COUNTDOWN

1. "Rights Group Demands End to Bias; Mayor Say All Is Fine," *Mississippi Free Press,* May 18, 1963, https://www.crmvet.org/docs/mfp/630518_mfp.pdf.

2. Myrlie Evers with William Peters, *For Us, the Living* (Garden City, NY: Doubleday, 1967), 270–71.
3. Joe Holley, "Memphis Norman Dies," *Washington Post,* January 28, 2005, https://www.washingtonpost.com/archive/local/2005/01/28/memphis-norman-dies/6b7b656b-3bd5-4939-b1a9-8f3cd1e603a4.
4. Adele Norris, "Anne Moody's Coming of Age in Mississippi: Seeing Anne's Struggles as Our Own," July 10, 2020, African American Intellectual History Society, Black Perspectives, https://www.aaihs.org/anne-moodys-coming-of-age-in-mississippi-seeing-annes-struggles-as-our-own.
5. Hunter Gray, as told to Erica Buist, "That's Me in the Picture: Hunter Gray Is Attacked at a Civil Rights Protest in Jackson, Mississippi, 28 May 1963," *Guardian,* March 27, 2015, https://www.theguardian.com/artanddesign/2015/mar/27/hunter-gray-1963-jackson-mississippi-sit-in.
6. Darrell Evers, interviewed by Orlando Bagwell, April 3, 1986, in *Eyes on the Prize: America's Civil Rights Years, 1954–1965,* Film and Media Archive, Washington University in St. Louis, American Archive of Public Broadcasting (GBH and the Library of Congress), Boston and Washington, D.C., http://americanarchive.org/catalog/cpb-aacip-151-cv4bn9xv7m.
7. Myrlie Evers-Williams and Manning Marable, *The Autobiography of Medgar Evers: A Hero's Life and Legacy Revealed Through His Writings, Letters and Speeches* (New York: Basic Civitas Books, 2005), 260.
8. Associated Press, "Another Negro Wins Ole Miss Admission," *Clarion-Ledger* (Jackson, MS), May 29, 1963, https://www.newspapers.com/image/185717254.
9. Andrew Szanton, "Cleve McDowell, Civil Rights Man," Medium, January 17, 2022, https://medium.com/@andrewszanton/cleve-mcdowell-civil-rights-man-b9ae8b43bb47.
10. M. Evers with Peters, *For Us, the Living,* 273–77.
11. Ibid.
12. Charles Evers and Andrew Szanton, *Have No Fear: The Charles Evers Story* (New York: John Wiley and Sons, 1997), 113.
13. M. Evers with Peters, *For Us, the Living,* 272.
14. Ibid., 278.
15. Ibid., 272.
16. *City of Jackson vs. John R. Salter, Jr. et al.* (1963) Salter v. City of Jackson, 253 Miss. 430, 176 So. 2d 63 (Miss. 1965).
17. M. Evers with Peters, *For Us, the Living,* 282.
18. Evers-Williams and Marable, *Autobiography of Medgar Evers,* 283–84.
19. Ibid., 284–85.
20. Associated Press, "Roy Wilkins Is Arrested at Jackson: NAACP Official Accused of Felony; D.C. Man Seized," *Washington Post* and *Times Herald* (Jackson, MS), June 2, 1963, reprinted in Evers-Williams and Marable, *Autobiography of Medgar Evers,* 284–86.
21. M. Evers with Peters, *For Us, the Living,* 280–81.
22. Myrlie Evers-Williams and Melinda Blau, *Watch Me Fly: What I Learned on the Way to Becoming the Woman I Was Meant to Be* (New York: Little, Brown, 1999), 76–77.
23. Ibid., 77.
24. Ibid.

25. Ibid., 76.
26. M. Evers with Peters, *For Us, the Living,* 286–89.
27. Evers-Williams and Marable, *Autobiography of Medgar Evers,* 287–88.
28. Ibid., 289.
29. Michael Vinson Williams, *Medgar Evers: Mississippi Martyr* (Fayetteville: University of Arkansas Press, 2011), 264.
30. M. Evers with Peters, *For Us, the Living,* 282–83.
31. Ibid., 284–85.
32. Ibid., 286–89.
33. Ibid.
34. Ibid.
35. Ibid., 292–93.
36. Ibid.
37. Ibid., 294–96.
38. Ibid.
39. Ibid.
40. Evers-Williams and Marable, *Autobiography of Medgar Evers,* 290.
41. M. Evers with Peters, *For Us, the Living,* 296–97.
42. Evers-Williams and Marable, *Autobiography of Medgar Evers,* 261.
43. Jack Mendelsohn, *The Martyrs: Sixteen Who Gave Their Lives for Racial Justice* (New York: Harper and Row, 1966), 71.
44. Williams, *Medgar Evers,* 279.
45. John R. Salter, Jr. (Hunter Gray), "Remembering Medgar Evers," *Against the Current,* no. 165, July–August 2013, https://againstthecurrent.org/atc165/p3935.
46. Mendelsohn, *Martyrs,* 71.
47. John F. Kennedy, "Radio and Television Report to the American People on Civil Rights, June 11, 1963," John F. Kennedy Presidential Library and Museum, https://www.jfklibrary.org/learn/about-jfk/historic-speeches/televised-address-to-the-nation-on-civil-rights.
48. Salter, "Remembering Medgar Evers."
49. C. Evers and Szanton, *Have No Fear,* 125.
50. Mendelsohn, *Martyrs,* 72.
51. Author interview with Myrlie Evers-Williams, 2021.
52. Jerry Mitchell, "Simply 'Daddy': Reena Evers-Everette Shares Memories of Medgar," *Clarion-Ledger* (Jackson, MS), June 1, 2015, https://www.clarionledger.com/story/magnolia/2015/06/01/reena-evers-everette-memories-medgar/28326495.
53. Author interview with Carolyn Wells, 2021.
54. Mitchell, "Simply 'Daddy.'"
55. Mendelsohn, *Martyrs,* 72–73.
56. M. Evers with Peters, *For Us, the Living,* 305.
57. Ibid., 302–3.
58. Mendelsohn, *Martyrs,* 73.
59. M. Evers with Peters, *For Us, the Living,* 304–5.
60. Ibid., 304.
61. Jerry Mitchell, "Medgar Evers: Assassin's Gun Forever Changed a Family," *Clarion-Ledger* (Jackson, MS), June 12, 2013, https://www.usatoday.com/story/news/2013/06/02/medgar-evers-family-legacy/2378631.

CHAPTER 8: HOW TO BE A CIVIL RIGHTS WIDOW

1. Myrlie Evers with William Peters, *For Us, the Living* (Garden City, NY: Doubleday, 1967), 306–7.
2. Ibid., 307–8.
3. "African Nationalist Urges Southern Negroes to Arm," *New York Times,* June 13, 1963, 12, https://timesmachine.nytimes.com/timesmachine/1963/06/13/89925521.html?pageNumber=12.
4. John R. Salter, Jr. (Hunter Gray), "Remembering Medgar Evers," *Against the Current,* no. 165, July–August 2013, https://againstthecurrent.org/atc165/p3935.
5. M. Evers with Peters, *For Us, the Living,* 309–10.
6. Ibid., 310.
7. Claude Sitton, "N.A.A.C.P. Leader Slain in Jackson: Protests Mount, Whites Alarmed," *New York Times,* June 13, 1963, 1, 12, https://timemachine.newyorktimes.com/ timemachine/1963/06/13/issue.html.
8. Quoted in "Funeral and National Response," National Parks Service, Medgar and Myrlie Evers Home National Monument, https://www.nps.gov/memy/lear/historyculture/funeral-and-national-response.htm.
9. Sitton, "N.A.A.C.P. Leader Slain."
10. "Not Forgotten: Medgar Evers, Whose Assassination Reverberated Through the Civil Rights Movement," *New York Times,* July 2, 2016, https://www.nytimes.com/interactive/projects/cp/obituaries/archives/medgar-evers-civil-rights.
11. M. Evers with Peters, *For Us, the Living,* 310–12.
12. Sitton, "N.A.A.C.P. Leader Slain."
13. "$5,000 Reward Offer Made as Youth Shot," *Clarion-Ledger* (Jackson, MS), June 16, 1963, https://www.newspapers.com/image/185676808.
14. M. Evers with Peters, *For Us, the Living,* 309.
15. Claude Sitton, "Whites Alarmed: Victim Is Shot from Ambush—158 Marchers Seized," *New York Times,* June 12, 1964, https://timesmachine.nytimes.com/timesmachine/1963/06/13/89925420.html?pageNumber=1.
16. "Evers, Medgar Wiley," Stanford University, The Martin Luther King, Jr. Research and Education Institute.
17. Film clip of Dr. Martin Luther King Jr. responding to a reporter's question about President John F. Kennedy's speech on civil rights and the murder of Medgar Evers, WSB-TV (Atlanta, Georgia), June 12, 1963, Digital Library of Georgia, https://dlg.usg.edu/record/ugabma_wsbn_wsbn40931.
18. Associated Press, "Evers Murder Rifle Found: Jackson Police Press Search As .30 .30 Spotted in Weeds," *Greenwood Commonwealth,* June 12, 1963, https://www.newspapers.com/image/255009330.
19. Author interview with Senator Michael Mitchell, April 2023.
20. M. Evers with Peters, *For Us, the Living,* 314.
21. *Salter v. City of Jackson,* opinion, June 7, 1963, Salter v. City of Jackson, 253 Miss. 430, 176 So. 2d 63 (Miss. 1965).
22. Author interview with Frank Figgers.
23. Author interview with Dennis Sweet III and Judge Denise Sweet Owens.
24. Darrell Evers, interviewed by Orlando Bagwell, April 3, 1986, in *Eyes on the Prize: America's Civil Rights Years, 1954–1965,* Film and Media Archive, Washington University in St. Louis, American Archive of Public Broadcasting (GBH and the

Library of Congress), Boston and Washington, D.C., http://americanarchive.org/catalog/cpb-aacip-151-cv4bn9xv7m.

25. M. Evers with Peters, *For Us, the Living,* 313.
26. Ibid., 314.
27. Myrlie Evers-Williams and Manning Marable, *The Autobiography of Medgar Evers: A Hero's Life and Legacy Revealed Through His Writings, Letters and Speeches* (New York: Basic Civitas Books, 2005), 299.
28. Charles Evers and Andrew Szanton, *Have No Fear: The Charles Evers Story* (New York: John Wiley and Sons, 1997), 134–35.
29. M. Evers with Peters, *For Us, the Living,* 315.
30. Ibid., 314–15.
31. Ibid., 315–16.
32. Salter, "Remembering Medgar Evers."
33. "Racial News Roundup: Protest Pace UP, Controls Tight," *Daily Press* (Newport News, VA), June 16, 1963, https://www.newspapers.com/image/232236931.
34. M. Evers with Peters, *For Us, the Living,* 315.
35. "Racial News Roundup."
36. Salter, "Remembering Medgar Evers."
37. Author interview with Rev. Ed King.
38. Salter, "Remembering Medgar Evers."
39. Rev. Edwin King, interview, in "Behind the Veil: Documenting African-American Life in the Jim Crow South." Duke University, John Hope Franklin Research Center, records 1940–1997 and undated, bulk 1993–1997.
40. M. Evers with Peters, *For Us, the Living,* 317.
41. Ibid.
42. C. Evers and Szanton, *Have No Fear,* 134.
43. Tom Dent, "Portrait of Three Heroes," *Freedomways,* Second Quarter, 1965.
44. M. Evers with Peters, *For Us, the Living,* 318.
45. "Funeral March Finishes in White-Led Agitation," *Clarion-Ledger* (Jackson, MS), June 16, 1963, https://www.newspapers.com/image/185676808.
46. M. Evers with Peters, *For Us, the Living,* 318.
47. Ibid.
48. Ibid.
49. C. Evers and Szanton, *Have No Fear,* 136.
50. Jackie Robinson, telegram to President John F. Kennedy, June 15, 1963, John F. Kennedy Presidential Library and Museum, Papers of John F. Kennedy, Presidential Papers, White House Central Name File, JFKWHCNF-2355-041, https://www.jfklibrary.org/asset-viewer/archives/JFKWHCNF/2355/JFKWHCNF-2355-041.
51. Salter, "Remembering Medgar Evers."
52. Ibid.
53. M. Evers with Peters, *For Us, the Living,* 319–21.
54. Ibid., 321–22.
55. Associated Press, "Evers' Funeral Sparks Violence in Mississippi," *Gazette and Daily* (York, PA), June 17, 1963, https://www.newspapers.com/image/390077961.
56. Evers-Williams and Marable, *Autobiography of Medgar Evers,* 302–4.
57. M. Evers with Peters, *For Us, the Living,* 323.
58. "Massive Turnout Urged to Greet Evers' Body at Washington D.C.," *Gazette*

and Daily (York, PA), June 17, 1963, https://www.newspapers.com/image/3900 77961.
59. M. Evers with Peters, *For Us, the Living,* 323–24.
60. Ibid.
61. National Parks Service, https://www.nps.gov/memy/learn/historyculture/funeral -and-national-response.htm.
62. M. Evers with Peters, *For Us, the Living,* 324.
63. Ibid.
64. C. Evers and Szanton, *Have No Fear,* 126.
65. "Funeral and National Response," https://www.nps.gov/memy/learn/historyculture /funeral-and-national-response.htm.
66. Jack Mendelsohn, *The Martyrs: Sixteen Who Gave Their Lives for Racial Justice* (New York: Harper and Row, 1966), 80.
67. M. Evers with Peters, *For Us, the Living,* 325–26.
68. Mendelsohn, *Martyrs,* 80–81.
69. M. Evers with Peters, *For Us, the Living,* 325.
70. Ibid., 326–27.
71. Ibid., 328.
72. Ibid., 328–29.
73. Ibid., 333.

CHAPTER 9: A TRISTATE CONSPIRACY?

1. Dudley Lehew, "Californian Is Charged with Murder of Evers: Suspect Transferred to Jail in Jackson," *Clarion-Ledger* (Jackson, MS), June 24, 1963, https:// www.newspapers.com/image/185707358.
2. From the Medgar and Myrlie Evers Papers, Mississippi Department of Archives and History, Mississippi Archives, Collection #Z/2231 000/S, Box 2.
3. Jack Mendelsohn, *The Martyrs: Sixteen Who Gave Their Lives for Racial Justice* (New York: Harper and Row, 1966), 81.
4. Ibid.
5. Ibid.
6. Rev. Dr. Martin Luther King Jr., Speech at the Great March in Detroit, Michigan. June 23, 1963. Source: Walter P. Reuther Library, https://reuther.wayne.edu /node/7858.
7. Lehew, "Californian Is Charged."
8. Ibid.
9. Ibid.
10. Associated Press, "Seek Others in Slaying of Evers," June 24, 1963, https://www .newspapers.com/image/799964313.
11. Jane Biggers, "Greenwood Shocked—Neighbors Recall Beckwith as Outspoken Marine Vet," *Clarion-Ledger* (Jackson, MS), June 24, 1963, https://www.newspapers .com/image/185707358.
12. Frank E. Smith, letter to Burke Marshall, June 26, 1963, John F. Kennedy Presidential Library and Museum, Papers of John F. Kennedy, Presidential Papers, White House Central Subject Files, HU: 2: ST 24: Mississippi: General, April 16, 1963, JFKWHCSF-0369-006-p0018, https://www.jfklibrary.org/asset-viewer/archives /JFKWHCSF/0369/JFKWHCSF-0369-006.

13. Ibid.
14. From the Medgar and Myrlie Evers Papers, Mississippi Archives, Collection #Z/2231 000/S, Box 2.
15. "Evers Suspect to Get Mental Tests," *Oakland Tribune*, July 26, 1963, https://www.newspapers.com/image/354477252.
16. From the Medgar and Myrlie Evers Papers, Mississippi Archives, Collection #Z/2231 000/S, Box 2, https://www.mdah.ms.gov/collections.
17. Ibid.
18. Ibid.
19. Ibid.
20. Ibid.
21. Don Whitehead, *Attack on Terror: The FBI Against the Ku Klux Klan in Mississippi* (Bronx, NY: Ishi Press International, 2012), 158.
22. "Evers Murdered: Civil Rights Leader Shot in Back," *Mississippi Free Press*, June 15, 1963, https://www.crmvet.org/docs/mfp/630615_mfp.pdf.
23. Ibid.
24. From the Medgar and Myrlie Evers Papers, Mississippi Archives, Collection #Z/2231 000/S, Box 2, https://www.mdah.ms.gov/collections.
25. Whitehead, *Attack on Terror*, 22.
26. Ibid.
27. Bernard LaFayette Jr. and Kathryn Lee Johnson, *In Peace and Freedom: My Journey to Selma* (Lexington: University Press of Kentucky, 2013), 76.
28. Author interview with Bernard Lafayette, 2021.
29. Ibid.
30. Associated Press, "Beckwith Indicted for Murder," *Times and Democrat* (Orangeburg, SC), July 3, 1963, https://www.newspapers.com/image/343888602.
31. Myrlie Evers with William Peters, *For Us, the Living* (Garden City, NY: Doubleday, 1967), 339.
32. Ibid., 338.
33. "NAACP Jeers Chicago's Mayor; Negro Clergyman Is Also Hooted at Rights Rally," *Baltimore Sun*, July 5, 1963, https://www.newspapers.com/image/376342583.
34. M. Evers with Peters, *For Us, the Living*, 338.
35. Ibid., 342.
36. Ibid., 339.
37. Mendelsohn, *Martyrs*, 82.
38. M. Evers with Peters, *For Us, the Living*, 344–47.
39. Myrlie Evers-Williams and Melinda Blau, *Watch Me Fly: What I Learned on the Way to Becoming the Woman I Was Meant to Be* (New York: Little, Brown, 1999), 78.
40. Ibid.
41. Ibid.
42. M. Evers with Peters, *For Us, the Living*, 340.
43. Evers-Williams and Blau, *Watch Me Fly*, 78.
44. "An Oral History of the March on Washington," interviews by Michael Fletcher, videos by Ryan R. Reed, *Smithsonian Magazine*, July 2013, https://www.smithsonianmag.com/history/oral-history-march-washington-180953863.
45. Ted Gittinger and Allen Fisher, "LBJ Champions the Civil Rights Act of 1964," National Archives, *Prologue* 36, no. 2 (Summer 2004), https://www.archives.gov/publications/prologue/2004/summer.

46. "Oral History of the March on Washington."
47. M. Evers with Peters, *For Us, the Living*, 340–41.
48. Coretta Scott King as told to the Rev. Dr. Barbara Reynolds, *My Life, My Love, My Legacy* (New York: Henry Holt, 2017), 115.
49. M. Evers with Peters, *For Us, the Living*, 347–49.
50. Ibid., 351–53.
51. Ibid.
52. FBI Files: Medgar Evers, File Number 157-901, Pages 1-5, FOIA, Web Archive, https://web.archive.org/web/20221114104650/https://vault.fbi.gov/Medgar%20Evers/Medgar%20Evers%20Part%201%20of%205.
53. Associated Press, "White Man Held Over at Jackson: Innocent Plea Made to Charge in Evers Slaying," *Montgomery Advertiser*, June 26, 1963, https://www.newspapers.com/image/256017038.
54. Medgar Evers, FBI files.
55. "Trials: Hung Jury," *Time*, February 14, 1964, https://content.time.com/time/subscriber/article/0,33009,870731,00.html.
56. M. Evers with Peters, *For Us, the Living*, 366–67.
57. Ibid., 368.
58. Ibid., 351.
59. An April 1963 assassination attempt against General Walker by Lee Harvey Oswald would later be cited by Oswald's widow, Marina, who called Walker "a very bad man and a fascist" as proof that Oswald very much wanted to kill someone, https://timesmachine.nytimes.com/timesmachine/1964/01/01/106930338.html?pageNumber=11.
60. United Press International, "New Lawyer Gets Beckwith's Case; Barnett's Partner in Charge—Jury Selection Continues," *New York Times*, April 8, 1964, https://timesmachine.nytimes.com/timesmachine/1964/04/08/97385690.html?pageNumber=30.
61. Medgar Evers, FBI file, April 14, 1963, report.
62. "Zinn—Mississippi 'Chronology,' 1963–1964," Wisconsin Historical Society, Howard Zinn Papers, 1956–1994, Archives Main Stacks, Mss 588, Box 1, Folder 22, 3, https://content.wisconsinhistory.org/digital/collection/p15932coll2/id/11455.
63. Jerry Mitchell and Beverly Pettigrew Kraft, "Ex-Jurors Remember Beckwith's 1964 Trials," *Clarion-Ledger* (Jackson, MS), January 31, 1994, https://www.newspapers.com/image/182664333.
64. M. Evers with Peters, *For Us, the Living*, 369.
65. "Beckwith's 2d Trial Ends in Hung Jury," *New York Times*, April 18, 1964.
66. Don Whitehead, *Attack on Terror: The FBI Against the Ku Klux Klan in Mississippi* (Bronx, NY: Ishi Press International, 2012), 157–60.
67. M. Evers with Peters, *For Us, the Living*, 371–72.
68. Gittinger and Fisher, "LBJ Champions the Civil Rights Act of 1964," https://www.archives.gov/publications/prologue/2004/summer/civil-rights-act.
69. Evers-Williams and Blau, *Watch Me Fly*, 81.
70. Claude Sitton, "Rights Team's Burned Car Found in Mississippi Bog; Dulles to Aid Hunt for 3," *New York Times*, June 24, 1964, https://timesmachine.nytimes.com/timesmachine/1964/06/24/issue.html.
71. "N.A.A.C.P. Plans Protest," *New York Times*, June 24, 1964, https://timesmachine.nytimes.com/timesmachine/1964/06/24/100204725.html?pageNumber=21.

72. "President Acts: Sends Ex-C.I.A. Head to South After Seeing Parents of Youths," *New York Times,* June 24, 1964, https://timesmachine.nytimes.com/timesmachine/1964/06/24/100204451.html?pageNumber=1.
73. Whitehead, *Attack on Terror,* 157–62.
74. Jerry Mitchell, "Simply 'Daddy': Reena Evers-Everette Shares Memories of Medgar," *Clarion-Ledger* (Jackson, MS), June 1, 2015, https://www.clarionledger.com/story/magnolia/2015/06/01/reena-evers-everette-memories-medgar/28326495.
75. Evers-Williams and Blau, *Watch Me Fly,* 86–87.
76. Ibid., 88.
77. Ibid.
78. Mitchell, "Simply 'Daddy.'"
79. Author interview with Carolyn Wells.
80. Eric Norden, "The Playboy Interview with Charles Evers," *Playboy* (website), October 1, 1971, https://www.playboy.com/read/the-playboy-interview-with-charles-evers.
81. Evers-Williams and Blau, *Watch Me Fly,* 85.
82. Ibid.

CHAPTER 10: JUSTICE

1. Myrlie Evers-Williams and Melinda Blau, *Watch Me Fly: What I Learned on the Way to Becoming the Woman I Was Meant to Be* (New York: Little, Brown, 1999), 88–91.
2. Ibid., 92–93.
3. Ibid.
4. Myrlie Evers-Williams, foreword to *Betty Shabazz: Surviving Malcolm X—A Journey of Strength from Wife to Widow to Heroine,*by Russell J. Rickford (Naperville, IL: Sourcebooks, 2003), 400–402.
5. Evers-Williams and Blau, *Watch Me Fly,* 196
6. Lorraine Boissoneault, "Martin Luther King Jr.'s Assassination Sparked Uprisings in Cities Across America," *Smithsonian Magazine* (website), April 4, 2018, https://www.smithsonianmag.com/history/martin-luther-king-jrs-assassination-sparked-uprisings-cities-across-america-180968665.
7. Charles Evers and Andrew Szanton, *Have No Fear: The Charles Evers Story* (New York: John Wiley and Sons, 1997), 229.
8. Ibid., 227–29.
9. Ibid., 229.
10. Larry Tye, "The Most Trusted White Man in Black America," *Politico,* July 7, 2016, https://www.politico.com/magazine/story/2016/07/robert-f-kennedy-race-relations-martin-luther-king-assassination-214021.
11. "James Baldwin: How to Cool It," *Esquire,* July 1968, https://www.esquire.com/news-politics/a23960/james-baldwin-cool-it.
12. Myrlie Evers-Williams, foreword to *Betty Shabazz: Surviving Malcolm X,* x.
13. Rickford, *Betty Shabazz: Surviving Malcolm X,* 402–3.
14. Ibid.
15. Ibid.
16. Evers-Williams and Blau, *Watch Me Fly,* 120–25.
17. "Mrs. Evers to Run for Congress Seat," *New York Times,* March 17, 1970, 32,

https://timesmachine.nytimes.com/timesmachine/1970/03/17/76716164.html?pageNumber=32.

18. Evers-Williams and Blau, *Watch Me Fly*, 235.
19. Rickford, *Betty Shabazz: Surviving Malcolm X*, 400–402.
20. Ibid.
21. Ibid.
22. Ibid.
23. Jerry Mitchell, "Myrlie Evers Sees Vision of Her Late Husband, Medgar," *Clarion-Ledger* (Jackson, MS), June 14, 2014, https://www.clarionledger.com/story/journeytojustice/2014/06/14/medgar-evers-walter-williams/10532219.
24. Author interview with Myrlie Evers-Williams.
25. Evers-Williams and Blau, *Watch Me Fly*, 282–83.
26. Ibid.
27. "Bomb in Car 'Astounds' de la Beckwith," *South Mississippi Sun*, January 18, 1974, https://www.newspapers.com/image/737086961.
28. Evers-Williams and Blau, *Watch Me Fly*, 197.
29. Ibid.
30. Author interview with Myrlie Evers-Williams.
31. Judith Cummings, "Los Angeles Council Election Seen as a Test for the Mayor," *New York Times*, April 13, 1987, https://timesmachine.nytimes.com/timesmachine/1987/04/13/998487.html?pageNumber=15.
32. Victor Merina, "10th District Race a Test for Bradley, 13 Hopefuls," *Los Angeles Times*, March 23, 1987, https://www.latimes.com/archives/la-xpm-1987-03-23-me-8983-story.html.
33. Associated Press, "Evers Widow Loses Bid for Los Angeles Post," *New York Times*, April 16, 1987, https://timesmachine.nytimes.com/timesmachine/1987/04/16/737687.html?pageNumber=19.
34. Evers-Williams and Blau, *Watch Me Fly*, 198–99.
35. Ibid.
36. "Myrlie Evers-Williams, Wife of Civil Rights Leader Killed in 1963, Sells 'Magnificent' Home in Bend," *Oregonian*, January 28, 2013, https://www.oregonlive.com/politics/2013/01/myrlie_evers-williams_wife_of.html.
37. Evers-Williams and Blau, *Watch Me Fly*, 200.
38. Ibid.
39. Ibid., 203.
40. Author interview with Jerry Mitchell.
41. Associated Press, "Medgar Evers' Body Exhumed for Autopsy," June 6, 1991, *Los Angeles Times*, https://www.latimes.com/archives/la-xpm-1991-06-06-mn-271-story.html.
42. Associated Press, "New Evers Autopsy Replaces Original, Reported as Missing," *New York Times*, June 7, 1991, https://timesmachine.nytimes.com/timesmachine/1991/06/07/016191.html?pageNumber=16.
43. Evers-Williams and Blau, *Watch Me Fly*, 208.
44. Alan Huffman, "Gun, Under Glass," *Oxford American*, no. 100 (Spring 2018), https://oxfordamerican.org/magazine/issue-100-spring-2018/gun-under-glass.
45. *Byron De La Beckwith v. State of Mississippi*, dissent by Chief Justice Dan Lee, March 26, 1998, De La Beckwith v. State, 707 So. 2d 547, 94 KA 402 (Miss. 1998).

46. Ibid.
47. Ibid.
48. Ibid.
49. Ibid.
50. Ibid.
51. Ibid.
52. Ibid.
53. Ibid.
54. Ibid.
55. Ron Harrist, "Urgent: White Supremacist Byron De La Beckwith Convicted of Medgar Evers' Murder," February 5,1994, https://webarchive.org/20230422142609/https://apnews.com/article/c18776f9f3cd1b5b312627ec5542dd84.
56. Associated Press, "Beckwith Convicted of Killing Medgar Evers," *Daily Advertiser,* February 5, 1994, 7, https://www.newspapers.com/image/539926994/?terms=Beckwith%20Convicted%20Of%20Killing%20Medgar%20Evers&match=1.
57. Ibid.
58. Ibid.
59. Ibid.
60. Ibid.
61. Ibid.
62. Associated Press, "Dr. William F. Gibson; Civil Rights Leader, 69," May 6, 2002, *New York Times,* https://www.nytimes.com/2002/05/06/us/dr-william-f-gibson-civil-rights-leader-69.html.
63. Dana Priest, "Evers-Williams Vows to Revive NAACP," *Washington Post,* February 19, 1995, https://www.washingtonpost.com/archive/politics/1995/02/19/evers-williams-vows-to-revive-naacp/a17b622e-1d97-40c7-92bc-98ce9c2a13f4.
64. Evers-Williams and Blau, *Watch Me Fly,* 249–50.
65. Author interview with Joe Madison.
66. Priest, "Evers-Williams Vows to Revive NAACP.".
67. Sam Fulwood III, "NAACP Elects Evers' Widow to Top Post: Civil Rights: Myrlie Evers-Williams Wins by One Vote, Ousting William Gibson as Chairman. Change Is Seen as Opportunity to Redirect Group's Focus. 'It Is Time to Heal Our Wounds,' She Says," *Los Angeles Times,* February 19, 1995, https://www.latimes.com/archives/la-xpm-1995-02-19-mn-33896-story.html.
68. Sam Fulwood III, "Saving the NAACP: Myrlie Evers-Williams Goes Way Back with the NAACP. Now That She's Talen Over, Can She Make It Important Again?," *Los Angeles Times,* June 25, 1995.
69. Fulwood, "NAACP Elects Evers' Widow to Top Post."
70. Evers-Williams and Blau, *Watch Me Fly,* 249–50.
71. Ibid.
72. Krissah Thompson, "Myrlie Evers-Williams Leaves the NAACP Board After 30 Years. What Will She Do Next?" *Washington Post,* February 13, 2014, https://www.washingtonpost.com/blogs/she-the-people/wp/2014/02/13/myrlie-evers-williams-leaves-the-naacp-board-after-30-years-what-will-she-do-next.
73. Priest, "Evers-Williams Vows to Revive NAACP."
74. "Evers-Williams Sworn In to Lead NAACP," *Tampa Bay Times,* May 15, 1995, https://www.tampabay.com/archive/1995/05/15/evers-williams-sworn-in-to-lead-naacp.

75. Ruben Castaneda, "Donations and Goodwill Flow as NAACP Inducts Chairman," *Washington Post,* May 15, 1995, https://www.washingtonpost.com/archive/local/1995/05/15/donations-and-goodwill-flow-as-naacp-inducts-chairman/142a9dc6-1482-44b4-8a78-660d5aaaf6ef.
76. Associated Press, "NAACP Has Retired Its Debt and Is Rebuilding," *Deseret News,* October 20, 1996, https://www.deseret.com/1996/10/20/19272543/naacp-has-retired-its-debt-and-is-rebuilding.
77. Coretta Scott King as told to the Rev. Dr. Barbara Reynolds, *My Life, My Love, My Legacy* (New York: Henry Holt, 2017), 322.
78. Author interview with Dr. Bernice King, March 4, 2022.
79. C. Evers and Szanton, *Have No Fear,* 227–29.
80. Scott King and Reynolds, *My Life, My Love, My Legacy,* 323.
81. Rickford, *Betty Shabazz: Surviving Malcolm X,* 530.
82. Scott King and Reynolds, *My Life, My Love, My Legacy,* 323.
83. Rickford, *Betty Shabazz: Surviving Malcolm X,* 530.
84. Evers-Williams and Blau, *Watch Me Fly,* 304.
85. Ibid.
86. New York Times News Service, "Grandson, 12, Admits Killing Shabazz but He Says Her Death Was Not Intended," *Baltimore Sun,* July 11, 1997, https://www.baltimoresun.com/news/bs-xpm-1997-07-11-1997192109-story.html.
87. Myrlie Evers-Williams, foreword to *Betty Shabazz: Surviving Malcolm X,* x–xii.
88. Ibid.
89. Michael A. Fletcher, "Evers-Williams to Step Down as NAACP Chairman," *Washington Post,* February 11, 1998, https://www.washingtonpost.com/archive/politics/1998/02/11/evers-williams-to-step-down-as-naacp-chairman/979f755d-0cd6-499c-8470-21f3b2cb9dfd.

CHAPTER 11: CARNEGIE HALL

1. Author interview with Jerry Mitchell, 2021.
2. Ibid.
3. Author interview with Myrlie Evers-Williams, 2021.
4. Ibid.
5. Associated Press, "New Navy Ship to Be Named for Slain Civil Rights Pioneer," *New York Times,* October 10, 2009, https://www.nytimes.com/2009/10/11/us/11evers.html.
6. Larry Tye, "The Most Trusted White Man in Black America," *Politico,* July 7, 2016, https://www.politico.com/magazine/story/2016/07/robert-f-kennedy-race-relations-martin-luther-king-assassination-214021.
7. Myrlie Evers-Williams, interviewed by Michel Martin, in "Civil Rights Leaders React to Obama's Win," *Tell Me More,* NPR, November 5, 2008, https://www.npr.org/templates/story/story.php?storyId=96645057.
8. Associated Press, "Darrell Evers; Slain Civil Rights Leader's Son," *Los Angeles Times,* February 19, 2001, https://www.latimes.com/archives/la-xpm-2001-feb-19-me-27399-story.html.
9. Bruce Bennett, "A Civil Rights Heroine Carries Her Torch Song to the Stage," *Wall Street Journal,* January 23, 2013, https://www.wsj.com/articles/SB10001424127887324539304578260030290569810.

10. Ibid.
11. Ibid.
12. Ibid.
13. Ashley Southall, "Paying Tribute to a Seeker of Justice, 50 Years After His Assassination," *New York Times,* June 5, 2013, https://www.nytimes.com/2013/06/06/us/paying-tribute-to-a-seeker-of-justice-50-years-after-his-assassination.html.
14. Joy-Ann Reid, "Myrlie Evers-Williams: NAACP Apologized for Denying Security Detail for Medgar," *theGrio,* June 16, 2013, https://thegrio.com/2013/06/16/myrlie-evers-naacp-apologized-for-denying-security-detail-for-medgar.
15. RT McNedd, "Myrlie Evers Meets with President Obama," *Michigan Chronicle,* June 4, 2013, https://michiganchronicle.com/2013/06/04/fifty-years-after-the-assassination-of-civil-rights-activist-medgar-evers-president-obama-met-with-evers-widow-myrlie-evers.
16. Ibid.
17. Author interview with Myrlie Evers-Williams, 2021.

Index

ABOUT MARINER BOOKS

Mariner Books traces its beginnings to 1832 when William Ticknor cofounded the Old Corner Bookstore in Boston, from which he would run the legendary firm Ticknor and Fields, publisher of Ralph Waldo Emerson, Harriet Beecher Stowe, Nathaniel Hawthorne, and Henry David Thoreau. Following Ticknor's death, Henry Oscar Houghton acquired Ticknor and Fields and, in 1880, formed Houghton Mifflin, which later merged with venerable Harcourt Publishing to form Houghton Mifflin Harcourt. HarperCollins purchased HMH's trade publishing business in 2021 and reestablished their storied lists and editorial team under the name Mariner Books.

Uniting the legacies of Houghton Mifflin, Harcourt Brace, and Ticknor and Fields, Mariner Books continues one of the great traditions in American bookselling. Our imprints have introduced an incomparable roster of enduring classics, including Hawthorne's *The Scarlet Letter,* Thoreau's *Walden,* Willa Cather's *O Pioneers!,* Virginia Woolf's *To the Lighthouse,* W. E. B. Du Bois's *Black Reconstruction,* J. R. R. Tolkien's *The Lord of the Rings,* Carson McCullers's *The Heart Is a Lonely Hunter,* Ann Petry's *The Narrows,* George Orwell's *Animal Farm* and *Nineteen Eighty-Four,* Rachel Carson's *Silent Spring,* Margaret Walker's *Jubilee,* Italo Calvino's *Invisible Cities,* Alice Walker's *The Color Purple,* Margaret Atwood's *The Handmaid's Tale,* Tim O'Brien's *The Things They Carried,* Philip Roth's *The Plot Against America,* Jhumpa Lahiri's *Interpreter of Maladies,* and many others. Today Mariner Books remains proudly committed to the craft of fine publishing established nearly two centuries ago at the Old Corner Bookstore.

EXPLORE MORE BY #1 *NEW YORK TIMES* BESTSELLING AUTHOR

JOY-ANN REID

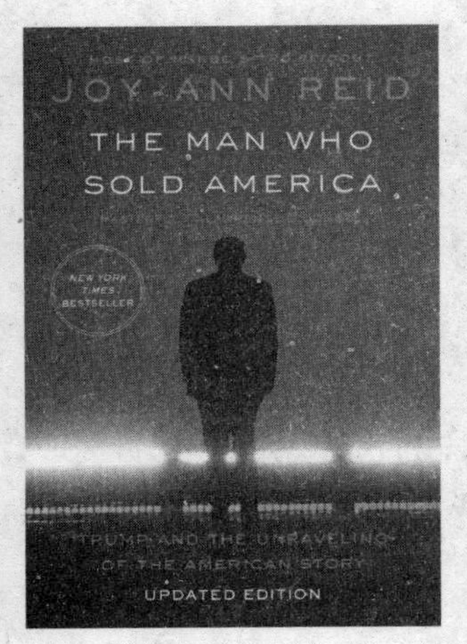

A *NEW YORK TIMES* BESTSELLER

MSNBC'S Joy-Ann Reid calculates the true price of the Trump presidency, now updated with a new afterword.

"The host of [*The ReidOut*] on MSNBC argues that President Trump's administration is characterized by grift and venality that demeans the office and diminishes America."
—*New York Times Book Review*

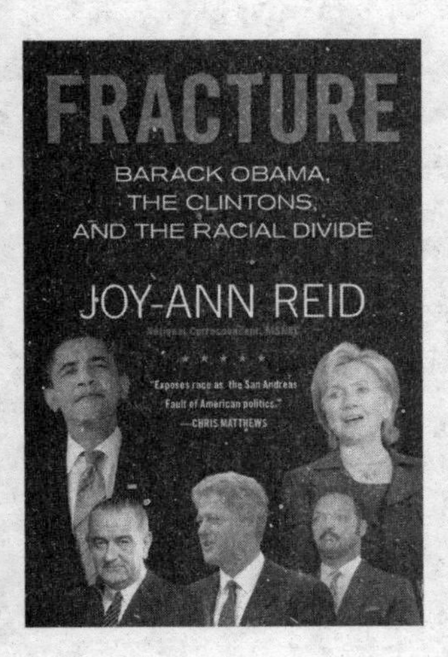

Barack Obama's speech on the Edmund Pettus Bridge to mark the fiftieth anniversary of the Selma to Montgomery marches should have represented the culmination of Martin Luther King Jr.'s dream of racial unity. Yet, in *Fracture*, MSNBC national correspondent Joy-Ann Reid shows that, despite the progress we have made, we are still a nation divided—as seen recently in headline-making tragedies such as police killings of Black citizens and uprisings across the country.

"Written with grace, eloquence, and vibrant prose, *Fracture* is a luminous and cautionary tale about the aspirations and limits of national politics when race, class, and gender have their say."
— Michael Eric Dyson, author of *The Black Presidency: Barack Obama and the Politics of Race in America*